AN INTRODUCTION TO

Eighteenth-Century

DRAMA

1700–1780

SIR PETER TEAZLE
(*Thomas King*)

LADY TEAZLE
(*Mrs. Abington*)

CHARLES SURFACE
(*William Smith*)

JOSEPH SURFACE
(*John Palmer*)

The Screen Scene in *The School for Scandal*, with the original cast, painted by
James Roberts, 1777

AN INTRODUCTION TO
Eighteenth-Century
DRAMA
1700—1780

BY

FREDERICK S. *Samuel* BOAS

M.A., Hon. LL.D., Hon. D.Litt., F.R.S.L.

GREENWOOD PRESS, PUBLISHERS
WESTPORT, CONNECTICUT

Library of Congress Cataloging in Publication Data

Boas, Frederick Samuel, 1862-1957.
    An introduction to eighteenth-century drama, 1700-
1780.

    Reprint of the 1953 ed. published at the Clarendon
Press, Oxford.
    Includes index.
    1. English drama--18th century--History and
criticism. I. Title.
[PR701.B6 1978]   822'.5'09   77-27612
ISBN 0-313-20193-5

Oxford University Press 1953

This reprint has been authorized by the Oxford University Press

Reprinted in 1978 by Greenwood Press, Inc.,
51 Riverside Avenue
Westport, CT. 06880

Printed in the United States of America

10 9 8 7 6 5 4 3 2 1

PREFACE

THE kind reception that has been given to my *Introduction to Tudor Drama* and *Introduction to Stuart Drama* has led me to think that a similar *Introduction to Eighteenth-Century Drama* might have its use. I have passed over Restoration Drama not from any lack of appreciation but because it has found in recent years well-qualified and sympathetic interpreters. On the other hand, the more favourable attitude of late towards eighteenth-century literature in general has only in a limited degree extended to its drama. This is, I believe, in part due to its almost bewildering profusion of output, especially in the middle years, varying remarkably in quality and type.

It has seemed to me, therefore, that it might be of service to single out the more representative figures, with a discussion of their chief plays. And in what is an introductory study I have found it advisable in the case of many of these plays to give an analysis, with carefully chosen quotations, of their frequently complicated plots. Otherwise, for readers unfamiliar with them any criticism must be merely in the air. This does not apply, of course, to *She Stoops to Conquer*, *The Rivals*, or *The School for Scandal*, which have kept their place in the theatrical repertory. A few other eighteenth-century plays such as Farquhar's *The Beaux' Stratagem*, Home's *Douglas*, and Colman's and Garrick's *The Clandestine Marriage* have recently been revived. In the pages that follow I have suggested several others as deserving similar honour.

No century in any of the arts can be cut off sharply at either end. Among the Restoration dramatists Dryden died conveniently in 1700 and Congreve virtually ended his dramatic career in the same year. On the other hand,

Vanbrugh and Farquhar wrote for the stage both before
and after that date, but the work of the former seems
more typical of the close of an era, and that of the latter
of the beginning of another. At the other extreme, to
keep this study within reasonable limits, it has seemed
advisable to take as a terminus the decade 1770–80, in
which the eighteenth-century drama reached its fine
flower in the plays of Goldsmith and Sheridan. This
means no disrespect to the work of Holcroft and others.

My chief attention has been naturally given to straight
plays, tragic or comic. Next in interest has been comic
opera in the hands of Gay and his followers. But farce,
pantomime, and miscellaneous entertainments, though
of importance to the historian of the theatre, have been
lightly treated. While recognizing fully the fundamental
connexion between drama and stage, of which this
study, I hope, gives sufficient proof, I have not attempted
a direct outline of the development of the playhouses of
the period and of the companies which performed in
them. To do this adequately would almost need a
supplementary volume. Chief among the theatres was
Drury Lane, which included among its successive
managers Rich, Steele, Cibber, Garrick, and Sheridan.
Next in importance after 1732 was Covent Garden
under Rich till 1761. In addition there were the two
successive theatres in Lincoln's Inn Fields and in the
Haymarket (the King's Theatre and the Little Theatre),
Goodman's Fields, and others of minor account. For a
detailed classification of the plays performed in them,
with their dates, reference should be made to the in-
valuable lists in Professor Allardyce Nicoll's *Histories of
Early Eighteenth Century Drama* and *Late Eighteenth Century
Drama,* to which I here acknowledge my debt. The companies in the different playhouses varied from time to

time, and on occasion the performers, especially in opera, were foreigners. But never since the heyday of Burbage and Alleyn, Tarlton and Kempe, had there been so brilliant a set of actors, reinforced by an equally talented bevy of actresses, taking the place of the Elizabethan boys for the female parts. Betterton, Verbruggen, Cibber, Booth, Quin, King, Garrick; Mrs. Bracegirdle, Mrs. Verbruggen, Mrs. Barry, Mrs. Abington, Mrs. Oldfield, and Kitty Clive are shining names in the resplendent roll-call.

It has indeed been contended, with some truth, that the period was one of players rather than of playwrights. But an unprejudiced study of the plays here discussed will, as I seek to show, reveal in a number of them more of merit than has been generally recognized. In addition there is the interest of watching the interplay of contending forces. The immoral wit of Restoration comedy, battered by the powerful attack of Jeremy Collier, yields place, though not fully, to the sentimentalism of Steele and his followers. This, in its turn, becoming stereotyped, meets with the satire which reaches its peak in *The School for Scandal*. With a middle-class audience more and more taking the place of the Court circles of Restoration days Lillo takes the initiative in catering for their tastes, and Goldsmith defies convention by introducing 'low' scenes. Heroic tragedy merges into the neo-classical type which is burlesqued by Fielding and Sheridan. The vogue of Continental opera on the English stage is successfully challenged by the ballad-operas of Gay and his school.

But, as will be seen, English eighteenth-century drama, especially in its earlier phases, owed much to European influences. The legends of Greek and Roman history furnished subjects for plots. Not only plots but technique and style were indebted to France, Italy, and

Spain, especially the former. Nevertheless, eighteenth-century drama never declined into the position of a satellite. There was a strong undercurrent of national spirit, sometimes taking the form of political propaganda. Even legendary British and Anglo-Saxon history was pressed into the service of the stage. Through John Home's *Douglas* the early annals of Scotland made a notable contribution. The figure of Shakespeare, even when transformed by Garrick and others, still loomed large before aspiring dramatists. But the most striking of all the aspects of the theatre during this period, from Farquhar and Steele to Goldsmith and Sheridan, is the predominant mastery of men of Irish birth.

Apart from their dramatic significance the plays here surveyed are of importance to the social and political historian. They throw light on the eighteenth-century attitude towards such vexed questions as duelling, divorce, gambling, both public and private, the game-laws, recruiting for the army and the naval press-gang. Successive political parties, Whigs and Tories, supporters of Walpole and of Frederick, Prince of Wales, followers and enemies of Lord Bute, made use of the stage for their own ends. Much of this is now *vieux jeu*.

But there is one aspect which is singularly, almost ominously, relevant to the world situation of our own day. Time after time, often under some thin disguise, the eighteenth-century dramatists represent Britain as the champion of freedom against, in their eyes, two enslaving forces, the French monarchy and the Roman Catholic Church. Today the places of these three are taken by the Atlantic community of nations, the power behind the Iron Curtain, and international Communism. Readers will find it of interest to make their own application of some of the salient passages in the plays.

November, 1952   F. S. B.

CONTENTS

CONTENTS

I

NICHOLAS ROWE

NICHOLAS ROWE, for a variety of reasons, forms a natural stepping-stone from Elizabethan and Restoration drama to that of the eighteenth century. He was the first to edit Shakespeare's works (though uncritically from the fourth folio) with a life and a preface. He chose as the hero of a play the Scythian conqueror whom Marlowe had glorified, and he made a complete version of Lucan's *Pharsalia*, of which Marlowe had translated the first Book. Among his other subjects were some which had already been handled by Heywood, Massinger, and Field. And he chose blank verse as his instrument instead of the rhymed couplet on which Dryden had set his seal. On the other hand, the whole atmosphere and sentiment of his plays were those of heroic tragedy. And by a chance the first of these coincided with the opening year of the eighteenth century.

Rowe was born at Little Barford in Bedfordshire on 20 June 1674. His father, John Rowe, was a barrister of good position who rose to be a Serjeant-at-Law. He sent Nicholas to a private school in Highgate and afterwards to Westminster, when he was twelve, as a King's Scholar. At sixteen he proceeded to the Middle Temple where, according to Johnson, 'he endeavoured to comprehend law, not as a series of precedents or collection of positive precepts, but as a system of rational government, and impartial justice'. But like so many members of the Inns of Court before and since, Rowe's interests were literary more than legal, and the death of his father on 30 April 1692 left him sufficiently independent to follow his main bent. His first play, *The Ambitious Stepmother*, was acted at Lincoln's Inn Fields Theatre towards the end of 1700 and was first published in quarto in January 1701.[1]

The prologue appeals for the sympathy of the tender, especially those of the feminine, hearts among the audience.

> If dying lovers yet deserve a tear,
> If a sad story of a maid's despair
> Yet move compassion in the pitying fair:
> This day the poet does his arts employ
> The soft accesses of your soul to try.
>
> .　.　.　.　.　.　.
>
> O could this age's writers hope to find
> An audience to compassion thus inclin'd,
> The stage would need no farce, nor song, nor dance,
> Nor capering Monsieur brought from active France.
>
> .　.　.　.　.　.　.　.
>
> Majestic tragedy would once again
> In purple pomp adorn the swelling scene.

Rowe thus started with high aims, but 'majestic' was too lofty an epithet for tragedy as presented by him. *The Ambitious Stepmother* carries on the tradition of heroic drama and is set against the exotic Oriental background characteristic of the type. When the play opens Arsaces, the aged Persian king, is on his death-bed. Real power is in the hands of his second wife, Artemisa. Infatuated by a chance sight of her beauty he had contrived to have her husband entrapped to death and had then wedded her. By her scheming arts she had gained full ascendancy over the king, who had sent into exile his elder son Artaxerxes with his loyal companion, the veteran

[1] The dates throughout this volume are according to the modern calendar, the year beginning on 1 January.

general, Memnon. They have just returned to Persepolis that Artaxerxes, as rightful heir, may make his claim to the succession. But Artemisa is determined to secure this for her own son Artaban. She finds a supporter in the scheming courtier Mirza who had offered his daughter, Cleone, as a bride to Artaxerxes only to have her rejected in favour of Memnon's daughter, Amestris. He has another cause of quarrel with Memnon, whom he declares his brother Cleander's murderer, though the general had only killed him in a duel provoked by Cleander in a drunken fit. Mirza confides a plan for estranging Artaxerxes and Memnon to Magus, a hypocritical priest of the Sun.

> *Mag.* That's a difficulty next to impossible.
> *Mir.* Cease to think so.
> The wise and active conquer difficulties
> By daring to attempt 'em. Sloth and folly
> Shiver and shrink at sight of toil and hazard,
> And make th' impossibility they fear.

It is in such reflective passages that Rowe's verse is usually most effective, though it also pulses powerfully in Artemisa's protest in her opening speech, which gives the key to her character:

> Ye diviner Powers
> By whom, 'tis said, we are, from whose bright beings
> These active sparks were struck which move our clay,
> I feel, and I confess th' ethereal energy,
> That busy restless principle, whose appetite
> Is only pleased with greatness like your own:
> Why have you clogg'd it then with this dull mass
> And shut it up in woman? Why debas'd it
> To an inferior part of the creation?
> Since your own heavenly hands mistook my lot,
> 'Tis you have err'd, not I.

Imperiously she bars the way of Artaxerxes to his dying father's bedside, and she only restrains Artaban from combat with his brother for fear of popular support for the rightful heir. Intermixed with the harsher tones of plot and wrangling are the softer strains promised in the prologue. Artaxerxes woos Amestris, and coyly she paints an idyllic picture:

> Had fate allotted us some obscure village,
> Where only blest with life's necessities,
> We might have pass'd in peace our happy days,
> Far from the cares which crowns and empires bring;
> There no step-mother, no ambitious brother,
> No wicked statesman, would with impious arts
> Have strove to wrest from us our small inheritance.

Even when in the Temple of the Sun she becomes his bride, she still trembles in suspense between 'unruly joys and chilling fears'. Yet there is one who is all envious of her fortune. Cleone, though rejected by Artaxerxes, is consumed by a hopeless passion for him which makes her deaf to Artaban's avowals of love and her father's desires. It is Mirza who, after his first scheme has failed, devises the plot to overpower his and the Queen's enemies. At the Festival of the Sun, when all the worshippers come unarmed to the temple to do sacrifice, the unsuspecting Artaxerxes, Memnon, and Amestris are seized by guards; the two men are hurried to a prison in the temple, while Amestris is torn from them to Mirza's palace.

It is Mirza's and the Queen's intent that Artaxerxes and Memnon shall be executed on the morrow. But they have not taken into account two persons. Artaban, to his mother's amazement, refuses to owe his crown to a treacherous and sacrilegious act:

> The conscious virtue
> That witnesses within my head for glory
> Points me to greatness by the paths of honour,
> And urges me to do as a king ought,
> That would not wear his purple as the gift
> Of impious treachery.

Cleone dons masculine dress, and visiting by night, with a dark lantern and a master-key, the two prisoners, offers them the chance of escape through Mirza's palace. That villainous name excites their suspicion, which is not allayed even when she declares that she is his daughter's messenger:

> She charg'd me guide you,
> When midnight sleep had clos'd observing eyes,
> Safe through her father's palace with this key—
> And if I met with any that durst bar
> Your passage forth, she bid me greet him thus—
>   (*Stabs herself*)
>
> *Artax.* (*catching her as she falls*)
> What hast thou done, rash boy?
> *Cleo.*   Giv'n you the last
> And only proof remain'd that could convince you
> I held your life much dearer than my own.

Her secret is revealed, and as she gives the key, and hears Artaxerxes call her 'sweet saint', she dies blessed and blessing.

This genuinely pathetic scene is followed unfortunately by one that is both unplausible and repellent. Mirza makes lustful advances to Amestris, now confined within his palace, and when repulsed attempts a rape. In the struggle between them she stabs him with his own poniard, and as he lies dying he hears from the captain of the guard, Orchanes, the amazing news of Cleone's death and the flight of the two prisoners. In

a last revengeful outburst he bids Orchanes drag
Amestris near him, and he stabs her. As she lies dying
Artaxerxes and Memnon enter to hear the tale of her
wrongs and her last appeal to her lover:

> O hold me fast! death shall not tear me from you.

Artaxerxes echoes her words as he lies down beside her
dead form:

> Wait for me, gentle spirit, since the stars
> Together must receive us.

He stabs himself, murmuring,

> How foolish is the coward's fear of death!
> Of death, the greatest—surest way to peace.

It is scarcely, however, as a 'way to peace' that Memnon, in mad horror, seeks his end by suicide. Well may
Artaban bid his mother, as they enter,

> Look on that scene of blood: the dire effects
> Of cruel female arts.

> .　　.　　.　　.　　.　　.　　.　　.
> By our bright Gods, I swear, I will assert
> The majesty of manly government,
> Nor wear again your chains.

Considering that to the last the Queen is unrepentant,
and that the innocent have suffered with the guilty,
Artaban's final verdict on the happenings of the fatal
night is unduly complacent:

> The gods are great and just. Well have you mark'd,
> Celestial powers, your righteous detestation
> Of sacrilege, of base and bloody treachery.
> May this example guide my future sway:
> Let honour, truth and justice crown my reign.

As Rowe acknowledges in his dedication of the printed
play to the Lord Chamberlain, the Earl of Jersey, critics

of the play had objected that 'the catastrophe in the fifth act is barbarous, and shocks the audience', and that Artaxerxes and Amestris ought to have been preserved, and 'a more noble and instructive moral drawn that way'. Rowe's plea in defence is that he was following Aristotle's precept that terror and pity are the ends of tragedy, of which his own application was that 'the audience should be struck with terror in several parts of the play, but always conclude and go away with pity'. Aristotle might not have accepted such an interpretation. A misjudgement to which Rowe pleaded guilty, and which was a mark of his 'prentice hand, was the excessive length of the play for performance. Hence on the stage there had to be a cut of 600 lines which, as he admits, 'left dark and intricate' to the audience parts of the ingenious but unhistorical and too complicated plot.

These contemporary criticisms are not the only ones to which Rowe's first tragedy seems today to be liable. The characterization is for the most part wanting in depth. Though Queen Artemisa gives the title to the play it is the melodramatic schemer Mirza who is the centrepiece of the action. Artaxerxes and Memnon are adequate stock figures of the dispossessed rightful heir and the loyal veteran. But it is Artaban, rebellious against his mother's treachery, though on his own behalf, who is more of an original creation, to whose love Cleone might well have responded instead of becoming Amestris's hopeless rival for that of Artaxerxes.

Why then, in spite of its shortcomings, could Rowe justly claim that 'the town has not received this play ill', and be encouraged to pursue his career as a dramatist? *The Ambitious Stepmother* provided some half-dozen good acting parts for the talented Lincoln's Inn company. The dialogue, though maintained throughout at a too uniformly hectic level, is expressed in fluent and clear verse. Above all, the play provided various theatrically effective scenes. The contentions in the Persian royal palace were conducted against a background of oriental pomp. The festival in the temple of the sun-god had its spectacular solemnity enhanced by the singing of the fine hymn, 'Hail, light, that doubly glads our sphere', composed by Rowe's friend, William Shippen. In striking contrast was the night scene where Cleone with her dark lantern steals her way to the imprisoned Artaxerxes and Memnon, to become the first of the holocaust with which the play closes.

For his second play, *Tamerlane*, Rowe again chose an oriental theme. Probably, like Charles Saunders, author of *Tamerlane the Great* (1681), he could have declared, 'I never heard of any play on the same subject until my own was acted.' In any case his play is of so completely a different pattern from Marlowe's *Tamburlaine* that comparison between them would be futile. With a violent perversion of historical fact Rowe presented the Scythian conqueror as the prototype of the ideal sovereign, William III. As he declared in his dedicatory letter to the Duke of Devonshire:

There are many features . . . in that great man's life not unlike his Majesty. His courage, his piety, his moderation, his justice, and his fatherly love of his people, but, above all, his hate of tyranny and oppression, and his zealous care for the common good of mankind, carry a large resemblance of him.

A similar note is struck in the prologue:

Our author makes a pious Prince his theme.

. . . .

Safe under him his happy people sate,
And griev'd at distance for their neighbours' fate.

Whilst with success a Turkish Monarch crown'd,
Like spreading flame deform'd the nations round:
With sword and fire he forc'd his impious way
To lawless pow'r, and universal sway.

If Tamerlane typified William III, the implication was
evident that Bajazet stood for the imperialistic Louis
XIV. The action takes place throughout within or
before Tamerlane's camp in Galatia, where battle is
about to be joined between him and Bajazet. His opening speech proclaims him a soldier only by necessity for
righteous ends.

O thou fell monster, war! that in a moment
Lay'st waste the noblest part of the creation,
The boast and master piece of the Great Maker,
That wears in vain th' impression of his image,
Unprivileged from thee.

When the contest, completely off the stage between
Acts I and II, goes in his favour, he takes no personal
pride in victory:

Can we call conquest ours?
Shall man, this pigmy, with a giant's pride,
Vaunt of himself and say 'thus have I done this'?
Oh! vain pretence to greatness! Like the moon
We borrow all the brightness which we boast,
Dark in ourselves and useless.

.   .   .   .

If I boast of aught,
Be it to have been Heaven's happy instrument,
The means of good to all my fellow creatures.
This is a King's best praise.

Bajazet, brought in chains before him, defies him as a
'preaching dervish' and proclaims his own megalo-
maniac conception of sovereignty:

Can a King want a cause when empire bids
Go on? what is he born for but ambition?
It is his hunger, 'tis his call of nature,
The noble appetite which will be satisfy'd,
And, like the food of Gods, make him immortal.

Yet Tamerlane magnanimously frees him from his
chains and restores to him his captive Queen Arpasia,
and her attendant Haly. So great is his religious tolerance that he, a disciple of Mahomet, takes into his
council the Christian Italian Prince Axalla, thus in-
flaming the wrath of a fanatical dervish. In the scene
between them Rowe reaches one of his higher flights
in the skilful use of argumentative and reflective
dialogue.

> *Tam.* Thou nam'st a man beyond a monk's discerning,
> Virtuous and great, a warrior and a Prince.
> *Der.* He is a Christian; there our law condemns him,
> Altho' he were even all thou speak'st, and more.
> *Tam.* 'Tis false: no law divine condemns the virtuous
> For differing from the rules your schools devise.
> Look round, how Providence bestows alike
> Sunshine and rain, to bless the fruitful year,
> On different nations, all of different faiths;
> And (tho' by several names and titles worship'd)
> Heav'n takes the various tribute of their praise;
> Since all agree to own, at least to mean,
> One best, one greatest, only Lord of all.

The dervish then delivers what he claims to be Mahomet's command to Tamerlane.

> Go on, and wheresoe'er thy arms shall prosper,
> Plant there the Prophet's name; with sword and fire
> Drive out all other faiths, and let the world
> Confess him only.
> *Tam.*   Had he but commanded

My sword to conquer all, to make the world
Know but one Lord, the task were not so hard.

.   .   .   .

But to subdue th' unconquerable mind,
To make one reason have the same effect
Upon all apprehensions; to force this
Or this man just to think as thou and I do:
Impossible! unless souls were alike
In all, which differ now like human faces.

Unable to prevail by argument, the dervish attempts
to stab Tamerlane with a concealed dagger which he
wrests from the assassin's grasp. Even this outrage the
conqueror forgives. But the dervish, unappeased, finds
an ally in the Tartar general Omar who has supported
Tamerlane in his rise to power but who is now enraged
with him because the conqueror has debarred him from
having as a prize of victory Bajazet's daughter, Selima.
She has given her love to the Italian commander Axalla.
Omar, with his soldiery, arrests them both, and Bajazet,
furious with Selima for giving the preference to a
Christian wooer, attempts to kill her, but she is saved
by the arrival of Tamerlane with Axalla, who has
escaped in the disguise of a slave.

Another pair of lovers meet a more tragic doom.
Bajazet, before his overthrow, had forced as a bride into
his harem the beautiful Greek maiden, Arpasia, who
had been contracted to her countryman of royal lineage,
Moneses. He appeals to Tamerlane to undo the wrong.
But Tamerlane, in his role of idealist, upholds the
sanctity of marriage—even to Bajazet.

Unhappy, royal youth, why dost thou ask
What honour must deny? Ha! is she not
His wife, whom he has wedded, whom enjoy'd?
And would'st thou have my partial friendship break

> The holy knot which, ty'd once, all mankind
> Agree to hold sacred and indissolvable?

To Arpasia he can only offer pity which she disdains:

> Think, I am born a Greek, nor doubt my virtue.
> A Greek, from whose fam'd ancestors of old
> Rome drew the patterns of her boasted heroes.
> They must be mighty evils that can vanquish
> A Spartan courage and a Christian faith.

Mighty evils soon follow to test her brave words. Bajazet's mutes enter with a bowstring for Moneses. As they
struggle with him she cries:

> I have a thousand, thousand things to utter,
> A thousand more to hear yet. Barbarous villains!
> Give me a minute, Speak to me, Moneses.
> *Mon.* Speak to thee? 'Tis the business of my life,
> 'Tis all the use I have for vital air.
> .   .   .   .
>   Only death,
> And the last night can shut out my Arpasia.

And as he is strangled she sinks in a fatal swoon.

In its command of effective, though often too long-
spun-out, dialogue *Tamerlane* is at least on a par with
The Ambitious Stepmother. But its scenes are less impressive
theatrically, and the contrast is too crude between the
high-souled hero, Tamerlane, and the human monster
Bajazet. Yet its implicit political allusion secured it a
half-century of popularity. First produced at the Lincoln's Inn Theatre towards the end of 1701, it was
printed in quarto in this and the next two years. It was
acted at various London playhouses, usually on 4 November, William III's birthday, till 1749[1] and in Dublin on
the same date till 1750.

[1] See the list in Nicoll, *Early Eighteenth Century Drama*, pp. 351-2.

With his next play, *The Fair Penitent,* Rowe shifted the scene from the Orient to Genoa and replaced royal personages with those of lower rank. As the prologue declared:

> Long has the fate of kings and empires been
> The common bus'ness of the tragic scene,
> As if misfortune made the throne her seat,
> And none could be unhappy but the great.
>
> .   .   .   .
>
> Stories like these with wonder we may hear,
> But far remote, and in a higher sphere,
> We ne'er can pity what we ne'er can share.
>
> .   .   .   .
>
> Therefore an humbler theme our author chose,
> A melancholy tale of private woes:
> No princes here lost royalty bemoan,
> But you shall meet with sorrows like your own.

Rowe here flatters the middle-class element in his audience, for his *dramatis personae* are of noble status, more highly placed than those in Massinger's and Field's *The Fatal Dowry* to which he was partly indebted, though he developed the plot on lines of his own.

Sciolto, a Genoese nobleman, had taken the place of the young Lord Altamont's father, who had died in exile, thrust out by his ungrateful State. Sciolto, when the play opens, is about to crown his benefactions by giving his beloved daughter Calista in marriage to Altamont. Trouble, however, mars the wooer's joy:

> When at your intercession,
> Last night Calista yielded to my happiness,
> Just e'er we parted, as I sealed my vows
> With rapture on her lips, I found her cold
> As a dead lover's statue on his tomb.

Calista had secretly given her heart to a rival suitor,

Lothario, an enemy of Altamont, and had let him seduce her. But to her entreaties that he should atone by marrying her he had turned a deaf ear. A letter that she sends to Lothario telling that through his cruelty and her father's insistence she has given her hand to Altamont, and asking for a last meeting between them, falls by accident into the hands of Altamont's friend Horatio, who thus learns her guilty secret. He is the husband of Altamont's sister, Lavinia, and their perfect union is the effective contrast to her brother's frustrated hopes. She seeks to share his grief, but for once in vain:

> *Hor.* Seek not to know what I would hide from all,
> But most from thee. I never knew a pleasure,
> Aught that was joyful, fortunate, or good,
> But straight I ran to bless thee with the tidings,
> And laid up all my happiness with thee.
> But wherefore, wherefore should I give thee pain?
> Then spare me, I conjure thee, ask no further.

Horatio determines to visit Calista and give her warning for the future. But she spurns him:

> *Cal.* Then all the boasted office of thy friendship
> Was but to tell Calista what a wretch she is:
> Alas what needed that?
> *Hor.*   Or rather say
> I came to tell her how she might be happy,
> To soothe the secret anguish of her soul,
> To comfort that fair mourner, that forlorn one,
> And teach her steps to know the paths of peace.
> *Cal.* Say then to whom this paradise is known,
> Where lies the blissful region? Mark my way to it,
> For oh! 'tis sure I long to be at rest.
> *Hor.* Then to be good is to be happy. Angels
> Are happier than mankind because they are better.

It is one of Rowe's most striking epigrams, but even

when Horatio tells her that popular talk couples her
name with Lothario's, and when he shows her own
letter to her, she declares it forged. When Altamont
enters she denounces Horatio as her slanderer till he is
forced to reveal to her husband that she has been

Dishonoured by the man you hate—Lothario.

Altamont strikes him and they fight till Lavinia runs
between their swords and parts them. Soon his sword is
again drawn to better purpose. He surprises Lothario
and Calista in a last assignation and in a duel kills his
wife's betrayer. In desperation she seizes Lothario's
sword wherewith to kill herself, but Altamont wrests it
from her, and he also stays the uplifted arm of Sciolto
against his daughter. But she cries:

Yes! yes, my father, I applaud thy justice,
Strike home, and I will bless thee for the blow;
Be merciful, and free me from my pain.

Sciolto recoils for the time from a rash revenge, but
he visits his daughter by night in a room hung with
black, with Lothario's body on a bier on one side and
a table with a skull and other bones, a book, and a lamp
on the other. These grisly trappings and a song invoking
midnight phantoms are ominous of further woe to come.
Sciolto offers his daughter a dagger, but as she lifts it
against herself he stays her arm.

A moment—give me yet a moment's space,
The stern, the rigid judge has been obliged:
Now nature and the father claim their turns.
.   .   .   .
Thou art my daughter still.
Cal.   For that kind word
Then let me fall thus humbly to the earth,
Weep on your feet and bless you for this goodness.

As Sciolto goes forth Altamont enters, as she thinks, to
urge the wrongs she has done him. But with him too
feeling has conquered, and 'fondness has prevailed upon
revenge'.

Again Calista succumbs:

> O, Altamont, 'tis hard for souls like mine,
> Haughty and fierce, to yield they have done amiss.
> But oh! behold my proud, disdainful heart
> Bends to thy gentler virtue,

But repentance cannot now halt catastrophe. Horatio
rushes in to announce that Sciolto has been attacked by
Lothario's revengeful faction and is dying. At the news
Calista, crying,

> Rest, thou world,
> This parricide shall be thy plague no more,
> Thus, thus, I set thee free,

stabs herself. When Sciolto is borne in she begs his
blessing, which he gives:

> Rest in peace!
>
> . . . .
>
> And may'st thou find with Heaven the same forgiveness
> As with thy father here—Die and be happy!
> *Cal.* Celestial sounds! Peace dawns upon my soul,
> And ev'ry pain grows less—O gentle Altamont,
> Think not too hardly of me when I'm gone,
> But pity me!

She dies with her eyes fixed on him as 'their last dear
object', and Sciolto with his latest breath blesses him for
his filial piety.

The Fair Penitent, produced at Lincoln's Inn Fields
Theatre in the early summer of 1703, with Mrs. Barry
in the titular part, had an even more enduring success
than *Tamerlane*. It was printed in the same year in quarto

and octavo and continued to be staged at Drury Lane, Covent Garden, and elsewhere for a long period. It was adapted into French, and Lothario has become proverbial as the equivalent of a rake. Yet he lacks the fascination of Richardson's Lovelace, who was apparently modelled on him. Still less can Calista compare with Clarissa. Her brazen persistence in denying her sin, and her delay of penitence till her last hour, forfeit our sympathy in an age less sentimental than the earlier eighteenth century. But the play still rightly attracts in other ways. Wedded love shines at its brightest in Horatio and Lavinia. The struggle between friendship and duty in Horatio, and between fatherly love and justice in Sciolto, is feelingly presented. In sententious and descriptive passages Rowe at times casts a spell.

Having succeeded with three tragedies containing neither a turn of humour nor a line of prose Rowe suddenly, in December 1704, tried his hand at a comedy in prose, *The Biter*. The title appears to have been a catchword at the time for a malicious deceiver. The scene is laid in Croydon during fair-time, and the play is for the most part on conventional lines—young lovers outwitting a senile amorist, a vain pursuing widow, and a bumpkin squire. But one character stands out as an original creation, Sir Timothy Tallapoy, who has made his fortune in the China trade in the East Indies and now 'makes himself be dress'd and serv'd exactly after the Chinese manner'. He calls the suitor favoured by his daughter 'a profane wretch, who sold his stock out of the old East India Company'. He tells him 'I am no friend to anything in the West, and am positively resolv'd, Sir, never to have anything to do with Westminster, West-Chester, West-Smithfield and the West-Indies. . . . I don't think there is a good moral man on this side the

Cape of Good Hope.' He calls himself a Mandarin and lards his talk with references to 'the most excellent Confucius' and 'the most glorious and wise city of Peking'. It is doubtful whether in 1704 a theatre audience would have been sufficiently versed in oriental happenings and customs to appreciate fully this burlesque, which might have appealed more to later, more sophisticated generations. Though Sir Timothy was acted by Betterton, and a quarto edition appeared in the year of the play's performance, it fell flat.

In 1705 Rowe returned to tragedy in the form of a pseudo-Homeric play, *Ulysses*. Once again, as in the Horatio–Lavinia episode in *The Fair Penitent*, he presents on the stage, as the prologue to *Ulysses* announces, a picture of constant wedded love. It had a special application while the war against France separated husbands and wives.

> To-night, in honour of the married life,
> Our author treats you with a virtuous wife:
> A lady, who for twenty years withstood
> The pressing instances of flesh and blood.
>   .   .   .   .   .   .
> Our English wives shall prove this story true.
> We have our chaste Penelopes who mourn
> Their widow'd beds and wait their lords' return.
> We have our heroes too who bravely bear,
> Far from their home, the dangers of the war.

But in going to 'old Homer' for a source Rowe was misguided. The noble simplicity of *The Odyssey* did not lend itself to the glittering embroidery of heroic drama. And as so often in Rowe's hands it is not the titular part which is the centre of interest. Ulysses, returning to Ithaca in disguise as the wanderer Æthon, poses, to test his wife, as a tool of Eurymachus, king of Samos, in his

wooing of the supposedly widowed Penelope. Eurymachus has one powerful card to play. Telemachus, the
son of Ulysses, is deeply enamoured of the Samian king's
daughter, Semanthe, whom he has just wedded, but
who looks back wistfully to her vow to be a virgin in the
goddess Cynthia's train. When Penelope proves deaf to
the plea of Eurymachus that they should be united in
marriage that same night, he at last forces her unwilling
consent by threatening the life of Telemachus. But before nightfall she declares to Aethon,

> One remedy alone is left to save me,
> And tell Eurymachus I find it—here.

She tries to stab herself, but Aethon prevents her and re-
enters as Ulysses 'magnificently armed and habited', to
hear her cry in amazement:

> Son of Laertes! King! my Lord! Ulysses!
>
> .   .   .   .
>
> O ecstasy!—But all that I can know
> Is that I wake and live, and thou art here.

But danger still threatens, and when Ulysses has revealed himself to Telemachus he bids him swear that he
will guard that night the entrance to the Queen's apartment against any of the 'cursed foreign tyrants'. This
leads to the best scene in the play where Eurymachus,
hastening to the joys of a bridal night, finds his way
barred by Telemachus, faithful to his oath, even against
the father of his beloved Semanthe. At last Eurymachus
draws his sword to force a passage, and as they fight he
falls wounded, to be found lying bloody and pale by
Semanthe, who kneels and pleads:

> Speak to me, say who,
> What cursed hand has done this dreadful deed,
> That with my cries I may call out for justice,

> Call on the Gods, and to my dear Telemachus
> For justice on my royal father's murderer.

To her amazement he mutters with his dying breath,

> It is Telemachus—on whom revenge me!

In vain the Prince tells how for her sake he held his hand until

> My royal father's honour and my own,
> The pledges of eternal fame or infamy,
> United urg'd, and call'd upon my sword.
> *Sem.* What is this vain, fantastic pageant, honour,
> This busy, angry thing that scatters discord
> Amongst the angry Princes of the earth,
> And sets the madding nations in an uproar?

She too will obey its command and, to avenge her father, will set the Samian arms to pour destruction on Ithaca. She departs crying, 'Detested be the name of love for ever!' But unforeseen entanglements occur. Another suitor, Antinous, betraying the trustful friendship of Telemachus, carries off Penelope. Crushed by this last blow the Prince throws himself on the ground and bids Semanthe

> Fly from the moan, the cry of the afflicted,
> From the complaining of a wounded spirit
> Lest my contagious griefs take hold on thee.

But the extremity of his anguish moves the heart of Semanthe:

> Tho' piety and honour urg'd me on,
> Tho' rage and grief had wrought me to distraction,
> I durst not, could not, would not, once accuse thee.

She confesses that she still loves him, though they must part for ever and she rejoin the haunts of the mountain-nymphs. And as a last proof of her devotion, she de-

nounces not him but Antinous as her father's murderer
to the Samian soldiers, and thus incites them against
the traitor who counts on despoiling Ulysses of both
his queen and his throne. The sage Mentor draws the
moral:

> Heav'n has approv'd the fraud of fond affection,
> The just deceit, a falsehood fair as truth,
> Since 'tis to that alone we owe your safety.

But the audience can scarcely have echoed this tribute
to Semanthe as *splendide mendax*. It is a highly equivocal
close to the tortuous story of the love between her and
Telemachus which on the stage goes far to 'steal the
show' from Ulysses and Penelope. Nor did this Greek
tragedy contain many of the reflective passages in which
Rowe had previously shown to advantage. Downes
speaks of it as having a 'successful run', but this did not
extend to more than seven performances in November
and December 1705.

From legendary Greece Rowe turned in 1707 in *The
Royal Convert* to legendary Britain, with 'the scene in
Kent, about twenty years after the first invasion of
Britain by the Saxons'. There is conflict between the
two races and their religions, Christianity and heathen
worship. But this only serves as a background to a
tragedy of rival fraternal loves. Aribert, younger brother
of the second Hengist, now King of Kent, had been
forced in his youth by his father to swear never to take
a Christian wife. But he had secretly married Ethelinda,
the daughter of a British chief, of that faith, and had
been converted by her:

> I heard her with an eloquence divine
> Reason of holy and mysterious truths:
> Of Heav'n's most righteous doom, of man's injustice;

> Of laws to curb the will, and bind the passions,
> Of life, of death, of immortality;
> Of gnashing fiends beneath, and pain eternal;
> Of starry thrones and endless joys above.

Hengist was betrothed to Rodogune, sister of the warrior Saxon Prince Offa, but on the wedding morning had forbidden the ceremony. He had found that Rodogune, haughty and cold to him, was in love with Aribert, to whom he now offers her as a bride, with partnership in his throne. Meanwhile Hengist, in this tangle of cross-loves, had by chance come upon Ethelinda in her hidden country retreat, become enamoured of her, and borne her to his castle, whence she appears to the at first incredulous Aribert:

> It cannot be.—No! 'tis illusion all.
> Some mimic phantom wears the lovely form,
> Has learnt the music of her voice to mock me.

The momentary joy of reunion is darkened by fears of what is to come, though Ethelinda bids Aribert find support in their religious creed.

> O lift thy eyes up to that holy pow'r,
> Whose wondrous truths and majesty divine
> Thy Ethelinda taught thee first to know:
> There fix thy faith and triumph o'er the world,
> For who can help, or who can save besides?

Soon the test comes. With the help of a confidant, Seofrid, Ethelinda escapes and is on the way to her brother in the British camp. Furious at her flight Hengist orders that Aribert shall be made a victim on the altar of the gods whom he has renounced. But as he is led in bonds to the altar the news comes that Offa with his 'crowding ensigns' and Rodogune with a 'chosen band' are attacking the palace, and Aribert is released. But

Ethelinda, on her way to the British camp, has been
captured by Saxon soldiers and is led in to be confronted
by the passionately jealous Rodogune, who sentences her
as a traitress to death. Amazed she kneels and pleads:

> Tho' now this moment to my eyes first known,
> To you I bend, to you I will appeal,
> And learn my crime from you.
> *Ari.*   Learn it from me.
> I am thy crime, 'tis Aribert destroys thee.

It is one of Rowe's most pregnantly forceful lines. Aribert, too, pleads in vain for her life.

> *Rod.* I swear she dies, my hated rival dies.
> *Ari.* Then I have only one request to make,
> Which sha' not be denied: to share one fate,
> And die with her I love.
>
> .   .   .   .
>
> *Rod.* Then take thy wish, and let both die together.
> Yes, I will tear thee out of my remembrance,
> And be at ease for ever.

Again Ethelinda seeks in her Christian creed consolation
for her husband's anguish.

> Why dost thou mourn when that good time is come
> When we shall meet no more, but live for ever
> In that dear place where no misfortunes come,
> Where age and want and sickness are not known,
> And where this wicked world shall cease from troubling?

Even when bound to the rack by the heathen priests,
under Rodogune's eyes, she is still constant. But there
comes a sudden Aristotelian περιπέτεια. Hengist, determined once more to carry off Ethelinda, is fatally
wounded by a soldier on guard, bids her be unbound,
and dies at her feet, bequeathing to Aribert his crown
and hers.

> She shall be thine.
> That—that's too much. The world has nothing in it
> Beyond to give—the next may have—I know not.

Rodogune, baffled and storming, departs with curses on the whole sex of men.

Her passions and Hengist's are throughout too uniformly volcanic, and the denouement is too abrupt. But in Ethelinda, a martyr in will, if not in deed, Rowe created a truly appealing figure, and the scenes in the heathen temple were theatrically effective. After seven performances at the King's Theatre in the Haymarket between November 1707 and January 1708 it had revivals in 1724 and 1739.

After an interval of about six years Rowe returned to the tragic stage with *Jane Shore*, produced at Drury Lane in February 1714. He announced in the prologue that the audience would be treated to 'a downright English feast', drawn from the homely 'recording ballads' of an earlier period and served up 'in imitation of Shakespeare's style'.

> In such an age immortal Shakespeare wrote,
> By no quaint rules nor hampering critics taught;
> With rough majestic force he mov'd the heart,
> And strength and nature made amends for art.
> Our humble author does his steps pursue,
> He owns he had the mighty bard in view;
> And in these scenes has made it more his care
> To rouse the passions than to charm the ear.

It cannot be said that in technique and versification *Jane Shore* has more of Shakespearian quality than Rowe's previous tragedies, nor has it a trace of his exemplar's humour. But in its historical background and in the figures of the Duke of Gloster, Hastings, and others the play trenches on the field of *Richard III*. It is

not, however, with the Duke's ruthless ambition but
with the fatal consequences of ill-starred and contending loves that Rowe is once again concerned. Jane, the
once highly-placed royal mistress, has fallen low. As
Gloster declares:

> Marry! the times are badly changed with her
> From Edward's days to these. Then all was jollity,
> Feasting and mirth, light wantonness and laughter,
> Piping and playing, minstrelsy and masquing,
> Till life fled from us like an idle dream.

Yet she is not without friends in her faithful neighbour,
Belmour, her confidante, Alicia, and the powerful Lord
Hastings. But Hastings has betrayed the love of Alicia
who turns on him with fury and vows revenge. As she
flies from him, his exclamation might apply to all the
women crossed in love in Rowe's tragedies:

> How fierce a fiend is passion! With what wildness,
> What tyranny untamed it reigns in women!
> Unhappy sex! whose easy yielding temper
> Gives way to ev'ry appetite alike;
> And love in their weak bosoms is a rage,
> As terrible as hate, and as destructive.

But it is not only in one sex that passion rules. Hastings
has thrown over Alicia for Jane. When she is deaf to his
vows he seeks to force her to his desires, but she is saved
by Dumont, whom Belmour has brought into her service, and who disarms Hastings.

As Gloster passes in procession Alicia seizes the oppor-
tunity for a double revenge. By a trick she substitutes for
the petition which Jane thinks she is presenting to the
Protector a paper warning him against Hastings, whom
'Shore's bewitching wife' draws to the side of King
Edward's sons. Gloster tempts Hastings to an outburst

against anyone 'whose damn'd ambition' would renew the horrors of the Civil War, but feigns approval and embraces him. To Jane he reveals his real feeling. He tells her that the State has resolved to set aside the 'unavailing infancy' of Edward's sons and to 'vest the sovereign rule in abler hands':

> This, though of great importance to the public,
> Hastings, for very peevishness and spleen,
> Does stubbornly oppose.
> *Jane.*   Does he? Does Hastings?
> *Glos.* Ay, Hastings.
> *Jane.* Reward him for the noble deed, just Heaven!

She continues to plead passionately the cause of injured innocence till the infuriated Protector bids two of his followers

>   turn the strumpet forth,
> Spurn her into the street; there let her perish,
> And rot upon a dunghill. Through the city
> See it proclaim'd that none, on pain of death,
> Presume to give her comfort, food, or harbour.

And knowing that Jane will not influence Hastings in his favour he arrests him at the next Council meeting for high treason, and orders his instant execution. But before this can take place Alicia rushes in frantically crying, 'I cannot speak, but I have murder'd thee.' In the reply of Hastings Rowe achieves one of his most pregnant sayings:

>   Oh! speak and leave me,
> For I have business would employ an age,
> And but a minute's time to get it done in.

There follows a scene of mutual forgiveness, embittered for Alicia by his solicitude that she should not let her hate wrong Jane.

His last thoughts hung on her,
And, as he parted, left a blessing for her,
Shall she be blest, and I be curst, for ever?

Thus when Jane, faint with hunger, begs at her door for
mercy she turns her ruthlessly away, and rushes off
raving, in pursuit of a vision of Hastings's headless trunk.
But unforeseen help comes to Jane. It was her husband,
Shore, who had served her as Dumont, and who now,
stripped of his disguise, raises her from the ground
and grants her the forgiveness with which she dies in
peace.

It may be questioned whether *Jane Shore* fully deserves its traditionally high rank among Rowe's plays.
The fortunes of the titular heroine are, during part of
the action, overshadowed by those of Alicia and Hastings. Jane's reckless defiance of Gloster on behalf of the
children of the King, to whom she had been not wife but
mistress, lacks plausibility. And though Penelope might
not recognize Ulysses after twenty years of war and
wandering the same excuse will not serve for Jane's
failure to see through Dumont's disguise. But the downfall of this royal mistress, with its legendary exaggera-
tion, had the same fascination for the eighteenth-century
playgoers as that of Nelson's Emma, similarly exaggerated, has had for cinema patrons in our own day.
The play, with a succession of leading actresses in the
name part, rivalled the success of *The Fair Penitent* and
was adapted for the French stage.

The success of *Jane Shore* prompted Rowe, in *Lady
Jane Gray* (as he spells her name), produced at Drury
Lane in April 1715, to dramatize a later, more fully
authentic, historical episode. Again there is the theme
of a disputed succession to the crown, but it now occu-
pies the foreground of the play and is complicated by

a bitter religious feud. Edward VI is dying, and there is rivalry as to his heir between the supporters of Lady Jane, the Protestant great-grand-daughter of Henry VII, and Mary, the Roman Catholic, his grand-daughter. Jane had been the young king's intimate companion.

> In every innocent delight they shared,
> They sung, and danc'd, and sat, and walk'd together,
> Nay, in the graver business of his youth,
> When books and learning call'd him from his sports,
> Ev'n there the princely maid was his companion.
> She left the shining Court to share his toil,
> To turn with him the grave historian's page,
> And taste the rapture of the poet's song.

So speaks the Duke of Northumberland, bent on marry-ing his son, Guilford Dudley, to Lady Jane, whom Edward had nominated as his successor. Northumber-land is seconded by the Duchess of Suffolk, Jane's mother:

> Daughter, receive this Lord as one whom I,
> Your father, and his own, ordain your husband.

The weeping girl's whole thoughts are with the dying Edward, but on Guilford's promise that he will forgo a bridegroom's right and will join in her mourning she consents to an immediate wedding. Jane has another lover in the Earl of Pembroke, hitherto Guilford's bosom friend, but who, thinking he has been out-manœuvred in his suit, denounces him as a betrayer. He confides his wrongs to Gardiner, Bishop of Win-chester, Mary's chief supporter, who bids him bide his time till 'these gospellers' have had their day and Mary mounts the throne. But the sight of Jane and Guilford following together the Lords of the Council to a meeting in the Tower wrings from Pembroke an impressively imaginative outburst:

> Methinks I go like our first wretched father,
> When from his blissful garden he was driven,
> Like me he went despairing, and, like me,
> Thus at the gate stopt short for one last view;
> Then with the cheerless partner of his woe,
> He turn'd him to the world that lay below:
> There for his Eden's happy plains beheld
> A barren, wild, uncomfortable field.
> He saw 'twas vain the ruin to deplore,
> He tried to give the sad remembrance o'er:
> The sad remembrance still return'd again,
> And his lost Paradise renew'd his pain.

The woman whom he has lost is in no less miserable case. Her mother, who has forced her into a sudden marriage, now greets her with the amazing news that she is to wear England's crown. The Lords of the Council, including her father and father-in-law, kneeling before her, salute her as 'Our liege, our sovereign, our lady, and our Queen'. She cannot credit it.

> What means this mock, this masquing show of greatness?
> Why do you hang these pageant glories on me,
> And dress me up in honours not my own?

Even when Northumberland paints in glowing colours the glories of her sovereign rule she turns weeping away.

> Is it, to be a Queen, to sit aloft
> In solemn, dull, uncomfortable state,
> The flatter'd idol of a servile Court?
> .   .   .   .   .   .
>   Is it not
> To live a life of care and, when I die,
> Have more to answer for before my Judge
> Than any of my subjects?

But at last she is persuaded to take unwillingly 'this fatal crown' to save England 'from tyranny and Rome'. All too soon Jane's fears are justified. The London crowd that had acclaimed her veers round to Mary's side.

Northumberland's army deserts and he is arrested as a traitor. Gardiner is appointed Chancellor and orders that Jane and Guilford be made prisoners in the Tower and kept apart.

> *Lady Jane.* Yet surely we shall meet again.
> *Guil.* Oh, where?
> *Lady Jane.* If not on earth, among yon golden stars,
> Where other suns arise on other earths,
> And happier beings rest on happier seats;
> When, with a reach enlarg'd, our souls shall view
> The great Creator's never-ceasing hand
> Pour forth new worlds to all eternity,
> And people the infinity of space.

It is a sublime vision, Miltonic in its range.

There is a momentary dawn of hope. During his brief tenure of power Guilford had regained Pembroke's friendship by helping to save his life. He makes repayment by procuring from Mary a pardon for Jane and her husband, which he announces to them joyfully. But on Gardiner's intervention this is made conditional on their renouncing their heresy. Else they must die that day: Guilford turns to Jane.

> By thee instructed, to the fatal block
> I bend my head with joy, and think it happiness
> To give my life a ransom for my faith.
>
> .   .   .   .
>
> *Lady Jane.* Oh, gloriously resolv'd! Heaven is my witness,
> My heart rejoices in thee more ev'n now,
> Thus constant as thou art, in death thus faithful,

Than when the holy priest first join'd our hands,
And knit the sacred knot of bridal love.

Even after Guilford's execution Gardiner pleads with
Jane to recant. But she is steadfast, and with farewell
words and gifts to her weeping attendants she mounts
the scaffold, praying to Heaven,

Raise up a monarch of the royal blood,
Brave, pious, equitable, wise, and good:
In thy due season let the hero come
To save the altars from the rage of Rome.

Thus the play ends as it began, on a defiantly Protestant
note. This doubtless appealed to the audience in 1715,
the year of the first Jacobite movement. But it did not
secure for *Lady Jane Gray*, though it was revived from
time to time, so conspicuous a success as *The Fair Penitent* or *Jane Shore*. Yet it can claim to be their superior
in dramatic technique. Instead of the interest being
dispersed it is concentrated on Lady Jane. As Ethelinda
in *The Royal Convert* had nobly embodied the martyr
in will, so in Jane Gray Rowe presented a strikingly
appealing picture of a martyr in deed, with the added
wistful charm of innocent girlhood.

With *Lady Jane Gray* Rowe's work for the stage came
to an end in 1715. It was the coping-stone to his sustained
dramatic achievement which, whatever its shortcomings,
by its idealism and breadth of range justified his appointment in the same year as Poet Laureate. Thenceforward he filled various official posts till his death on
6 December 1718, followed by burial in Westminster
Abbey.

II

GEORGE FARQUHAR

As Rowe forms a bridge between Restoration and eighteenth-century tragedy, George Farquhar acts as a similar link in the sphere of comedy. He was born in Londonderry in 1677, a younger son of a clerical father, Prebendary of Raphoe. George was educated at the Londonderry Grammar School, was probably a refugee during the siege of the city, April–July 1689, and volunteered for service under William III in the Battle of the Boyne, July 1690. In July 1694 he matriculated as a sizar in Trinity College, Dublin, and later won an exhibition. But he preferred reading Shakespeare, especially *Hamlet*, to the prescribed academic studies, and the Smock Alley Theatre was a powerful magnet to draw him outside the college precincts. He bade a final farewell to these, without a degree, at an unspecified date after February 1696. After a short spell as a printer's proof-reader he was accepted as an actor in the Smock Alley company by the manager, Joseph Astbury. This was largely owing to the good offices of the talented comedian, Robert Wilks, with whom Farquhar was to have a life-long connexion. His acting career, which began, to his surprise, with the title-role in *Othello*, ended early in 1697 when in the part of Guyomar in Dryden's *Indian Emperor* he accidentally severely wounded his fellow actor Price. Determined not to act again, he was advised by Wilks to try playwriting instead and to seek the judgement not of Dublin but of London, whither, with the proceeds of a benefit performance in his pocket, he soon set forth.

He arrived in the English capital with the double asset of a university education and practical stage experience. But he was ignorant of London life, and he wisely waited for more than a year and a half before testing public favour with a play. Meanwhile an almost epoch-making event had occurred, the publication in March 1698 of Jeremy Collier's broadside, *A Short View of the Immorality and Profaneness of the English Stage*, which was to have a far-reaching influence. But at first sight little of this appeared in Farquhar's first play, *Love and a Bottle*, produced at Drury Lane Theatre in December 1598. The chief character, George Roebuck, 'an Irish gentleman, of a wild roving temper', modelled on Farquhar himself, is a thorough-paced rake, not worthy of the devotion of Leanthe who, to be near him, dons a page's disguise and, after a confusing series of mistaken identities, becomes his bride. Yet it may be a concession to Collier when Leanthe says of him, 'Wild as winds, and unconfined as air. Yet I may reclaim him. . . . How charming would virtue look on him, whose behaviour can add a grace to the unseemliness of vice.' In her efforts at reforming Roebuck she has an ally in her 'sober and modest' brother Lovewell, whose merits are rewarded by union with Lucinda, 'a lady of considerable fortune'. Yet today none of the lovers has as much interest as Lyrick, the poet, in whom Farquhar personifies another aspect of himself. In Lyrick's dialogue with his landlady, Mrs. Bulfinch (Act III, sc. 2), the dramatist turns to adroit use meditations which he was later to embody in his *Discourse on Comedy*:

Lyr. There's more trouble in a play than you imagine, Madam.

Bul. There's more trouble in a lodger than you think, Mr. Lyrick.

Lyr. First, there's the decorum of time.

Bul. Which you never observe, for you keep the worst hours of any lodger in town.

Lyr. Then there's the exactness of characters—

Bul. And you have the most scandalous one I ever heard.

Lyr. Then there's laying the drama—

Bul. Then you foul my napkins and towels.

Lyr. Then there are preparations of incidents, working the passions, beauty of expression, closeness of plot, justness of place, turn of language, opening the catastrophe—

Bul. Then you wear out my sheets, burn my fire and candle, dirty my house, eat my meat, destroy my drink, wear out my furniture.

As I read this it carries me forward to exactly two centuries later, when in Pinero's *Trelawny of the Wells* Tom Wrench, occupying the garret in Mrs. Mossop's theatrical lodgings, discourses on the novel technique of the play on which he is engaged. In Act IV, Sc. 2 Lyrick, in more cynical vein, expounds further to Lovewell his views on the current stage productions:

Love. Well, you saw the new tragedy last night: how did it please you?

Lyr. Very well: it made me laugh heartily.

Love. What, laugh at a tragedy!

Lyr. I laugh to see the ladies cry; to see so many weep at the death of the fabulous hero, who wou'd but laugh if the poet that made 'em were hang'd.

. . . . . .

Love. But what relish have you of comedy?

Lyr. No satisfactory one—My curiosity is forestall'd by a foreknowledge of what shall happen. . . . As the catastrophe of all tragedies is death, so the end of comedies is marriage.

Love. And some think that the most tragical conclusion of the two.

For a new play by an unknown author *Love and a*

Bottle had a creditable success. It had the more-than-average run of nine nights, which secured for Farquhar his share of the takings from his two benefits at the third and sixth performances. Before writing his second comedy he did the theatre a service of a different kind. On a visit to the Mitre Tavern he was struck by hearing the voice of a girl reading Beaumont and Fletcher's *The Scornful Lady*. She was Anne Oldfield, aged sixteen, the niece of the hostess. Farquhar brought her to the notice of Vanbrugh who got Rich, the manager of Drury Lane, to give her a first engagement, the prelude to a brilliant stage career. He also persuaded Rich to bring over Wilks by the offer of a double salary from Dublin to London.

Farquhar had meanwhile been engaged upon transforming into a romance of London life a novel by Antoine Furetière, *Le Roman bourgeois*. It had been translated into English as *The City Romance*, which Farquhar proceeded to adapt, partly from his own experiences, as *Adventures of Covent Garden*, published in 1699. It was a series of amorous entanglements with disguises and mistakes of identity.[1] These helped to furnish Farquhar with incidents in his second play *The Constant Couple, or a Trip to the Jubilee*, which opened at Drury Lane on 28 November 1699. Neither title was happily chosen. Lady Lurewell, when an innocent girl of fifteen, had been seduced by a nameless roving Oxford undergraduate. In revenge she had sworn hostility to all the male sex and delights in fooling to the top of their bent the motley group of suitors who are paying court to her. Among them is Colonel Standard, 'brave and generous', who has been disbanded after the peace of Ryswick in 1697 and who talks of being off to Hungary. But he would be loyal to another

---

[1] For an analysis of its plot see Willard Connely's *The Young George Farquhar* (1949), pp. 68–72.

call by his country. 'Let but a single drum beat up for volunteers between Ludgate and Charing Cross, and I shall undoubtedly hear it at the walls of Buda.' He has sympathy with the plight of his disbanded brother officers: 'I met yesterday a broken lieutenant, he was ashamed to own that he wanted a dinner, but begged eighteenpence of me to buy a new sheath for his sword.' So also with his men: 'This very morning in Hyde Park, my brave regiment, a thousand men that looked like lions yesterday, were scattered, and looked as poor and simple as the herd of deer that grazed beside 'em.'

The crowning blow of his unemployment is that it discredits him as a suitor. As he tells Lady Lurewell, 'This commission, madam, was my passport to the fair; adding a nobleness to my passion, it stamped a value on my love; 'twas once the life of honour, but now its hearse, and with it must my love be buried.' So disinterested is his further avowal that Lady Lurewell murmurs to herself, 'Now were he any other creature but a man, I could love him.' The Colonel is so incensed by Sir Harry Wildair's boasts of favours from Lady Lurewell that he gives him an unaccepted challenge to a duel, and as a further test lends him a ring engraved with the words 'Love and Honour' to present to her. Her furious outburst at its sight leads to the revelation that she had given it as a pledge to her youthful lover, whom the Colonel now proclaims himself to have been, and embraces her, crying, 'the blest remembrance fires my soul with transport. I know the rest—you are the charming she, and I the happy man.' He excuses his long absence by enforced continental travel and military service abroad, and Lady Lurewell utters a recantation, 'then men are still most generous and brave'. But it is not a convincing example of a 'constant couple', and the

interest lies for us in Farquhar's first full-length portraiture of a professional soldier in Colonel Brandon.

The town fastened on the sub-title of the play, *A Trip
to the Jubilee*, though this, too, was a misnomer. Clincher
senior, an apprentice, who after inheriting his father's
estate aspires to be a beau, tells his country bumpkin
brother that he is going to the 1700 Jubilee in Rome;
it 'is the same thing with our Lord Mayor's day in the
City; there will be pageants and squibs, and raree-
shows, and all that'. He has provided himself with
pocket-pistols against bravoes, and a swimming-girdle in
case of shipwreck. But he never sets out on his trip. To
make his escape from a fictitious husband of Lady Lurewell to whom he is paying court he changes his coat, in
a scene based on *The Adventures of Covent Garden*, with
a porter, Tom Gerrard, whose wife accuses Clincher
of murder. When he is searched and the pistols are
found on him, a constable orders him off at once to
Newgate.

Tom, in his turn, is accused of murdering Clincher,
and when his brother, delighted at the prospect of becoming heir, offers him half-a-crown to confess, he
declares 'I did kill him.' But Clincher junior wants to be
satisfied that his senior is 'dead in law', and sends Tom
'to swear positively before a magistrate that you killed
him dead, that I may enter upon the estate without any
trouble'. Tom instead hastens to Newgate to get back
his coat from Clincher senior, who on his release re-
enters in a blanket, while his astonished junior cries
'A ghost! a ghost!—Send for the Dean and chapter
presently', and persists, 'were you ghost, or brother, or
devil, I will go to the Jubilee'. This prompts Colonel
Standard to a sarcastic attack on the Englishman abroad
which has not yet entirely lost its sting.

Go to the Jubilee! go to the bear-garden! The travel of such fools as you doubly injures our country; you expose our native follies, which ridicules us among strangers; and return fraught only with their vices, which you vend here for fashionable gallantry.

He bids the pair go back to their native plough and cart, while Sir Harry Wildair interposes, 'Let 'em alone, Colonel, their folly will be now diverting.' And diverting it still remains today, while the main action, of which Sir Harry is the central figure, has lost most of its appeal. He is designed as a more light-hearted counterpart of Roebuck in *Love and a Bottle*, who has shown bravery in the Flanders campaign, has a plentiful estate, 'a genteel and easy education', and turns 'all passions into gaiety of humour'. But he scarcely lives up to this flattering introduction. He has just come back from Paris, where he has been charmed by Lady Lurewell and has followed her to London. But till he can find out where she lives he asks the hypocritical Vizard, another of her suitors, to recommend him to another pretty mistress. Out of spite Vizard sends him to his cousin Angelica, a girl of sixteen, telling him that she is a harlot, and her mother, posing as Lady Darling, is a bawd. Sir Harry begins by offering Angelica twenty guineas, to be told that 'when you have learned more wit and manners you shall be welcome here again'; whereupon he rejoins, 'Egad, now I conceive there is a great deal of wit and manners in twenty guineas.' On a second visit his high-flown compliments provoke her to anger; which he thinks is only affected because her frowns are becoming.

Ang. Think what strict modesty should bear, then judge of my resentments.

Sir. Har. Strict modesty should bear! Why, faith, madam,

I believe the strictest modesty may bear fifty guineas, and I don't believe 'twill bear one farthing more.

Ang. What d'ye mean, sir?

Sir Har. Nay, madam, what do you mean? If you go to that, I think now fifty guineas is a very fine offer for your strict modesty, as you call it.

Angelica flounces out, but undaunted Sir Harry returns for a third visit, fortified by fifteen bumpers of burgundy. She calls her footmen to take hold of him, but when they scramble for coins which he throws among them, he pelts them out, and seizes her. In lofty tones she declares that innocence shines in her face and appeals to the 'something generous' in his soul. His retort has an echo of Falstaff's meditation on 'honour' on the field of Shrewsbury:

Can your virtue bespeak you a front row in the boxes? No; for the players can't live upon virtue. Can your virtue keep you a coach and six? No, no, your virtuous woman walks a-foot. Can your virtue hire you a pew in a church? Why, the very sexton will tell you, no. Can your virtue stake for you at picquet? No. Then what business has a woman with virtue? Come, come, madam, I offered you fifty guineas: there's a hundred.—The devil! Virtuous still!

When Angelica throws down and stamps upon the purse he offers, Sir Harry decides to make his market with her mother, but finds her equally resentful. In his defence he turns to quote from Vizard's letter, only to find that he has been completely befooled. Lady Darling offers him the choice of a duel with Vizard or a marriage with Angelica, what he calls a very pretty dilemma.

I must commit murder or commit matrimony. Which is best now? . . . If I kill my man, the law hangs me: if I marry my woman, I shall hang myself.—But, damn it! Cowards dare fight; I'll marry. That's the most daring action of the two.

For readers or playgoers today it needs more than a glib jest to wipe out the scandal of the scenes in which Sir Harry has made an ascending scale of bids for Angelica's favours; or be reconciled to her instant acceptance of his hand. But it was otherwise with the audience in Drury Lane. A brilliant company of actors headed by Wilks as Sir Harry Wildair and Mrs. Verbruggen as Lady Lurewell secured for the play a triumph. It was performed fifty-three times in its first season, and Farquhar was given four benefit nights. In the flush of his success he began, during a visit to Holland, a sequel called *Sir Harry Wildair*, which was produced at Drury Lane on 1 May 1701.

But, as has been previously noted with other of Farquhar's plays, the title is not entirely apt. Sir Harry does not appear on the stage till Act II, scene 2. The play opens with a dialogue between Colonel Standard and a new character, his brother Fireball, a Captain in the Navy who has just returned from an expedition to the Baltic. As he says himself, 'we seamen speak plain', and when the Colonel tells him that he has married a fine lady, Fireball draws an ironical picture of the type.

A fine lady can laugh at the death of her husband, and cry for the loss of her lap-dog. A fine lady is angry without a cause and pleas'd without a reason. A fine lady has the vapours all the morning and the cholic all the afternoon.... A fine lady goes to church for fashion's sake, and to the basset-table with devotion.

He adds that it is talk of the town that Lurewell is a coquette and Standard a cuckold.

Stan. She's an angel in herself, and a paradise to me.
Fire. She's an Eve in herself and a devil to you.
Stan. She's all truth, and the world a liar.

Here, perhaps influenced by Collier, Farquhar strikes a new note on the blessings of matrimony which blends not very harmoniously with other elements of the play. Stung by Fireball's further taunts Standard bribes his wife's waiting-woman to keep watch on her and report to him. When Lady Lurewell appears it is in forbidding guise. She abuses and strikes her servants, she throws back to a tailor the stays that he has made for her, though she cannot find a fault in them. When the Colonel greets her with 'Good morrow, dearest angel', she upbraids him for coming in with dirty feet. When he asks her to welcome four officers and men of honour whom he has invited to dinner, she retorts:

Officers and men of honour! That is, they will daub the stairs with their feet, stain all the rooms with their wine, talk bawdy to my woman, rail at the Parliament, then at one another, fall to cutting of throats, and break all my china.

Even when he tells her that his brother has come ashore and wishes to pay his respects to her, she declares that she will 'not be at leisure to entertain a person of his Wapping education'.

Yet surprisingly he is among the company with her in the next scene who have lost all their money at cards to Sir Harry, who now makes his entrance. And we are reminded of his least attractive aspect in *The Constant Couple* when he makes use of his winnings to offer to Lady Lurewell 'a French pocket book with some remarks upon the new way of making love', which she finds to be a bank bill for a hundred pounds. Among the losers at cards is a French marquis who is determined to have revenge. Sir Harry, soon after his wedding, had taken it into his head to go to Rome for the Jubilee. His wife had followed him as far as Montpellier, where she had fallen ill, and it was reported that she had died and been secretly buried. The Marquis shows Lurewell a picture of Angelica, which he vows she had let him have after he had seduced her, and also declares that his brother had lent her 'ten thousand livres' which Sir Harry must repay. It is repellent that Lurewell, now the wife of Standard, should rejoice in hearing what she believes to be the lapse of a woman who had posed as a model of virtue. She assails Sir Harry with the repeated question, Was his wife virtuous? His answer is an even more rapturous glorification of matrimony than that of Standard:

There was never such a pattern of unity. Her wants were still prevented by my supplies: my own heart whisper'd me her desires 'cause she herself was there. . . . We never felt the yoke of matrimony because our inclinations made us one: a power superior to the forms of wedlock.

If this is another concession to Collier it does not square with Sir Harry's Jubilee journey apart from his bride nor with his advances to Lurewell. But on Angelica's side it is justified. She had given out a report of her death in order to test her husband's fidelity and had in masculine dress assumed the part of his younger brother, Beau Banker, a scholar of Oxford where (the Trinity College, Dublin, dramatist unkindly suggests) he cannot have got his elegant dress nor learned to dance and speak French. In a further masquerade she appears as her own ghost to warn Lurewell against defaming her, and against betraying Standard's bed. Then she enters to Sir Harry as the spirit of his departed wife, and when he asks whether she is alive or dead, she cries 'Alive, alive', and embraces him.

Wild. Look ye, madam, I hate to converse so familiarly with spirits. Pray, keep your distance.

Ang. I am alive, indeed I am.
Wild. I don't believe a word on 't.

He moves away, whereupon Angelica weeps and declares she will die in earnest. Sir Harry bids her not be angry, as she has taken him unprovided. 'If I don't welcome you home with raptures more natural and more moving than all the plays in Christendom—I'll say no more.'

Among Lurewell's devotees Clincher senior reappears, no longer with 'the travelling maggot' in his head, but running stark mad after news and politics. He pumps Fireball about his Baltic expedition and asks what sort of a man is the 'pretty, dear, sweet, pretty King of Sweden', a strange description of the warrior, Charles XII. When Fireball takes him off to a tavern, he wants to drink a health to the Spanish Succession by which Louis XIV had secured the crown for his grandson Philip, and which Fireball refuses to toast as it means 'confusion to our trade, religion, and liberties'.

When Clincher has been made drunk he is carried to Lurewell's apartment, where Standard finds him and bids his wife compare the two pictures of this 'monkey' and himself. Again Standard speaks for the ideal of conjugal devotion:

I love you next to Heav'n, and by that Heav'n I swear the constant study of my days and nights have been to please my dearest wife. Your pleasures never met control from me, nor your desires a frown.

Whereupon Lurewell sobs, 'Generous, generous man!' Thus belatedly she qualifies to take a part in the quartet with her husband, Angelica, and Sir Harry, which ends the play with rules to keep husbands and wives happy, Angelica being deservedly acclaimed by Sir Harry as answering the definition of a good wife.

The Drury Lane audience may not, after its experience of Restoration comedy, have been sufficiently prepared for such edifying domestic precepts, or they may
have thought them unfitting to the lips of Wildair and
Lurewell. In this sequel Wilks and Mrs. Verbruggen
and many others of the accomplished company resumed
their former parts, with the addition of Colley Cibber
as the French marquis, but the play ran for only nine
nights.

The comparative failure of *Sir Harry Wildair* may have
prompted Farquhar to try a different venture by re-
calling Fletcher's popular play *The Wild Goose Chase* as
The Inconstant. He was attracted to it because the chief
character Mirabel was of the same type as Roebuck and
Wildair. Into this Farquhar grafted in a newly devised
Act V some experiences of the French Chevalier de
Chastillon as told by him in *Les Amours d'Armide*. Thus
Oriana finally wins the hand of Mirabel not, as in *The
Wild Goose Chase*, by posing as an Italian heiress, but by
rescuing him from a plot against his life. The two friends
of Oriana who gain their husbands by affecting to
treat them scornfully are replaced effectively by a new
character, Bisarre, who deals with her serious-minded
lover Duretete after the same fashion. Another new
character is Oriana's brother Dugard, anxious for her
welfare and her happiness in wedlock.

But neither Farquhar's ingenuity as an adapter nor
Wilks's performance as Mirabel could ensure success
for *The Inconstant*. A noisy claque interrupted the first
night's performance and the death of William III on
8 March 1702 plunged London into mourning. After
six nights the play had to be taken off. A very acid
comment on it is contained in a dialogue published on
14 April between Rambler and Sullen, two playgoers,

and Chagrin a critic.[1] Sullen says that he has heard that
a play is in rehearsal at Drury Lane by the author of
The Trip to the Jubilee:

Ramb. Pray, what is it?

Sull. I have not heard the name, but am told it is entirely
Fletcher's.

Ramb. 'Tis a sign his Muse is at an ebb, but if he alters it,
'tis a thousand to one he spoils it. Which of Fletcher's, pray?

Sull. *The Wild Goose Chase.*

Ramb. But why that? I have seen it acted with good
applause, and needed no alteration.

Sull. No matter for that; he vamps it up, and with some
wretched interpolations of his own passes it for new.

With his next venture Farquhar trusted mainly to his
own invention, though, as he acknowledged in his preface to *The Twin Rivals* when published, he was indebted to a fellow countryman, William Longueville,
treasurer of the Middle Temple, for the suggestion of
a plot turning upon the contest over an inheritance
between twin brothers, and some lines spoken by two
minor characters. When the play opens the elder
brother, Hermes Wouldbe, has been abroad five years
and the younger, Benjamin, a hunchback, is bankrupt.
As he laments to his boon-companion, the rake Richmore, 'My twin-brother! Ay 'twas his crowding me that
spoiled my shape, and his coming half an hour before
me that ruined my fortune.'

Now news comes that his father, a peer, has died.
Here is his opportunity: 'My father dead! and my elder
brother abroad! If necessity was the mother of invention,
she was never more pregnant than with me.' He will find
an instrument to dispossess his brother in Mrs. Man-

[1] In *A Comparison Between the Two Stages* (Drury Lane and Lincoln's
Inn Fields), reprinted and edited by S. B. Wells (1942).

drake, who combines the two vocations of a bawd and a midwife, and who was present at his birth. She arranges that a letter is to be delivered to the steward of the estate announcing the death of Hermes Wouldbe in a duel in Germany, and that a will is to be forged by her nephew, the lawyer Subtleman, leaving the title and seven thousand pounds a year to Benjamin. 'Go, get into possession, possession, I say; let us have but the estate to back the suit, and you'll find the law too strong for justice, I warrant you.' And thrown in with the estate will be the charming Constance, beloved of Hermes: 'She's engaged to marry no man but my lord Wouldbe's son and heir; now you being the person she's recoverable by law.' But this does not suit Benjamin. 'Marry her! No, no! She's contracted to him; 'twere injustice to rob a brother of his wife—an easier favour will satisfy me.'

If Farquhar wanted to show that it was his aim, as he says in his preface, to improve upon Collier's invective, he would have been better advised not to parade in the opening scenes of his play such a villainous gang. Even when Constance enters, walking in the Park with her sprightly friend Aurelia, their talk is at first of the unfortunate plight of Clelia (who never appears in person) who has been seduced by Richmore. They catch sight of his nephew, Captain Trueman, in whom Aurelia has found an admirer. 'He's a pretty fellow. But, then, he's a soldier, and must share his time with his mistress, Honour, in Flanders.' None the less he is to play an important part in the action.

The plot on Benjamin's behalf succeeds just long enough for him to show how unworthy he is of such good fortune. He holds a levee in his dressing-room of suitors to whom he makes hypocritical promises of securing their advancement. He keeps poor tradesmen waiting for their money, but pays at once 50 guineas, lost at cards, as a debt of honour. 'Your father thought otherwise', protests his steward, 'and was used to say that nothing was honourable but what was honest.'

But it is a short-lived triumph. Hermes Wouldbe arrives from abroad to hear the astonishing news that he is dead, and to see his brother carried across the stage in a chair with a number of attendant footmen. Hermes has one servant, with the generic Irish name of Teague made popular by Sir Robert Howard in his *The Committee* (1663). But with his intimate familiarity with different classes of Irishmen Farquhar has given a uniquely lifelike portrait. His Teague is at once simple and shrewd, a servant and yet 'a shentleman bred and born'; hungry for a good meal but with a native eloquence of speech, the birthright of one whose 'grandfader was an Irish poet'. He is the progenitor of the figures made familiar to us in our own day by Synge and Sean O'Casey.

He is too complex for Subtleman to appreciate when for a tavern dinner he procures him as a witness to the forged will. When Hermes visits Benjamin to claim the estate and is confronted with the will he insists on the two witnesses being produced. One of them, to his amazement, is Teague, who makes it clear that he has been a victim of bribery. Benjamin's case would be lost but for Mrs. Mandrake, who swears, falsely, that she was present as midwife when he was the first-born. As Hermes draws his sword, Subtleman accuses him of an assault upon the body of a peer, and hands him over to a squad of constables, who carry him off in custody to a meanly furnished sponging-house, which his fancy converts into the Tower. But his deliverance is swift. He is visited by Constance, who had already given proof of her fidelity, and by Trueman, who warns the constable in charge, 'you're drawn into a wrong cause, and it may prove your destruction if you don't change sides immediately'. He also borrows the coat, wig, and staff of the constable, who willingly assents, when he learns that his prisoner is a lord.

Thus disguised Trueman visits Benjamin to announce that his brother has hanged himself, because Constance would not come to him, while a letter in her name invites him to call on her that evening. Still in his disguise, and led out of his way by Teague, 'a vanderer ever since he was born', he arrives before Mrs. Mandrake's house in time to rescue Aurelia from a rape by Richmore. He draws from Richmore, who vaunts himself as a justice of the peace, an acknowledgement that a man who has made a woman with child and promised her marriage, is bound in law to fulfil this. Then throwing off his disguise he extracts from Richmore by the logic of his own exposition of the law a promise to make amends to Clelia, who still loves him. When Benjamin appears in answer to Constance's supposed invitation he finds himself rejected, and his brother's claim as the elder born finally certified by Mrs. Mandrake, under the threat of punishment for her wickedness. Then Aurelia, finding that her deliverer the 'honest constable' is no other than Trueman, with genteel blood in his veins, suggests that they should follow the good example set by their leaders, Hermes and Constance.

Once again Farquhar's hopes were to be disappointed. The *Twin Rivals* ran for only thirteen nights after its production at Drury Lane, 2 December 1702, and the galleries, on which he had chiefly relied for a middle-class audience, were only thinly filled. In the preface to the printed version of the play he sought to throw the blame for the play's comparative failure on the public. They resented as an innovation a comedy which substituted for old poetic licence the strictness of poetical justice. The ladies had been scared off beforehand by formidable stories of a midwife. Richmore had been identified with a particular person. Above all the play had been accused of transgressing the legitimate bounds of comedy, whose function, as Jonson had declared (though not consistently observing it himself), was 'to sport with human follies not with crimes'. To this objection Farquhar makes a conclusive answer.

'Tis said, I must own, that the business of comedy is chiefly to ridicule folly; and that the punishment of vice falls rather into the province of tragedy; but if there be a middle sort of wickedness, too high for the sock and too low for the buskin, is there any reason that it should go unpunished? What are more obnoxious to human society than the villainies exposed in this play, the frauds, plots and contrivances upon the fortunes of men, and the virtue of women? But the persons are too mean for the heroic; then what must we do with them? Why, they must of necessity drop into comedy.

These comments are of interest as illustrations of Farquhar's conception of his role as a dramatist, but the Drury Lane audience was doubtless largely influenced by less theoretical considerations. The villains, as already mentioned, monopolized the earlier scenes too long. Mrs. Mandrake (played by a man, William Bullock) made up as a bawd for what rumour had anticipated from her as a midwife. The fluctuations in the fortunes of the twin brothers were somewhat tortuously spun out. And with three heroines, including the invisible Clelia, sharing the love-interest, it became unduly entangled in the last act.

E

On the other hand, what are to us the most attractive features of the play, the life-like portraiture of Teague, the presentation of Trueman as the loyal and resourceful soldier, the idealism of the dialogue between Hermes, unrecognized, and the goldsmith Fairbank, counted for less than they do today. Of the deceased father of the twins Fairbank tells: 'The noble lord, the truly noble lord, held his estate, his honour, and his house, as if they were only lent upon the interest of doing good to others. He kept a porter, not to exclude, but serve, the poor.' And when he follows his patron's example in extending hospitality, Hermes declares, 'Surely, if Justice were an herald, she would give this tradesman a nobler coat of arms than my brother'. These are not the accents of the Caroline age and Court.

At the suggestion of Wilks Farquhar again tried his hand at adaptation. He remodelled *Les Carosses d'Orléans* by Jean de la Chapelle into a farcical comedy, *The Stage-Coach*. With the help of the French refugee playwright, Pierre Motteux, he arranged with Betterton for its production at Lincoln's Inn Fields towards the close of 1703. With Barton Booth and Thomas Doggett in the two chief parts, a captain and a country booby, it had a favourable reception and was frequently revived.[1]

But Farquhar now needed a more stable source of income than his uncertain earnings as a dramatist. Early in 1703 he had contracted an improvident marriage with Margaret Pennell, widow of an army officer, with two dependent children and ten years his senior. It was therefore a piece of good fortune that early in 1704 the Duke of Ormonde, Lord Lieutenant of Ireland,

[1] For a full account of the adaptation see W. Connely, op. cit. 211–19.

granted him a commission as Lieutenant of Grenadiers, the regiment of which the Earl of Orrery was Colonel. The Duke also attended a performance of *A Trip to the Jubilee* at the Smock Alley Theatre, in which Farquhar, during a visit to Dublin, played the part of Sir Harry Wildair. He failed as an actor but the performance, under Viceregal patronage, brought him the unprecedented sum of £100.

Though at first Farquhar's new military duties left him less leisure for playwriting they proved of benefit to him as a dramatist. He was stationed as a recruiting officer first at Lichfield and then at Shrewsbury. Hitherto, except in his boyhood, his experience had been of life in the two capitals, Dublin and London. He now for the first time came into close touch with the society of two important provincial towns and the neighbouring countryside, providing new types for his *dramatis personae*. He had already shown a marked predilection for military figures. He was now to view the life of the army from inside, and in his special office to become familiar with one of its seamier sides. This was to furnish the divertingly realistic scenes in his next play, *The Recruiting Officer*.

The play opens with Kite, drawn from Farquhar's sergeant, wheedling recruits into the service in Shrewsbury market-place and reporting to Captain Plume, modelled on Farquhar himself, that in a week he has secured five, including a lawyer whom Plume rejects because he can write and draw petitions. In a later scene Kite's methods of recruiting are vividly illustrated. He comes on with two yokels, Pearmain and Appletree, whom he has befuddled with drink, and asks them if they have ever seen the Queen's picture, to which they answer 'No, no, no'.

Kite. I wonder at that; I have two of 'em, set in gold, and as like her Majesty, God bless the mark!—See, here they are, set in gold.

Gives each a broad piece

Apple. The wonderful works of Nature!

Pear. What's this written about? Here's a posy, I believe —*Car-o-lus.* What's that, sergeant?

Kite. Oh, *Carolus!* Why, *Carolus* is Latin for Queen Anne, —that's all.

Pear. 'Tis a fine thing to be a scollard. Sergeant, will you part with this? I'll buy it on you, if it come within the compass of a crown.

Kite. A crown! Never talk of buying; 'tis the same thing among friends, you know; I'll present them to you; you shall give me as good a thing.

Thus the pair, without knowing it, have received their enlistment money and are presented by Kite to Plume as 'a couple of honest brave fellows that are willing to serve the Queen'. When they indignantly deny this, and declare they have nothing but the Queen's picture, Plume tells them the worth of the gold pieces and that they are fairly enlisted. But when Pearmain asks to be taken to the Mayor, Plume, to prevent the trick being exposed, pretends to be angry with Kite, beats him off the stage, and assures the pair, 'I came among you as an officer to list soldiers, not as a kidnapper to steal slaves.' He tells them that they are at liberty, and by flattering promises backed by a bribe wins the assent of Pearmain, from whom Appletree, though doubting, cannot bear to be separated. Never since Shakespeare had shown Falstaff with his ragged followers near Coventry had there been such a picture of the damnable misuse of the King's or the Queen's press.

It is not only the one sex with which Plume's smooth tongue prevails. A country girl, Rose, enters with her brother Bullock who sells corn. She has a basket of young and tender chickens which she is crying for sale. Plume offers to take the lot at a guinea, and when Rose protests that she cannot give change, he retorts, 'Indeed, indeed, but you can: my lodging is hard by, chicken, and we'll make change there.' The words are equivocal from one who has been a rake, but on Rose's own report all that he has asked for the chickens and his presents of lace and a snuff-box is 'to have my brother for a soldier, and two or three sweethearts that I have in the country; they shall all go with the Captain'.

The resourceful Kite has further irregular methods of recruiting. Disguised as an astrologer he beguiles a smith into enlisting by telling him that it is the decree of the stars that he will 'be made captain of the forges to the grand train of artillery'. Similarly a butcher is assured that he will be appointed surgeon-general of the whole army. Later, when three Justices of the Peace sit on the bench to carry out the provisions of the Mutiny and Impressment Acts it is Kite who presses the case for the Crown against the scruples of two of the Justices. The third, Mr. Balance, orders a man to be enlisted though he has a wife and five children, because he keeps a gun, and kills hares and partridges, and another, who works in the coal-pits, because he 'has no visible means of liveli-hood, for he works underground'.

Balance forms a link with the love-plot. His daughter Sylvia is in love with Plume and her father favours him till, by his son's death, Sylvia becomes heir to his estate and thus, in his view, suitable for a loftier match. Her cousin Melinda, already a lady of fortune, is playing fast and loose with her civilian admirer, Mr. Worthy, whose name betokens his character, and who is a friend of Plume. In a pique after a quarrel with Sylvia she sends a letter to Balance telling him that she has heard from Worthy that Plume has dishonourable designs upon his daughter. Balance, who has already sent Sylvia into the country, tears up the letter in presence of Worthy, who recognizes the hand of Melinda and picks up the pieces for further use. He has a rival for Melinda's favour in an affected coxcomb, Captain Brazen, whose manner of salutation to all and sundry is 'My dear, I am your servant and so forth'. As Worthy describes him, 'his impudence were a prodigy were not his ignorance proportionable'. He claims to know everybody and to have performed miracles of valour. When he asks Balance his name, and is told, 'very laconic, sir', he responds, 'Laconic! a very good name, truly; I have known several of the Laconics abroad.—Poor Jack Laconic! he was killed at the battle of Landon, in which battle I had two and twenty horses killed under me.' Brazen may embody some features from Farquhar's own observation but he makes the impression of a belated version of the classical *miles gloriosus*.

Further complications soon follow. In particular Sylvia dons masculine dress and offers herself as a recruit, under the name of Jack Wilful. Plume and Brazen compete for her till she declares, 'I will list with Captain Plume. I am a freeborn Englishman and will be a slave my own way.' This leads to a series of entanglements including her appearance before her father on the bench who is so provoked by her home thrusts that he calls to Plume, 'Captain, if you don't list him this minute, I'll leave the court.' It is only when he learns from his steward that Sylvia is missing, and that the white suit trimmed with silver belonging to her dead brother is not to be found, that he realizes the truth. He astonishes Plume by asking him to write the discharge of his young

gentleman soldier, and Sylvia is equally surprised when
Plume greets her, 'Now you are at liberty—I have discharged you.'

Sylv. Discharged me?
Bal. Yes, sir, and you must once more go home to your
father.
Sylv. My father! Then I am discovered. O sir (*kneeling*), I
expect no pardon.
Bal. No, no, child, your crime shall be your punishment.
Here, Captain, I deliver her over to the conjugal power for
her chastisement; since she will be a wife, be you a husband,
a very husband.

. . . .

Plume. Why then I have saved my legs and arms, and lost
my liberty.... Sir, my liberty, and hopes of being a general,
are much dearer to me than your twelve hundred pound
a year.—But to your love, madam, I resign my freedom, and
to your beauty my ambition: greater in obeying at your feet
than commanding at the head of an army.

Farquhar could not throw round Sylvia the idyllic
charm of Fletcher's love-lorn heroines masquerading as
youths, but he skilfully adapted the type to the conditions of his own period. Melinda goes through varying
moods till she consults the mock astrologer Kite, who
warns her, 'To-morrow morning you will be saluted by a
gentleman, who will come to take his leave of you, being
designed for travel.... If the gentleman travels he will
die abroad; and if he does you will die before he comes
home.' Melinda takes this to apply to Worthy, who,
with Plume, is hidden behind a screen. After some intricate business concerning the respective handwritings of
Melinda and her pert maid Lucy, Worthy proves to
Plume that it was Melinda who wrote the defamatory
letter to Balance. In repentant mood she confesses that

she has done her cousin an injury, and with Worthy she brings herself to square accounts: 'You have been barbarous to me, I have been cruel to you; put that and that together, and let one balance the other. Now if you will begin upon a new score . . . here's my hand, I'll use you as a gentleman should be.'

Yet one more trial awaits Worthy. The mischief-making Lucy, using a signature of Melinda, has made an appointment with Brazen to meet about half a mile out of town at the water-side, but she is to be masked lest she should be known by any of Worthy's friends. Brazen exultingly shows the signature to Plume who at once informs Worthy of Melinda's matrimonial intentions. In a fury Worthy dashes off to fight a duel with pistols, which Brazen declines as he is a foot-officer and never uses them. Lucy unmasks to stop the fray, and when Worthy cries 'Take her', Brazen retorts, 'The devil take me if I do'. Imperturbable to the last he invents reminiscences of an uncle of Balance who was governor of the Leeward Islands, and admits that he has not got a single recruit, whereupon Plume, resigning his commission, hands over to him the twenty that he has raised.

Disheartened by several failures to repeat the success of *The Trip to the Jubilee* Farquhar was so apprehensive of the fate of *The Recruiting Officer* that in an epilogue he promised to adapt some words to be sung to the Grenadier March,

for you'll all obey
Soft music's call, though you should damn his play.

His fears proved groundless. When the play was produced at Drury Lane on 8 April 1706, with Wilks and Cibber as Plume and Brazen, Richard Estcourt as Kite,

and Anne Oldfield as Sylvia, it scored a triumph, with
three benefit nights for the author. Lintot immediately
published it in book form, with Farquhar's dedication
'To all friends round the Wrekin', assuring them that it
was a comedy and not a libel.

Nevertheless Farquhar was still in financial straits.
He had returned from Shrewsbury to London, where he
lay ill, and found a fresh field for his military interest in
the composition of a jejune narrative poem *Barcelona* on
the capture of that town by the Earl of Peterborough.
Meanwhile a leading group of the Drury Lane company,
including Wilks and Anne Oldfield, had deserted Rich
in favour of Swiney, manager of the Haymarket Theatre.
The bizarre result was that both managers put on rival
performances of *The Recruiting Officer*. A more important
consequence was to follow. The faithful Wilks visited his
despondent friend and ordered him to write. 'Draw your
drama. I will call on you this day week to see it.' The
plot was outlined in due time, to the satisfaction of Wilks
and Swiney, and was filled in by the dramatist, working
at headlong speed, during the Christmas season 1706–7.
As Shrewsbury had furnished the scene and material of
The Recruiting Officer, so he drew them from Lichfield for
The Beaux' Stratagem. But it is surprising that except for
a French prisoner of war, Count Bellair, he introduces
no soldiers. The Lichfield figures hail from the city inn
or the county society. And the two beaux are interlopers
there, seeking to mend their broken fortunes. Aimwell is
brother to a lord and Archer is his boon companion.
After their own fashion they have made the best of their
opportunities.

Aim. We have lived justly, Archer; we can't say that we
have spent our fortunes but that we have enjoyed 'em.

Arch. Right! So much pleasure for so much money, we

have had our pennyworths; and had I millions, I would go
to the same market again.—O London, London!—Well, we
have had our share and let us be thankful.

Their stratagem takes the form of Aimwell posing as a
lord, with Archer as his footman. They put up at a Lichfield inn, of which the landlord, Boniface, is in league
with a gang of highwaymen. The unsuspecting Aimwell
entrusts him with a box containing their only assets
'somewhat above two hundred pound', and commands,
'Be sure you lay it where I may have it at a minute's
warning . . . and pray order your ostler to keep my
horses always saddled.' When Boniface repeats these
directions to his lively daughter Cherry, she at once
concludes that the guest is a highwayman, whereupon
her father adds, 'this box is some new purchased booty',
which they must get into their own hands by plying the
footman with drink and Cherry's endearments. 'I don't
think it lawful to harbour any rogues but my own.'

With Act II the scene passes to the country house of
Lady Bountiful, whose daughter Dorinda is having to
listen to her sister-in-law's Sunday morning impeach-
ment of her husband, Sullen. With a dowry of ten
thousand pounds she had a right to something better
than a silent sot as a mate and insufferable country
pleasures. As Sullen makes a brief appearance, calling
for a dram, his wife bursts out, 'I shall never ha' good
of the beast till I get him to town. London, dear London,
is the place for managing and breaking a husband.'
Meanwhile she is philandering with the French Count,
who is a prisoner of war.

Aimwell turns Sunday morning to his purpose by
going to the country church where 'the appearance of a
stranger draws as many gazers as a blazing star', and
where he can 'single out a beauty, rivet both my eyes to

hers'. The venture succeeds, for Dorinda is fascinated by
his bearing, 'no airs to set him off, no studied looks nor
artful posture—but nature did it all'. She tells Scrub,
Sullen's servant, to invite to drink a bottle of ale the
footman, who will disclose his master's identity. The
so-called footman has been winning the good graces of
Cherry, and Farquhar has written no more charming
dialogue than that in which Archer makes the girl
repeat the items of Love's catechism which he has
taught her, and from which she has learnt that 'your
discourse and your habit are contradictions and it would
be nonsense in me to believe you a footman any longer'.
So too when Archer as Scrub's guest entertains him and
afterwards the two ladies with fanciful reminiscences
and a song, Mrs. Sullen exclaims, 'The devil take him
for wearing that livery!' and confesses that she prefers
him to the Count. She arranges that her husband shall
be privy to a declaration of love to her by Bellair, which
she dismisses as merely an amusement on both sides.

In the mean time Aimwell at the inn has been in
company with two other counterfeit persons. One is
Gibbet, a highwayman, who has deposited his loot with
Cherry, and who is posing as a Captain in a marching
regiment. Taking Aimwell, on Boniface's assurance, to
be also on the road Gibbet confides to him that Captain
is only a good travelling name that stops a great many
foolish inquiries. His other conversationalist is Foigard,
chaplain to the captured French officers, who claims to
have been born in Brussels, and to be a subject of the
King of Spain, but whose speech betrays him to be Irish
and a subject of Queen Anne. Aimwell himself then
adds to the list of impostures by pretending to be seized
with a fit outside of Lady Bountiful's house, into which
he is carried to be treated with her hartshorn drops and

other remedies. Only Mrs. Sullen whispers to Dorinda, 'Love's his distemper, and you must be the physician.' To prevent his having a relapse in the air Lady Bountiful bids the ladies show him the house, especially the pictures. But he clings to Dorinda while Archer shows himself to Mrs. Sullen as a connoisseur of classical paintings and mistakes a picture of Venus as her portrait. He continues in the same rhapsodical strain when by an artifice he gains admission to Mrs. Sullen's bedchamber at night.

Mrs. Sull. In the name of wonder, whence came ye?
Arch. From the skies, madam. I'm a Jupiter in love, and you are my Alcmena.

When he seeks to carry her off she shrieks 'Thieves! thieves! murder!' at which Scrub rushes in echoing her cry, denouncing Archer as 'one of the rogues . . . they're broke into the house with fire and sword'. Gibbet, with two confederates, has made a raid, instructed by Boniface, on Lady Bountiful's treasures, and he now enters with a dark lantern and a pistol which is seized by Archer, who makes him a prisoner. The two other rogues, with swords drawn, drag in Lady Bountiful and Dorinda, but they are engaged by Aimwell, whom Cherry had warned of the raid, and who is seconded by Archer.

Farquhar has throughout shown Archer of inferior quality to Aimwell, but it is now that he stresses the difference. Archer still has designs on Mrs. Sullen's honour, as a recompense for his services to her, in which he has been wounded.

Was not this blood shed in your defence, and my life exposed for your protection? Look ye, madam, I'm none of your romantic fools, that fights giants and monsters for nothing; my valour is downright Swiss; I'm a soldier of fortune and must be paid.

She is saved by the opportune arrival of her brother, Sir Charles Freeman. Aimwell has brought Foigard to perform the marriage between himself and Dorinda, but he bids him retire, and confesses to her, 'Behold your lover and your proselyte, and judge of my passion by your conversion. I am all a lie, nor dare I give a fiction to your arms.' He tells her that he is brother to the man whose title he has usurped, and that he had come with a scandalous design to prey upon her fortune. Her reply is: 'Once I was proud, sir, of your wealth and title, but now am prouder that you want it; now I can show my love was justly levelled, and had no aim but love.' Yet she too dismisses Foigard and goes out, but soon returns with astonishing news.

This gentleman's honour obliged him to hide nothing from me; my justice engages me to conceal nothing from him. In short, sir, you are the person that you thought you counterfeited; you are the true Lord Viscount Aimwell, and I wish your lordship joy. Now, priest, you may be gone; if my lord is pleased now with the match, let his lordship marry me in the face of the whole world.

Sir Charles Freeman comes forward as witness that Aimwell's brother had died the day before he left London, and left him heir to his honour and estate. Aimwell is thus able to fulfil his bargain with Archer of letting him have half their winnings. He offers the choice of Dorinda or her ten thousand pounds, knowing that he will take the fortune.

It was a remarkable *tour de force* for Farquhar, lying on what was to be his death-bed, to keep the complicated factors of the plot moving to their solution throughout this last act. But its most surprising issue was held in reserve till the very end. It is probable that his own unfortunate domestic affairs had prompted Farquhar's reading of a more than sixty-year-old pamphlet—Milton's *The Doctrine and the Discipline of Divorce*. He there found it written of an ill-matched couple, 'Instead of being one flesh, they will be rather two carcases, chained unnaturally together, or, as it may happen, a living soul bound to a dead corpse.' These words are closely echoed in a wrangle between Sullen and his wife (Act III, Sc. 3), and later in the scene Mrs. Sullen expounds to Dorinda, in a paraphrase of Milton's argument, that 'natural hatred is a greater evil in marriage than the accident of adultery'. As she sums it up, 'Nature is the first lawgiver, and when she has set tempers opposite, not all the golden links of wedlock, nor iron manacles of the law can keep 'em fast.'[1]

But it needs the arrival of Sir Charles Freeman to find a way out for his sister. On hearing Sir Charles declare at dinner that minds as well as bodies must be united in matrimony, Sullen says, 'then 'tis plain we are two'.

> *Sir Char.* Why don't you part with her, Sir?
> *Sull.* Will you take her, Sir?
> *Sir Char.* With all my heart.
> *Sull.* You shall have her to-morrow morning, and a venison-pasty into the bargain.

Sir Charles reminds him of his promise next morning, when Sullen and his wife make a recital of the bars to their mutual contentment, and declare there is only one thing on which they can agree—to part. Thus for the first time in English drama was Milton's doctrine of

---

[1] For a fuller comparison of Farquhar's dialogue and Milton's prose, see W. Connely, op. cit., pp. 284–5.

divorce by consent seen in practice. And the epilogue makes it plain even to those who knew nothing of Milton's pleas:

> Both happy in their several states we find,
> Those parted by consent, and those conjoined.
> Consent, if mutual, saves the lawyer's fee,
> Consent is law enough to set you free.

Towards the end of January 1707 the play was finished. Lintot at once accepted it for publication and paid the needy author £30 in advance. Swiney arranged for its production at the Haymarket, with many of the former Drury Lane company headed by Wilks as Archer and Anne Oldfield as Mrs. Sullen. The first night was on 8th March, and Wilks, to whom Farquhar declared 'I owe chiefly the success of the play', hastened to his bedside to give him the news of its success. It was the start of a triumphant stage career during the following centuries with its climax in May 1949, when it was revived at the Phoenix Theatre with John Clements and Kay Hammond as principals.

But by the irony of fate Farquhar was to enjoy the fruits of his highest dramatic achievement for only less than two months. On 29 April, the date of the eleventh performance of *The Beaux' Stratagem*, and of an extra benefit performance, he died, and on 3 May was buried in St. Martin's-in-the-Fields. He was twenty-nine years of age, as was Christopher Marlowe when his life, too, came to a premature end. Nor was this the only parallel, if it be not pressed too closely, between the two dramatists. Each came to London with academic equipment to seek his fortune in the theatre. As the figure of Tamburlaine caught the public imagination in the late sixteenth century so did that of Sir Harry Wildair in the early eighteenth. Marlowe brought to tragedy new poetic enchantment, Farquhar to comedy a fresh spirit of geniality. Each was in the full maturity of his dramatic power and future promise when the 'fell sergeant', Death, decreed his final 'exit'.

III

SIR RICHARD STEELE

RICHARD STEELE was among the audience on the first night of *The Beaux' Stratagem* and suggested some cuts adopted in later performances. He must have had a fellow feeling with a dramatist with whom in his own earlier career he had so much in common. He was born in Dublin in March 1672, the son of an attorney who died when he was five years of age. His uncle by marriage, Henry Gascoigne, secretary to the Duke of Ormonde, took care of the youthful Richard, and through the Duke's influence obtained for him in 1684 a place on the foundation of the Charterhouse. Under the headmaster, Thomas Walker, he made progress, sometimes painful, in classical studies, and made the beginning of a lifelong friendship with Joseph Addison who entered the school in 1686, from which he proceeded to Queen's and afterwards Magdalen College, Oxford. Steele followed him in 1689 as a commoner at Christ Church, whence he migrated after two years to Merton as a postmaster. But to the high-spirited young Irishman the academic life offered no lasting attraction. In his own words, 'a drum passing by . . . I listed myself for a soldier'. He became a trooper in the Life Guards of the young Duke of Ormonde, grandson of his patron, in 1692 or 1693. On the death of Queen Mary on 28 December 1694 he wrote a poetic elegy *The Procession* which he dedicated to Lord Coutts, Colonel of the Coldstream Guards, who took him on to his personal staff and obtained for him an Ensign's commission in his own regiment. He soon rose to the rank of Captain. To the dashing Guardsman life in the capital had its temptations and pitfalls. He fought a duel, in which he nearly killed another officer, and had an illegitimate child. In repentant mood, while employed on guard at the Tower, he composed, first for his own use, a short treatise *The Christian Hero* of which the argument ran that 'no principles but those of religion are sufficient to make a great man'. In April 1701 he published it under his own name, and in July a second, amplified, edition was called for. But to his regimental comrades this edifying publication was an irritant and stirred them to mockery. 'From being reckoned no undelightful companion' Steele 'was soon reckoned a disagreeable fellow'. To regain their good will, 'as nothing can make the town so fond of a man as a successful play', he settled to try his hand at a comedy. Was there ever so singular a reason for a man setting out as a dramatist?

And it was odd that for a piece intended to enliven his character, as he put it, he should have chosen so lugubrious a title as *The Funeral, or Grief à-la-Mode*. Nor is the plot in itself either very original or convincing. Old Lord Brumpton has made a second marriage with a hard-hearted, intriguing young beauty with whom he is so infatuated that he lets her persuade him to disinherit in her favour his soldier son by his first wife, Lord Hardy. Lord Brumpton is believed to have died in a fit, but his steward Trusty has seen him wake from his 'lethargic slumber' and advises him to conceal himself so that he may watch the actions of his survivors. His supposed widow in her talk with her waiting-woman Tattleaid reveals herself as a heartless hypocrite, making in public a pretence of grief, but delighting in the anticipated joys of a rich widowhood. His son bears the injustice done him with dignity, hoping to repair his fortune with his sword, with 'a glorious war in an honest cause approaching'. Meanwhile he pays shy court to his father's ward, Lady Sharlot, while his more self-confident brother officer Campley lays strenuous siege to her high-spirited sister, Lady Harriot. She escapes with him from Lady Brumpton's sinister oversight, and astonishes a company of soldiers who, at Trusty's suggestion, have been ordered to seize Lord Brumpton's supposed corpse on its way to burial by leaping from the coffin when it is opened. Spectators in the theatre and readers of the play may well be equally mystified, and as a crowning surprise it now transpires that Lady Brumpton had made a secret marriage with her associate Cabinet six months before her wedding to Lord Brumpton, who suddenly reappears, and whose will is therefore invalid.

As the acute author of *A Comparison of the Two Stages*[1] was soon to point out, the plot has numerous weaknesses. But the merits of the play lie in its character-drawing, the comic realism of much of its dialogue, and its wholesome morality. As Farquhar had projected much of himself into his leading figures so Steele embodied in Lord Hardy his conception of himself, in idealized form. And Hardy's servant, Will Trim, 'the young man that attended him at Christ Church, Oxford, and followed him ever since' is evidently modelled on Steele's college scout, Will. Campley, though distinguished from Hardy by his vivacity and dominant spirit, has nothing in him of the Restoration rake. And the two gallants have their counterparts in the Ladies Sharlot and Harriot, contrasted but equally charming types of the womanhood which Steele was an adept in portraying.

But the outstanding attraction of the play is provided

[1] See p. 45 n., above.

by some of the incidental scenes. We see Sable, the undertaker, drilling his set of paid mourners.

... Put on your sad looks, and walk by me that I may sort you. Ha, you! a little more upon the dismal; this fellow has a good mortal look—place him near the corpse. ... Let's have no laughing now on any provocation. Look yonder, that hale, well-looking puppy. ... Did not I give you ten, then fifteen, now twenty shillings a week to be sorrowful? and the more I give you, I think, the gladder you are.

And when he finds that Lord Brumpton is still alive he threatens to reveal the secret unless he gets the whole money he was to have been paid for burying him.

When Lady Brumpton's scandalmongering friends come to condole with her she goes through the pretence of taking her waiting-woman for his ghost.

Lady B. Nay, my dear, dear lord, why do you look so pale, so ghastly at me? Wottoo, wottoo, fright thy own trembling, shivery wife?—

Tat. Nay, good madam, be comforted.

Lady B. Thou shalt not have me. (*pushes Tat.*)

Tat. Nay, good madam, 'tis I, 'tis I, your ladyship's own woman—'tis I, madam, that dress you and talk to you, and tell you all that's done in the house every day; 'tis I—

Lady B. Is it then possible? Is it then possible that I am left? Speak to me not—hold me not. ... Oh me! Alas! Alas! Oh! Oh. I swoon—I expire.

Steele is drawing on his own military experience when Hardy and Campley review the ragged fellows whom Trim has got together for the raid on the coffin. They are mostly old soldiers, one of whom, Matchlock, had saved Hardy's life in the battle of 'Steinkirk', but who had been whipped from constable to constable in coming from Cornwall to enlist.

Camp. But what pretence had they for using you so ill?

Match. I was found guilty of being poor.

Camp. Poor devil!

Lord H. Timothy Ragg! O Ragg, I thought when I gave you your discharge, just afore the peace, we should never have had you again. How came you to list now?

Ragg. To pull down the French king.

Lord H. Bravely resolved! But pull your shirt into your breeches in the meantime.

Similarly with Tatter, Clump, and Bumpkin, till Hardy declares, 'Well, I've seen enough of 'em.'

There is more of a burlesque touch here in peace-time than in the kindred scene in *The Recruiting Officer*[1] five years later, when the War of the Spanish Succession was in full blast.

Rich staged *The Funeral* towards the close of 1701. In his anxiety about its reception Steele arranged for a number of men from his regiment to be present as a *claque* on its first night. As he confessed in the closing couplet of his prologue

He knows his numerous friends; nay, knows they'll show it.
And for the fellow soldier, save the poet.

But his fears proved groundless. With Cibber as Hardy, Wilks as Campley, Pinkethman as Trim, and Anne Oldfield as Lady Sharlot, the play caught the taste of the town. It also secured the entry of 'his name, to be provided for in the last table-book' of William III, but the death of William in March 1702 disappointed his hopes. It was another disappointment that after the outbreak of war in the following May he was moved as Captain of a company from London to Landguard Fort, opposite Harwich. Even here creditors pursued him, and in the attempt to satisfy them he obtained from

[1] See pp. 51–52, above.

Rich an advance of £72 for a comedy, *The Election of Gotham*, of which nothing further is known. This was followed by *The Lying Lover, or The Ladies' Friendship* which was produced at Drury Lane on 2 December 1703. The play is adapted from Corneille's *Le Menteur* and follows it, often very closely, to Act IV, scene iii.[1] Young Bookwit has cast aside his Oxford gown and donned a soldier's uniform, the easier to win his way to female hearts. As he tells his friend Latine, who is posing as his footman, 'The name of soldier bids you better welcome. 'Tis valour and feats done in the field a man should be cried up for; nor is't so hard to achieve.' 'The fame of it, you mean', retorts Latine. When they introduce themselves to two ladies, Penelope and Victoria, in St. James's Park, Bookwit at once lays siege to the former with imaginary tales of his martial exploits. When they have departed he excites the jealousy of Lovemore, who has been for two years a suitor to Penelope, by further imaginary accounts of a magnificent water gala which he arranged in her honour.

Latine warns him that this 'may prove dangerous sport', but Bookwit has his answer ready in words of Steele's own mint.

Hush, hush, call it not lying. . . . My father has cramped me in a college while all the world has been in action. Then as to my lying to my mistress 'tis but what all the lovers upon earth do. Call it not then by that coarse name, a lie. 'Tis wit, 'tis fable, allegory, fiction, hyperbole—or be it what you call it, the world's made up almost of nothing else.

The first result of Bookwit's fabrications is that Lovemore accuses the bewildered Penelope of being out all night on the water with him, entertained with sym-

[1] In notes to the Mermaid edition of Steele's plays (1926) G. A. Aitken indicates the passages nearest to the French original.

phonies of music and sumptuous dishes. He flings away
from her crying, 'I'll print on thy favourite in his heart's
blood my revenge.' Jealousy also arises between
Penelope and Victoria, and before a further meeting
with Bookwit, each, under a pretence of giving friendly
help, spoils the other's appearance.

Vict. But indeed, my dear, you shan't go with your hood
so; it makes you look abominably with your head so forward. There (*displacing the hood*), that's something. You had
a fearful, silly, blushing look: now you command all hearts.

.   .   .   .

Pen. But alas, madam, who patched you to-day? Let me
see. It is the hardest thing in dress—I may say, without
vanity, I know a little of it. That so low on the cheek pulps
the flesh too much. Hold still, my dear, I'll place it just by
your eye—Now she downright squints. (*Aside.*)

And so forth, in an unusually diverting scene. But
after various complications things grow more serious.
Lovemore and Bookwit meet at midnight in Covent
Garden and they have a duel in which the former falls
and is left for dead. Bookwit is arrested by the watch
under the command of a self-important constable and is
lodged with Latine in Newgate. The scenes here are of
Steele's invention. Among the prisoners waiting to be
hanged is Storm, a highwayman, with his accomplice
Faggot. Bookwit salutes them understandingly. 'Your
spirits could not stoop to barter on the 'change, to sneer
in courts, to lie, to flatter, or to creep for bread. You
therefore chose rather to prey like lions than betray like
crocodiles, or fawn like dogs.'

Steele, in the vain hope of getting rich quickly, had
made some payments to an alchemist. He now presents
one of such practitioners, a Mr. Charcoal, among the
Newgate prisoners, who, 'having found out the

melioration of metals' which the ignorant call coining, is to meet his fate on Friday next. He apologizes to Bookwit: 'I'm very unhappy our acquaintance is to be short. I'm very sorry your business is not over, sir, that, if it must be, we might go together.'

Steele was ill inspired when in Act V for his racy prose he mainly substituted mediocre blank verse. Bookwit, still in Newgate, is distraught with the reflection on what he has done.

> I cannot bear the rushing of new thoughts;
> Fancy expands my senses to distraction,
> And my soul stretches to that boundless space
> To which I've sent my wretched, wretched friend.

When Latine assures him, 'Your honour was engaged', Bookwit, reverting to prose, becomes the mouthpiece of Steele's denunciation of the duelling of which he had had one bitter experience. 'Honour! The horrid application of that sacred word to a revenge against friendship, law and reason is a damned last shift of the damned envious foe of the human race.'

The soft pedal of the blank verse is again turned on when Bookwit, under a jailer's charge, is brought to Penelope's lodgings, and his old father is overcome by the sight. Bookwit exclaims:

> O best of fathers! Let me not see your tears,
> Don't double my afflictions by your woe—
> There's consolation when a friend laments us, but
> When a parent grieves, the anguish is too native,
> Too much our own to be called pity.

Herewith a new note of sentimentality is sounded in English comedy which was to furnish a distinctive designation for Steele's dramatic work. This becomes even more flagrant when the farcically indulgent jailer leads the others out to leave father and son alone, and the former, crying 'Oh, child, you've broke your father's heart', swoons. Thereupon Bookwit, running to him, exclaims:

He faints, he's cold, he's gone:
He's gone, and with his last breath called me parricide.
'You've broke your father's heart.' Oh, killing sound!
I'm all contagion; to pity me is death,
My griefs to all are mortal but myself.

With the re-entry of the rest of the company it is found that Old Bookwit has merely fainted, and now Latine, to save Bookwit, declares that it is by his hand that Lovemore has fallen. But Lovemore had recovered from his wound, and in the disguise of a serjeant-at-law had heard all that had passed. He now reveals himself. 'Lovemore still lives to adore your noble friendship, and begs a share in't.' It is more than friendship that he craves from Penelope who, knowing what proof he has given of his passion for her, now proclaims, 'My person and my mind are yours for ever.' And this leaves the prospect of a union between Bookwit and Victoria who promises to approve all the truth he tells her.

The play, as has been seen, throughout nearly the first four acts was a skilfully amusing adaptation and it had the advantage of being acted by most of the same company as the successful *The Funeral*. Yet it ran only six nights. The explanation is to be found in some of Steele's own words when *The Lying Lover* was published by Lintot in January 1704. In the dedication to the Duke of Ormonde he stated that 'the design of it is to banish out of conversation all entertainment which does not proceed from simplicity of mind, good nature, friendship and honour'. And more explicitly in the preface,

'I thought it would be an honest ambition to attempt a comedy which might be no improper entertainment in a Christian commonwealth'. He had overshot the mark with his Drury Lane audience. As he was to claim later, 'as a comic poet I have been a martyr and confessor for the Church: for this play was damned for its piety'.

It was not till 23 April 1705 that Steele's third play, *The Tender Husband, or The Accomplished Fools* was produced at Drury Lane. The first title covers the minor and less attractive part of the play. Clerimont's wife has not only adopted a domineering attitude but is ruining him by gambling. 'Oh the damned vice', cries her husband, voicing Steele's own view, 'that women can imagine all household care, regard to posterity, and fear of poverty, must be sacrificed to a game at cards!' After a tour on the Continent she has turned against her own country's ways. 'Abroad the people of quality go on so eternally, and still go on, and are gay and entertaining. In England discourse is made up of nothing but question and answer.' As the English are so saucy with their liberty, she'll have all her lower servants French, and when her spinet-master sings to her she wishes that he had given more into the French manner.

To test her further Clerimont encourages his own mistress, Fainlove, dressed as a pretty gentleman, to make amorous advances to her. Himself concealed, he sees her tempt Fainlove to kiss her lips, and then steps forth with sword drawn, bidding the invader of his bed and honour also draw. Mrs. Clerimont's alarm is all for 'the brave pretty creature', Fainlove, till her sex is revealed, when she cries, 'I'll be the death of her.' But it is for herself that she has to fear, as her husband again offers to draw his sword.

Mrs. Cler. Don't murder me impenitent; I'm wholly in your power as a criminal, but remember I have been so in a tender regard.

Cler. But how have you considered that regard?

Mrs. Cler. Is it possible you can forgive what you ensnared me into? . . . You laid that train, I'm sure, to alarm, not to betray my innocence. Mr. Clerimont, scorn such baseness. Therefore I kneel—I weep—I am convinced.

Cler. (*taking her up and embracing her*). Then kneel and weep no more, my fairest—my reconciled. Be so in a moment, for know I cannot (without wringing my own heart) give you the least compunction.

Once again, though less extravagantly than in *The Lying Lover*, sentimentality mars Steele's intended effect.

Against this has to be set the sparkling effervescence of what is technically the underplot, but which claims the major part of the dialogue. Its leading figure is a younger brother of Clerimont, a Captain, who has taken part in the victory of 'glorious Blenheim' in August 1704. With the aid of an astute lawyer, Pounce, brother of Fainlove, the Captain plans to make love to Biddy, niece of Tipkin, a Lombard Street banker, with a dowry of ten thousand pounds in money, five thousand in jewels, and a thousand in land a year. Unfortunately Pounce is already drawing up a marriage settlement between her and a country booby, Humphry Gubbin, son and heir of Sir Henry, and Biddy's cousin. But Pounce feels that a difficulty may be met and overcome. Humphry objects to marriage between cousins and has only been affianced to Biddy at the command of his tyrannical father. Pounce's first step, therefore, is to introduce him to Fainlove, with the tale that this supposed young gentleman has a sister, 'a prodigious fortune'.

Biddy herself sets suitors another problem. Isolated from society by a vigilant aunt, 'she has spent all her solitude', as Pounce warns Captain Clerimont, 'in reading romances; her head is full of shepherds, knights, flowery meads, groves and streams, so that if you talk like a man of this world to her, you do nothing'. The Captain assures him that 'I have been a great traveller in fairyland myself', and that the heroines of the fashionable novels are his intimate acquaintance.

It is torture to the heiress, as she complains to her aunt, that she has been christened Bridget. In the romances, as she truly declares, 'the heroine has always something soft and engaging in her name: something that gives us a notion of the sweetness of her beauty and behaviour; a name that glides through half-a-dozen tender syllables.' She protests against her aunt's idea that she should live comfortably, married to her cousin. When Pounce introduces in the Park the Captain with his arm in a scarf she is charmed by the elegance of his speech and his admiration of the landscape to which she responds in kind. She begs him to call her Parthenissa, the name of the heroine in Orrery's romance, but when he suggests that instead of her surname, Tipkin, he should put her in possession of Clerimont, she exclaims against his precipitancy.

O fie! Whither are you running? You know a lover should sigh in private and languish whole years before he reveals his passion; he should retire into some solitary grove, and make the woods and wild beasts his confidants. You should have told it to the echo half a year before you had discovered it, even to my handmaid.

Well may the Captain describe her to Pounce as 'a perfect Quixote in petticoats', who is ruled entirely by the precedents in romance. Pounce advises him to serenade her, but meanwhile his cause is being advanced by his rival Humphry who tells her that 'I thought it would be proper to see how I liked you, as not caring to buy a pig in a poke'. She treats him as a wild man, who has been caught in a forest, and had been suckled by a wolf. 'If thou hast yet learned the use of language, speak, monster.' He naturally takes her to be mad, and is delighted when she tells him that she hates him, as he doesn't care for her.

After the serenade Pounce brings in the Captain disguised as a painter to make a portrait of Biddy. He tells her that ladies may be drawn with three kinds of airs, the haughty, the mild, and the pensive, and that she seems most inclined to the last, delighting 'in the fall of waters, pastoral figures, or any rural view suitable to a fair lady who, with a delicate spleen, has retired from the world'.

Biddy. No; since there is room for fancy in a picture, I would be drawn like the Amazon Thalestris, with a spear in my hand, and a helmet on a table before me. At a distance behind let there be a dwarf, holding by the bridle a milk-white palfrey.

Captain. Madam, the thought is full of spirit, and if you please, there shall be a Cupid stealing away your helmet, to show that love should have a part in all gallant action.

Biddy. That circumstance may be very picturesque.

The Captain then tells of 'a late marriage between a young lady of great fortune and a younger brother of a good family', and beseeches Parthenissa to 'make the incident I feigned a real one'. The difficulty that she ought by the romance precedents to be seized by stealth is solved by her putting herself into the hands of Humphry, from whom the Captain is to carry her off, while Humphry astonishes everyone by announcing that he has married Fainlove.

Steele again owed something to France, especially in the painter scene to Molière's *Le Sicilien*. But his main debt was to Addison, to whom, when Tonson published the play in May 1705, he dedicated it as 'no improper memorial of an inviolable friendship'. Addison had written a prologue for the Drury Lane performance and, as Steele stated in no. 555 of *The Spectator*, had contributed 'many applauded strokes' to the play, about which there can be merely speculation. With the addition of Estcourt as Pounce to the distinguished cast *The Tender Husband* might have looked forward to a longer April run than five nights, but it was put on again in later months of 1705 and had many further revivals.

A long period was to follow before Steele was again to come forward as a dramatist. His two marriages, his official and political activities, his achievements in alliance with Addison as an essayist, diverted his attention from composition for the stage. Through his appointment by George I as Supervisor of Drury Lane and in other ways he kept in touch with theatrical affairs. But it was not till 1720 that he alluded to a play in preparation by 'a friend of mine', which was evidently his own comedy produced at Drury Lane on 7 November 1722 as *The Conscious Lovers*.

As in his earlier days Dick Steele had been indebted to Corneille and Molière, so now Sir Richard, knighted in 1715, went for a source to Rome—the *Andria* of Terence. In the Latin play the youthful Pamphilus has seduced Glycerium, supposed sister of Chrysis, a courtesan from Andros, who is about to give birth to a child and whom he has promised to marry. On the other hand the father of Pamphilus had arranged for his son to wed Philomena, daughter of his wealthy friend Chremes.

But at the cremation of Chrysis, Glycerium had gone
too near the flames and had been saved by Pamphilus,
whose excitement revealed that they were lovers. On
hearing of this Chremes broke off the match with his
daughter.

Steele, in his moralizing vein, gives an innocent complexion to the relations between Bevil and Indiana, as
he rechristens them. While on a continental tour, he has
met the girl, daughter of a Bristol merchant, Danvers,
at Toulon. With her father in the Indies, and her only
other surviving relative an Aunt Isabella, Bevil has
rescued her from an oppressor, brought her to England,
benefited her, but never yet told her of his love. It has,
however, been apparent when during a scuffle at a
masquerade, which Steele substitutes for the cremation,
then strange to England, she swoons and Bevil betrays
his feelings by clasping her in his arms.

The rich merchant Sealand then tells Sir John, Bevil's
father, that the wedding fixed for that very day with his
daughter Lucinda is off. Sir John, intent on out-
manœuvring Sealand, conceals the news, while Bevil,
most dutiful of sons, to humour his father parades in
a wedding garment as if attired for the ceremony.
Lucinda, from whom he is anxious to be free, has an
ardent suitor in his friend Myrtle (Charinus in *Andria*).
He has a rival, somewhat needlessly invented by Steele,
in Cimberton, called by Myrtle 'a formal, philosophical,
pedantic coxcomb . . . his strongest bias is avarice,
which is so predominant in him that he will examine the
limbs of his mistress with the caution of a jockey'. Her
mother, Sealand's second wife, without consulting him
or the girl, is having articles of marriage drawn up
between her and Cimberton.

Steele was better inspired in another way. Terence

never brings Glycerium on the stage. Steele shows Indiana being warned by her aunt that men are the destroyers of women, serpents who lie in wait for doves. When Bevil appears Indiana asks his opinion on her aunt's view 'that no man ever does any extraordinary kindness or service for a woman but for his own sake'. To her surprise he answers, 'Indeed I can't but be of her opinion.'

Ind. What, though he should maintain and support her, without demanding anything of her, on her part?

Bev. Why, madam, is making an expense in the service of a valuable woman (for such I must suppose her) though she should never do him any favour—nay, though she should never know who did her such service, such a mighty heroic business?

Ind. Certainly, I should think he must be a man of an uncommon mould.

When Bevil assures her that her hero 'is no more than every gentleman ought to be, and I believe very many are', we feel that it is the moralist rather than the play-wright who is giving the speaker his cue. On Steele's own admission this is even more patent in Act IV. In *Andria* Charinus, misled by the scheming of Davus, the *servus* of Pamphilus, had accused his friend of double-crossing him concerning marriage with Philomena, and there had been for a time a wordy quarrel. Steele had seen here an opportunity for sermonizing on a favourite topic. As he stated in the preface to the play when printed, 'the whole was writ for the sake of the scene of the fourth act, wherein Mr. Bevil evades the quarrel with his friend'. Myrtle in a letter challenges Bevil to a duel, and when the latter declines to take it up, taunts him with caring only for his own safety. Bevil's reply repeats in the most solemn tones the denunciation of duelling to which Steele had previously given expression in *The Lying Lover*.[1]

Sir, you know that I have often dared to disapprove of the decisions a tyrant custom has introduced, to the breach of all laws, both human and divine. . . . I have often told you, in confidence of heart, I abhorred the daring to offend the Author of life, and rushing into His presence—I say by the very same act to commit the crime against Him, and immediately to urge on to His tribunal.

Only when Myrtle makes mock of his dalliance with Indiana does he momentarily agree to meet him, but soon recollecting himself, shows a letter from Lucinda which sets forth her feelings and restores harmony between the friends.

For the final solution of the plot's entanglements Steele departs widely from his source. In *Andria* the mystery of Glycerium's birth is cleared up by Crito, a cousin of Chrysis, who arrives from Andros and relates that the girl in infancy had been shipwrecked with an uncle, since dead, whom Chremes recognizes to have been his brother. Thus Glycerium is his long-lost daughter whom he is now glad to unite, with a handsome dowry, to Pamphilus. Steele eliminates Crito. It is Sealand who, in order to find out for himself what Indiana is like, pays a visit to her and her aunt. Isabella at once recognizes him as her brother, and from Indiana's account of her 'strange, strange story' Sealand begins to suspect that she is his daughter by his first wife. Proof is forthcoming in a bracelet which he had bestowed on this wife and by Indiana's acknowledgement that her lost father's name was Danvers, as Sealand had been called before he made the change on going to the Indies. Thus Indiana and Lucinda are sisters, each of

[1] See p. 72, above.

whom has a title to half of their father's estate. This
is more than enough for such whole-hearted lovers as
Bevil and Myrtle, but for the avaricious Cimberton it
spells good-bye. 'I was in treaty for the whole but if that
is not to be come at, to be sure there can be no bargain.'

While Steele's adaptation of Terence's plot was in the
main skilful his dialogue had lost much of its earlier
sparkle, and was almost throughout on too uniformly a
sententious level. It is not surprising therefore that when
the manuscript of *The Conscious Lovers* was submitted to
Colley Cibber he found it too grave for a comedy and
suggested either (according to one account) the addition
or, more probably, the extension of the parts of Tom
and Phillis, the servants of Bevil and Lucinda. With the
very first words between them the dialogue takes on a
racier tone.

Phil. Lord, one is almost ashamed to pass along the streets!
The town is quite empty and nobody of fashion left in it. . . .
Alas, alas! it is a sad thing to walk. O fortune, fortune!
Tom. What! a sad thing to walk? Why, Madam Phillis,
do you wish yourself lame?
Phil. No, Mr. Tom, but I wish I were generally carried
in a coach or chair, and of a fortune neither to stand nor go,
but to totter, or slide, to be short-sighted or stare, to fleer
in the face, to look distant, to observe, to overlook. Yet all
become me. . . . Oh, Tom, Tom! is it not a pity that you
should be so great a coxcomb, and I so great a coquette, and
yet be such poor devils as we are?

In a later scene the coquette makes play with the
coxcomb. 'Since I am at leisure you may tell me when
you fell in love with me; how you fell in love with me,
and what you have suffered, or are ready to suffer for
me.' Here Steele dishes up again a scene of 'low love'
from *The Guardian*, 20 June 1713, in which a maid and

a footman breathe upon opposite sides of a pane which they are cleaning. Then Tom begs her to shorten his torment. 'Oh, Phillis, you don't know how many china cups and glasses my passion for you has made me break. You have broke my fortune as well as my heart.'

Cibber's zeal for the play included acting the part of Tom with Elizabeth Younger as Phillis. Barton Booth, who had been Pamphilus in the Westminster School production of *Andria*, played Bevil. Wilks as Myrtle and Anne Oldfield as Indiana also helped to ensure the success of *The Conscious Lovers*, which had an initial run of eighteen nights and eight further performances during the season. It was published by Tonson in December 1722 with a dedication to King George, who rewarded the dramatist with 500 guineas. Steele could thus afford to make light of some splenetic attacks upon the play headed by Dennis.

He was also encouraged to proceed farther with a play the main idea of which he had discussed with the actor Richard Estcourt in 1712, and which he now called *The School of Action*. Increasingly disabled by ill health he worked at it at intervals, partly in London, partly in the country, during 1723–5, but was able to complete only three acts and part of a fourth. It is preserved, with some leaves missing, in British Museum Add. MS. 5145 c. Severn, a barrister, with his Oxford friend Humber, is setting up a new playhouse with a School of Action, whose purpose Severn thus describes:

As all that reside in inns of courts and universities, though they do not enter into any of the learned professions, are yet better accomplished for any other ways of life by having the same education with those who go into them; so will all who come to our School of Action be better qualified in their own characters by being instructed among players, who are taught to become any part which shall be imposed upon them.

A country attorney, Pincers, with his wife and his ward Dolly, has mistaken the playhouse for an inn and they have been put up in the tiring-room. Severn is in love with Dolly and bent on frustrating a scheme by which her rascally guardian designs on her marriage to get for himself half of her estate. Severn has let Dolly into the secret by which the School of Action is to serve his purpose. An actor, Dotterell, who has hitherto played small parts, is told that in the new play he shall be a ghost. 'You shall come to the country gentleman who lay here last night in the figure of his deceased brother, a fat justice of the peace, who left all his money in his hands and he cheats him.' In Act II he appears to the trembling attorney demanding the return of his money and carrying off his wife through a trap-door. Another actor, Spider, is jealous, because Dotterell is to be a ghost while he is only to be a tapster, till Severn assures him, 'You are to be a tapster to the inn in which he is to be a ghost, so that he's in a manner in your keeping.' An actress, Mrs. Umbrage, is engaged, to show Dolly, who is 'mighty theatricall disposed', the pleasures and beauties of the house. Then candidates for the stage are interviewed, including Gwillyn, a Welshman, who recites Hamlet's soliloquy as 'To pee and not to pee', and Buskin who spouts a blank-verse speech and is put out of countenance when told to repeat it in undress. All this springs so spontaneously out of Steele's theatrical experience, and the dialogue has so much of his earlier verve, that one must lament that *The School of Action* was never finished.

The fragment, also in the same British Museum manuscript, which has been named *The Gentleman*, is of

interest in more than one way. The dialogue between
Sir Harry Severn and his man Tom is based on Steele's
description of high life below stairs in no. 88 of *The
Spectator*. The show, in honour of the marriage of the
landlord's daughter, at which Tom is a steward, is an
up-to-date version of the old folk-lore fight between
St. George and the Dragon, in which St. George, per-
sonated by the youth Dicky on a war-horse, is victor.
Then others in the show intervene:

Constable. Hold, hold, sir knight; the dragon's my neighbour—he's a tailor in my neighbourhood.

A Masquer. Open the dragon; open the dragon; keep the
peace; take out the tailor.

Lawyer Masquer. Take care what you do; take care what
you do. If he is a denizen, the law is very severe. Though
there are nine to make up a man, by a fiction of law it is
murder to kill any one of them; the law supposes him a
whole man.

Is not this dragon, with the tailor inside who must not
be injured, first cousin to the lion through whose neck
half the face of Snug the joiner was to appear?[1]

During the remaining few years Steele's activities
were crippled by illness, pressure of creditors, and legal
controversies till his death at Carmarthen on 1 September 1729. But with so manifold competing interests
in his eventful life one can be grateful that he left so
entertaining and wholesome a legacy to the English
comic stage.

[1] *The School of Action* and *The Gentleman* were first printed by John
Nichols in 1809. They are reproduced with introductory comments by
G. A. Aitken in his Mermaid edition of Steele's plays (1926).

IV

COLLEY CIBBER—MRS. CENTLIVRE

IN the preceding chapters Colley Cibber has from
time to time figured as an actor. He was also a
voluminous writer of plays, of which the most representative were akin to Steele's sentimental comedies.
Born in London on 6 November 1671 he was educated
at Grantham and served in 1688 in the force raised by
the Earl of Devonshire in aid of the Prince of Orange.
In 1690 he joined in a minor capacity the Drury Lane
Company, and thenceforward to the close of his life he
was in the fullest sense a man of the theatre.

His first comedy, *Love's Last Shift* (1696), was followed
by several others, by a tragedy, *Xerxes*, and *King Richard III*, adapted from Shakespeare's play. It was with *The
Careless Husband*, produced at Drury Lane on 7 December 1704, that he established his position as a dramatist.
The scene is laid at Windsor, and the title part is that
of Sir Charles Easy, who is carrying on intrigues with
Lady Graveairs and his wife's waiting-woman, Mrs.
Edging. To these at present Lady Easy turns a blind
eye, lest a display of 'jealousy may tease him to a fix'd
aversion; and hitherto, though he neglects, I cannot
think he hates me'.

Even Sir Charles's acid banter cannot provoke an
angry retort.

Sir Char. Nay, the deuce take me if I don't really confess
myself so bad that I have often wonder'd how any woman
of your sense, rank and person, could think it worth her
while to have so many useless good qualities.

.   .   .   .

L. Easy. I can't boast of my good qualities; nor, if I could, do I believe you think 'em useless.

Sir Char. Nay, I submit to you—Don't you find 'em so? Do you perceive that I am one tittle the better husband for your being so good a wife?

L. Easy. Pshaw! You jest with me.

Their dialogue is cut short by the news of the arrival in Windsor of Lord Morelove, in pursuit of the scornful Lady Betty Modish. As he confides to Sir Charles, he had ventured to criticize her conduct, whereupon

She told me I was rude, and that she would never believe any man could love a woman that thought her in the wrong in any thing that she had a mind to, at least if he dar'd so tell her . . . She desired to be alone, that I would take my odious proud heart along with me and trouble her no more.

He has not seen her since, but now repents of having contradicted her. Thereupon Sir Charles gives him the opportunity of meeting her at dinner, to which his wife has gone to invite her.

Lady Betty is in ecstasies over a new scarf she has just received from London. ''Tis all extravagance both in mode and fancy, my dear. I believe there's six thousand yards of edging in it. Then such an enchanting stoop from the elbow—something so neat, so lively, so noble, so coquet and charming!' But Lady Easy is in no mood for such frivolities. She warns Lady Betty that it is only the beauty of the mind, not of the outside, that has lasting value, and rebukes her for showing more favour to Lord Foppington, who loves all women alike, than to her faithful Lord Morelove. There is cynical shrewdness in Lady Betty's retort:

The men of sense, my dear, make the best fools in the world; their sincerity and good breeding throws them so entirely into one's power, and gives one such an agreeable thirst of using them ill to show that power—'tis impossible to quench it.

When Foppington, in the next scene, appears he is the typical vainglorious and affected coxcomb, interlarding his talk with French phrases, making light of the wife whom he married for her fortune, and boasting of the success of his amours.

The situation of a woman holding at arm's length and humiliating the lover to whom she is ultimately to yield has lost today most of the appeal which it had for play-goers in earlier times. The manœuvres by which Lady Betty irritates Morelove by paying attentions to Foppington, and Morelove, urged on by Sir Charles, seeks to excite her jealousy by courting Lady Carstairs, seem to us now too long drawn out. But they lead up to the admirable scene in Act IV where all the parties are assembled with sallies of wit passing to and fro (as Foppington puts it) as in tennis. It is here that Lady Betty gives her first sign of relenting when she asks Morelove to let her speak with him, and permits him to be her escort when the company make their exit in pairs.

Hitherto the duel between them has somewhat over-shadowed the relations between 'the careless husband' and his wife. But in Act V Cibber sees an opportunity of answering Jeremy Collier's attack, to which he makes a direct reference, on the immorality of plays.

L. More. Since the late short-sighted view of 'em vice may go on and prosper; the stage dares hardly show a vicious person speaking like himself, for fear of being call'd profane for exposing him.

L. Easy. 'Tis hard, indeed, when people won't distin-guish between what's meant for contempt, and what for example.

Lady Easy finds her husband and Mrs. Edging asleep together, and stirred into blank verse she for the moment utters threats:

> I'll throw the vizor of my patience off;
> Now wake him in his guilt,
> And barefac'd front him with my wrongs.

But then she thinks that she may be at fault, and as he is asleep without his wig Heaven may punish him with some languishing distemper. Murmuring 'Forbid it mercy, and forbid it love!', she takes a steinkirk (neck-cloth) off her neck and lays it gently on his head. When Sir Charles wakes he feels the steinkirk and knows that his wife must have seen him sleeping with her woman. He is stricken suddenly with remorse.

> How low an hypocrite to her must that sight have prov'd me! The thought has made me despicable even to myself. How mean a vice is lying! and how often have these empty pleasures lull'd my honour and my conscience to a lethargy, while I grossly have abus'd her, poorly skulking behind a thousand falsehoods. Now I reflect, this has not been the first of her discoveries. How contemptible a figure must I have made to her!

This speech marks a triumph for Collier's reforming influence and Cibber continues to press the moral home. Sir Charles surprises his wife by asking her why she ever ventured upon marriage with him, who never took pains to appear but what he was, 'a loose unheeded wretch . . . and, in my best of praise, but carelessly good-natur'd'.

Lady Easy. Your own words may answer you. Your having never seem'd to be but what you really were; and through that carelessness of temper there still shone forth to me an undesigning honesty I always doubted of in smoother faces:

thus, while I saw you took least pains to win me, you pleas'd and woo'd me most.

Sir Charles is startled by her understanding of him and after further exchange of confidences declares, 'Receive me then entire, at last, and take what yet no woman ever truly had, my conquer'd heart.' Whereupon Lady Easy exclaims, 'O the soft treasure! O the dear reward of long desiring love. . . . Thus, thus to have you mine is something more than happiness; 'tis double life and madness of abounding joy.' She even shows her absolute trust in him by refusing his request that she should at once discharge Mrs. Edging. In these speeches there is a riot of sentimentality surpassing anything in Steele's plays.

Here the play might well have come to a close. But Cibber again brings into the foreground the tension between Lady Betty and Lord Morelove, who begs pardon for the favour he has shown to Lady Graveairs. Sir Charles intervenes with a counter-check in a violent indictment of Lady Betty's treatment of Morelove and her flirtation with Foppington. At last this calculated manœuvre succeeds. Lady Betty confesses that she has been to blame, and assures Morelove of her 'utter detestation of any past or future gallantry that has or shall be offered by me to your uneasiness'. She begs Foppington's pardon for the freedom that she has taken with him, but he airily answers that he has lost a thousand fine women in his time, without being out of humour, and as he has contributed to her happiness, he asks leave to complete it by joining her and Morelove's hands. Even Lady Graveairs rushing in angrily is sufficiently mollified by Sir Charles to accept Lady Easy's invitation to join the company at supper followed by music and a song.

In our eyes today the conversion of the rake Sir

Charles is too sudden, and the surrender of Lady Betty
is too long delayed, to be convincing, but the play, with
its combination of Restoration and moralizing elements,
was an immediate and enduring success. Pope was to
pour scorn on those critics who would 'deny *The Careless
Husband* praise'.

In the dozen years that followed Cibber contributed
a number of plays of various types to Drury Lane or the
Haymarket, some of them adaptations. Among them
was a tragedy, *Perolla and Isadora* (1705); comedies, *The
Comical Lovers* (1707), *The Double Gallant, or The Sick
Lady's Cure* (1707), *The Lady's Last Stake, or The Wife's
Resentment* (1707); an entertainment, *Hob, or The Country
Wake* (1711), and masques, *Venus and Adonis* and *Myr-
tillo* (1715). Some of these proved popular, but were not
among his most significant productions.

Towards the end of 1717 Cibber seized on the opportunity of combining a sentimental comedy with a political onslaught. The Jacobite rebellion of 1715 was still
fresh in popular memory, and the faction that had re-
fused to swear allegiance to the sovereigns after the 1688
revolution was still troublesome. In his *Non-Juror*, produced at Drury Lane in December, Cibber hit upon the
idea of transforming Molière's Tartuffe into a hypocritical adherent of the lost Stuart cause, in the person
of the aptly named Wolf, Doctor of Divinity. This
schemer has been taken by Sir John Woodvil into his
house, where he has obtained complete ascendancy over
him. He has persuaded him that all who are not members of the Roman or English Catholic Church are
pagans. Hence Sir John has disinherited in Wolf's
favour his son, Colonel Woodvil, and designates him as
the bridegroom of his daughter Maria instead of her
faithful lover, Mr. Heartly.

Maria at first affects to be pleased when her brother gives her the news that her father opposes Heartly. She is like Lady Betty in *The Careless Husband* in rebuffing her admirer, but with less hauteur and more sprightliness. 'Now one has something to struggle for; there's difficulty, there's danger, there's the dear spirit of contradiction in it now. O, I like it mightily.' She asks her brother, 'Don't you know that I am a coquette?' and when he retorts, 'it's a hateful character', she jauntily answers,

Aye, it's no matter for that, it's violently pleasant, and there's no law against it that I know of. You had best advise your friend Heartly to bring in a bill to prevent it. . . . Take my word, coquetry has govern'd the world from the beginning, and will do so to the end on't.

When Heartly enters she banters him mercilessly, even refusing his request that she shall swear at least she'll never be another's. When she goes out laughing to have tea, the Colonel seeks to cheer him up, and confides his suspicions that the Doctor's desires are fixed, not upon Maria, but her mother. They are interrupted by Wolf's entry and his request that they will join the family prayers. Heartly accepts, provided he does not leave out the prayer for the Royal Family, to which Wolf gives an equivocal answer, followed by a threat against the Government, which provokes the Colonel into shaking him. He runs out to complain to Sir John, but soon returns preceded by Maria, whose dressing-room he has invaded at the desire of her father, who now appears, frowns at Heartly and carries Maria off.

There follows an admirable scene in which Sir John takes the girl to task for playing the fool to no purpose, while his wife mediates between them: 'Maria's of a cheerful temper, my dear, but I know you don't think she wants discretion.' Sir John insists that she must marry, and describes his chosen bridegroom, a staunch member of the English Catholic Church, sober and chaste, and aged almost forty-nine, to which Maria replies, 'You can no more bring me, sir, to endure a man of forty-nine than you can persuade my Lady to dance in a church to the organ.' Thereupon Sir John fires his final shot, 'In one word, the good and pious Doctor Wolf's the man I have decreed your husband.' When Maria greets this announcement with laughter he counters with the threat, 'if you expect a shilling from me, the Doctor is your husband, or I'm no more your father'. He becomes even more infatuated with Wolf after hearing from him in secret that the non-juring head-quarters at Avignon Lane has elected him Bishop of Thetford, after which Sir John scrupulously addresses him as 'my Lord'.

But Lady Woodvil has been alarmed by the prospect of her husband bestowing his estate upon Wolf, and in concert with the Colonel they prepare to frustrate this. They find an unexpected ally in Charles, who is acting as servant to Wolf. But, as he confides to Maria, with whom he too has fallen in love, he is a gentleman born who through Wolf's influence took part in the 1715 rebellion, and arriving in London as a refugee was taken into his house by Sir John and made an attendant on the Doctor. In proof of his repentance Charles hands over to Maria a deed, not yet signed and sealed, by which Sir John grants to Wolf 'in present four hundred pounds per annum of which this very house is part, and at your father's death invests him in the whole remainder of his free estate'. The Colonel is entirely disinherited and Maria is to lose four thousand pounds unless she marries with the Doctor's consent.

This leads to an ingeniously devised series of complications. Maria, together with Charles, hurries off to a lawyer, who draws up a facsimile of Sir John's conveyance, except that the Colonel's name is everywhere substituted for that of the Doctor. Heartly, hearing of her thus going to a lawyer's with the Doctor's servant, is racked with jealousy, and Maria keeps him further on tenterhooks by telling him that her business 'abroad', as he calls it, was a secret she cannot disclose till next morning. She keeps it also from her brother, but his main interest is now in revealing Wolf's hypocrisy. He brings Sir John to hear him making love to his wife, but the Doctor, catching sight of them in the background, astutely converts his amorous outpourings as if their object was Maria. The Colonel's plan has miscarried and Sir John's infatuation for Wolf is so fortified that he insists on signing what he thinks is the deed disinheriting his son immediately.

It is Lady Woodvil who, at the second time of asking, succeeds in trapping Wolf. At her suggestion her husband hides under a table and listens to the Doctor's fervid protestations of love to his wife, till he can bear no more and seizes him by the throat with a cry of 'Traitor'! The further working out in full of Sir John's disillusion and of Wolf's exposure, culminating in the revelation that he is a Popish priest in disguise, and his arrest for treason, has lost much of its appeal today. On the other hand it is doubtful if justice has been done to the artistry of Cibber's portrait of Maria. The high-spirited girl, who can torment the man to whom her heart is really given, shows delicate tenderness to her other lover, Charles, whose passion is hopeless. As she confesses to him, 'It loses you no merit with me, nor is it in my nature to use any one ill that loves me, unless

I lov'd that one again; then indeed there might be danger.' When he asks what is the charm by which his rival has secured her preference, her answer gives the clue not only to her own attitude but to many marriages since then at which the world has wondered.

The gentleness and modesty of your temper would make with mine but an unequal mixture: with you I should be ungovernable, nor know myself; your compliance would undo me. I am by nature vain, thoughtless, wild and wilful; therefore ask a higher spirit to control and lead me. For whatever outward airs I give myself, I am within convinc'd a woman makes a very wrong figure in happiness that does not think superiority best becomes her husband.

Heartly's generous intervention with the Government on behalf of Charles, resulting in his pardon and reconciliation with his father, brings her nearer to a confession of her feeling. After telling him that he is 'horrid silly', she adds, 'But since 'tis love that makes you such a dunce, poor Heartly, I forgive you.' And the Colonel clinches matters by making her give Heartly her hand, and showing herself 'consistent with that good sense I always thought you mistress of'. And she betrays something more than good sense when she at last tells her secret—how by the facsimile conveyance she has foiled Wolf's designs.

Anne Oldfield can never have had a more rewarding part than Maria. Cibber himself played the Doctor, with Booth as the Colonel and Wilks as Heartly. The sensation aroused by the play, with its political and religious implications, was proved not only by the issue of five editions of it in 1718 but by the feud of pamphlets, on either side, that it occasioned. A visit of King George to Drury Lane, to see the play, emboldened Cibber to

dedicate it to him, for which he received a reward of
200 guineas.

It was not till January 1728 that Cibber's next, and
last, important comedy was staged at Drury Lane. It
was a venturesome experiment, an adaptation of a piece
A Journey to London which Sir John Vanbrugh had left
unfinished at his death in 1726. It contained two loosely
connected plots. The journey to London had been
undertaken by a country gentleman, Sir Francis Head-
piece, with his wife, son, and daughter, as he had just
been elected a parliament man to Westminster. He was
thus in hopes of obtaining from the Government some
highly paid office. Meanwhile his wife starts on the
extravagant ways of a would-be woman of quality, his
oafish son begins a flirtation with their landlady's
daughter, and his pert daughter shows herself a regular
enfant terrible. Cibber's treatment of this plot was doubt-
fully inspired. He makes Sir Francis Wronghead (as he
calls him) speak with a country accent and have a
dubious claim to his seat in Parliament. He lets the girl
be almost trapped into a marriage with a *soi-disant*
Count, a forger, and the son similarly with the Count's
mistress, who exposes him. And it is in the vein of
sentimental comedy that, on condition of his immediately marrying her, the Count is pardoned and even
given £500, the amount of his forged bill, for honeymoon
expenses.

But, as Cibber's change of the main title to *The
Provok'd Husband* proves, it was the other plot in Vanbrugh's unfinished play that chiefly attracted him. He
even changes the names of its two leading figures from
Lord Loverule and Lady Arabella to Lord and Lady
Townly. While he takes over much of Vanbrugh's
dialogue between them he inserts passages of his own,

including one in the opening scene. The provoked husband asks his lady to tell him seriously why she married him and she answers:

Wives have infinite liberties in life that would be terrible in an unmarried woman to take. . . . In the morning a married woman may have men at her toilet; invite them to dinner; appoint them a party in the stage-box at the play, engross the conversation there, call them by their Christian names, talk louder than the players; from thence jaunt into the city, take a frolicsome supper at an India House, perhaps in her *gaieté de cœur* toast a pretty fellow; then clatter again to this end of the town, break, with the morning, into an assembly, crowd to the hazard-table.

It is the full-length programme of the twenty-four hours of an eighteenth-century woman of fashion which Lady Townly carries out completely. But, as Cibber makes clear, she does not violate her marriage vows. Her chief offences in her husband's eyes are her extravagance at the gaming-table and her unseemly late hours. Finally he can bear them no longer.

Lord Town. Whatever may be in your inclination, madam, I'll prevent your making me a beggar at least.

Lady Town. A beggar! Croesus! I am out of patience. I won't come home till four to-morrow morning.

Lord Town. That may be, madam, but I'll order the doors to be locked at twelve.

Lady Town. Then I won't come home till to-morrow night.

Lord Town. Then, madam, you shall never come home again.

Lady Town. What does he mean? I never heard such a word from him in my life before.

In a preface to the printed edition of *The Provok'd Husband* Cibber stated that Vanbrugh had intended in the catastrophe of the play to make the husband turn his wife out of doors, and thus to point a moral to vicious women. With Cibber sentiment had also to be taken into account—but not till the eleventh hour. The last straw is when he finds his wife turning away a tradesman unpaid, though he had given her a large sum to clear off her debts. She retorts that he has less to complain of than many husbands of equal rank. His reply must have startled not only her but many of the Drury Lane audience.

Death, madam! do you presume upon your corporal merit, that your person's less tainted than your mind? Is it there, there alone, an honest husband can be injured. Have you not every other vice that can debase your birth, or stain the heart of woman?

He deplores that the legislature has left no precedent of a divorce for 'this adultery of the mind as well as that of the person'. He summons his sister Lady Grace and his confidential friend Manly who were present at his wedding to be witnesses of his 'determined separation', though he acquits her of the least suspicion against the honour of his bed. Then at last Lady Townly breaks down and falls upon Lady Grace's neck, crying, 'Support me, save me, hide me from the world.'

Manly pleads with Townly not to leave her thus but to give a hearing to something that is labouring in her mind, whereupon she makes what she calls not her excuse but her confession. Infatuated with the homage paid to her beauty she had triumphed over all hearts, while insensitive herself to any, and had allowed her father to choose Townly as her husband.

Our hands were joined, but still my heart was wedded to its folly. My only joy was power, command, society, profuseness and to lead in pleasure. The husband's right to rule I thought a vulgar law which only the deformed or meanly spirited obeyed. I knew no directors but my passions, no master but my will. Even you, my Lord, some time o'ercome by love, were pleased with my delights, nor then foresaw this mad misuse of my indulgence. And though I call myself ungrateful while I own it, yet as a truth it cannot be denied that kind indulgence has undone me, it added strength to my habitual failings.

Time alone, she declares, can convince him of her future conduct, and not till then can she hope for pardon. But Townly, realizing that he has not been without fault, makes the surprising announcement, 'No, madam, your errors, thus renounced, this instant are forgiven', which brings the response, 'Oh, till this moment never did I know, my Lord, I had a heart to give you.' Well may Townly take Manly and his sister to witness, 'See here the bride of my desires! This may be called my wedding-day.' Townly's change of front is too abrupt to be convincing but it allows of a harmonious conclusion which Cibber substitutes for what, according to him, had been Vanbrugh's intended austere climax.

As with *The Non-Juror*, but now on literary not political grounds, the performance of *The Provok'd Husband* aroused a controversy. Cibber's enemies, ignorant of his share in the play, condemned 'the journey to London' part, which was mainly Vanbrugh's, and applauded loudly the Townly plot in which Cibber had the chief hand. In self-defence, when he published the comedy in 1728 with a dedication to Queen Caroline, he also printed *A Journey to London* from Vanbrugh's manuscript. The division of opinion has lasted into our own day. W. C. Ward, in his edition of Vanbrugh's dramatic works, rejected *The Provok'd Husband* as not worth including. Allardyce Nicoll, in his *History of Early*

Eighteenth Century Drama (1925), with more reason calls it one of the best comedies of the period.

A faction also interrupted the performance in January 1929 of Cibber's pastoral ballad-opera, *Love in a Riddle*, though on the second night the Prince of Wales was present. When from this *Damon and Phillida* was extracted it was not announced as by Cibber, was favourably received and constantly revived. His enemies had yet more occasion to blaspheme when in December 1730 he was appointed Poet Laureate. Thereafter he produced no more plays, but in 1740 he rendered a notable service to the history of the theatre by publishing the *Apology* for his life. This vivacious autobiography should have been enough to save Pope from his egregious blunder in the final edition of *The Dunciad* (1743) in replacing Theobald by Cibber on the throne of Dulness. Throughout his career of eighty-six years, ending on 11 December 1757, Colley Cibber as dramatist, actor, and manager established a reputation proof against satirical attack.

MRS. CENTLIVRE

THE place of Mrs. Centlivre as the representative of her sex among early eighteenth-century dramatists corresponds broadly with that of Mrs. Aphra Behn among their Restoration predecessors. In both cases, too, some of the details of their lives are obscure. Her father appears to have been a Mr. Freeman of Holbeach in Lincolnshire whose estate was confiscated after the Restoration and who migrated to Ireland, where his daughter Susannah may have been born. Little is known of her early life except that she came to London, and

became associated in marriage or otherwise with an
officer named Carroll. After his death in a duel she
became an actress in a strolling company. While playing
at Windsor she attracted Joseph Centlivre, chief cook to
Queen Anne and George I, whom she married, and with
whom she lived till her death on 1 December 1723.

As early as 1700 she had begun to write for the stage
with a blank-verse tragedy, *The Perjur'd Husband*, which
was followed by several comedies of no special distinction. It was with *The Busy-Body*, performed at Drury
Lane in May 1709, that Mrs. Centlivre made her first
and greatest hit. The play takes its title from Marplot,
who is described among the *dramatis personae* as 'a sort
of a silly fellow, cowardly, but very inquisitive to know
everybody's business, generally spoils all he undertakes,
yet without design'. As one of the characters in the play
says of him: 'He is pressing to be employ'd, and willing
to execute, but some ill fate generally attends all he
undertakes and he oftener spoils an intrigue than helps
it.' He is a less malicious forerunner of Gilbert's 'disagreeable man' in *Princess Ida*:

> A charitable action I can skilfully dissect;
> And interested motives I'm delighted to detect;
> I know everybody's income and what everybody earns,
> And I carefully compare it with the income-tax returns.

A complicated situation offers a fine opportunity for his
meddling. He and the heiress Miranda are both wards
of the surly Sir Francis Gripe who wants to marry
Miranda, who pretends to consent, though she is secretly
in love with a gentleman of fortune, Sir George Airy.
Gripe has driven out his son Charles, friend of Airy, who
loves and is loved by Isabinda, daughter of the merchant
Sir Jealous Traffic, who after some years of residence in

Spain intends that the girl shall marry a Don from that country about to arrive in England. He locks the girl up, and in accordance with Spanish custom gives her a woman called Patch as a duenna, who, however, is in league with Charles's servant, Whisper. They arrange for Charles to visit Isabinda when her father is away, but during their interview he unexpectedly returns; and Marplot, who has followed Charles to the house, to find out his secret, gives it away and infuriates Gripe by threats if the gentleman 'comes not as safe out of your house as he went in'.

Meanwhile Gripe is so confident of his hold over Miranda that he agrees to an offer by Airy to pay a hundred pounds to have an hour with her. He stipulates that he must be present, and there is a diverting scene, where she keeps silent to Airy's protestations of love, but lets him kiss and embrace her, to which her guardian objects as 'contrary to the articles'.

Marplot arrives soon afterwards to reproach her for allowing Airy to fling away a hundred pounds upon 'your dumb ladyship'. She bids him return with a message that she has chosen Sir Francis to have and to hold, and then adds:

Advise him to keep from the garden gate on the left hand, for if he dare to saunter there about the hour of eight, as he used to do, he shall be saluted with a pistol or blunderbuss. . . . Tell him he shall find a warm reception if he comes this night.

Mar. Pistols and Blunderbusses! Egad, a warm reception indeed. I shall take care to inform him of your kindness, and advise him to keep further off.

Miranda (*aside*). I hope he will understand my meaning better than to follow your advice.

Marplot fails to realize that Miranda is thus ingeniously making him her instrument of an assignation with Airy. It is one of Mrs. Centlivre's deftest strokes. Sir George grasps the import of the message and proposes a toast to the garden-gate. He is punctual at the rendezvous, and is delighted when Miranda asks, 'Do you think we can agree on that same terrible bugbear, Matrimony, without heartily repenting on both sides?' There is a sudden end to their bliss when Gripe is announced. He has been stopped when starting on an errand to Epsom by Marplot, who has brought him back in the belief that Miranda might cause trouble by shooting an intruder. And there is further mischief by Marplot. Sir George takes refuge behind the chimney-board, and to prevent Sir Francis lifting it Miranda declares that she has a pet monkey there. Marplot cannot resist peeping and discovers Sir George, who runs off, throwing down some china which Gripe is told was broken by the monkey.

Meanwhile Charles has made a second attempt to see Isabinda, climbing by a rope ladder through her closet window, but through the accident of a dropped letter her father is put on his guard and catches sight of him. In his fury Sir Jealous turns Patch out of doors and locks Isabinda in his own room, swearing 'she shall see neither sun nor moon till she is Don Diego Babinetta's wife, who arrived last night'. There is no time to lose and Patch urges Charles, who understands Spanish, to personate the Don. He appears for the wedding ceremony in a Spanish habit accompanied by Airy dressed as an English merchant, Mr. Meanwell, a friend of the Don's family. Sir Jealous drags in Isabinda, whose agonized feelings burst into blank verse, equivalent to the accompaniment of slow music in the thrilling parts of some modern plays.

O hear me, sir! hear me but speak one word.
Do not destroy my everlasting peace.
My soul abhors this Spaniard you have chose,
Nor can I wed him without being curst.

Sir Jealous remains obdurate, and in an admirably written scene Charles can scarcely help giving himself away while 'Meanwell', affecting to bring the girl to reason, whispers to her that the supposed Spanish bridegroom is Charles, and gets her enraptured consent to the union. But Marplot nearly spoils all by his crowning piece of busy-bodying. He asks at the door whether there is a gentleman within in a Spanish habit, and then tells Sir Jealous that it is Charles, who 'might have been here in a masquerade'. Sir Jealous, realizing that he may have been tricked, tries to get to the officiating clergyman and to stop the wedding. But Airy bars the way with his sword drawn till Charles and Isabinda appear as man and wife.

Sir George and Miranda have also out-manœuvred her guardian, and are similarly joined. To complete the discomfiture of Sir Francis Miranda hands to Charles deeds entitling him to the legacy of his uncle's estate which his father has kept from him for three years. With an imprecation, 'Confound you all', Sir Francis stalks away. Sir Jealous, on the other hand, with an abrupt change of mood, gives the pair who have outwitted him his blessing. 'When a thing was past I ever had philosophy enough to be easy.' In the general atmosphere of reconciliation blundering but honest Marplot is not forgotten. Charles forgives him and Airy undertakes that Sir Francis shall make him master of his rightful estate.

It is an edifying close to a skilfully handled series of complications. The play at once caught the fancy of the town. It was performed both at Drury Lane and the Haymarket in 1710 and was frequently revived in other theatres also.

Mrs. Centlivre was thus tempted to try the always risky experiment of a second Part, *Marplot in Lisbon*. She probably chose Portugal as the scene of this Part instead of Spain, so dear to Sir Jealous Traffic in *The Busy-Body*, because Portugal was an ally of England in the War of the Spanish Succession. Otherwise it is strange that Charles should have come to Lisbon instead of Madrid as executor for Sir Jealous who has just died. Detained for the lack of some legal papers, as he tells Colonel Ravelin, an English officer, he passes the time 'very insipidly'. As a diversion he has begun an affair with a lady who has given him a sign by waving a handkerchief from her window. The Colonel warns him to be cautious as the Portuguese women are revengeful. 'If you manage your intrigue so closely to escape the husband and relations, 'tis odds but your mistress finds some pretence to employ her bravoes, fellows that will dispatch a dozen men for a moidore.' Charles answers that he goes well armed, understands the language, and will not easily fall a victim. But that the Colonel was justified in his warning is at once proved when Marplot, who has come with Charles to Lisbon, rushes in pursued by two bravoes who are beaten off. 'I had a mind', he explains, 'to see where that lady liv'd that shook her handkerchief at you, and out of no other design than to inform you, I protest, Charles, when immediately these two scoundrels came slap upon me.'

The lady of the handkerchief is Donna Perriera, the young, well-born wife of an old, ugly merchant. Her fiery brother, Don Lopez, a grandee, looks on her marriage as a dishonour to their family, and accuses her husband of tamely bearing the disgrace of being a cuckold. The taunt seems to be only premature. Donna Perriera makes hypocritical protestations of love and loyalty to her husband, while she is expecting a visit from Charles, who has bribed her duenna, Margaritta, to be his agent. When Charles comes and after high-flown speeches tries to embrace her she startles him by holding up a dagger. To his astonished queries she explains, 'By this I would imprint on your mind the danger which we are both expos'd to, if we are not both discreet; favours in Portugal must not be boasted of.' Charles assures her, as a man of honour, of secrecy, she throws the dagger away, and a door is opened for them to go into the more private next room, when all are astounded by seeing Marplot tumbling down from the chimney. Charles draws his sword, the women shriek 'Thieves!' and 'Murder!', while Marplot cries that it is a pure accident and that he never thought of finding Charles. This is true, for Marplot was on the track of another intrigue between Colonel Ravelin and an affected French lady, Mademoiselle Janeton. To spy upon them he had climbed into the chimney of the Colonel's lodgings, and seeing nobody had scrambled down the next-door chimney which was that of the Perrieras' house.

When at the women's screams the Don rushes in and threatens Marplot he declares that he has seen a friend of his in the room. To save her mistress Margaritta whispers to him, 'Recall what you have said, not one word more of the man you saw here, as you hope to live two hours.' Thereupon Marplot proves that, though a blunderer, he is no fool by ingeniously explaining that when he said a friend he meant himself, 'there needs no logic to prove a man's best friend is himself'. The Don

disbelieves his tale and sends for the Corregidor to im-
part the secrets of the laws in Portugal to this heretic
dog. Marplot seizes on this good hint, and (no doubt
to the gratification of the Drury Lane theatre Protestant
audience) declares, 'I'll pretend to turn Papist.' He begs
to be recommended to some saint to take care of him in
the other world, and the Don, feeling it to be a merito-
rious action to have regard to the heretic's poor soul,
agrees to send for a priest to give him religious instruc-
tion. But Marplot has touched the heart of Margaritta
who helps him to escape. It is only, however, to fall into
fresh danger. A bravo hands him a letter addressed to
an Englishman which he opens. It is a challenge to his
sister's lover by Don Lopez, who follows it up by an
assault on Marplot from which he is rescued by the
opportune arrival of Charles and Ravelin.

Marplot is the cause of further complications and
surprises till at last Charles and Donna Perriera are
found together by her husband and brother, who send
for two priests to confess them before they are put to
death. Here Mrs. Centlivre puts an excessive strain
upon her audience. She has brought Isabinda to Lisbon,
dressed as a boy, with the papers needed by her husband, with whom she has already had an interview
without his recognizing her. She even has to hear him
describe her to the Colonel as 'a poor good-natur'd tit,
and I lov'd her heartily till I married her'. When Marplot adds, 'Nature abhors constraint', and the Colonel
echoes, 'Aye, Aye, inconstancy is a fault in Nature, and
who can help it?' the play strikes a pre-Collier note for
which the almost incredible magnanimity of Isabinda
can only partially atone. To save her husband she puts
on the habit of one of the priests, which she transfers to
Charles, who thus disguised walks out with the other

priest. Isabinda is now in feminine dress and the priest reproaches Perriera for summoning them when there is no male thing in the room. At once credulous of his wife's innocence the Don abjectly begs her forgiveness. There is a final scene in which Marplot makes his last blunder, but which ends with general reconciliation.

Though *Marplot* has its merits, it is uneven, and especially in the later acts has unconvincing episodes. The Drury Lane audience showed its discrimination in giving it much shorter shrift than to *The Busy-Body*. Produced on 30 December 1710 it ran for only a few performances.

Another play in which the scene is laid in Portugal is *The Wonder: A Woman Keeps a Secret* produced at Drury Lane on 27 April 1714. This gives the opportunity for stressing the difference in their political and social attitudes between the English and the Portuguese. The former, as one character describes them, 'are by nature what the ancient Romans were by discipline, courageous, bold, hardy, and in love with liberty. Liberty is the idol of the English, under whose banner all the nation lists.' In strong contrast is the despotic claim of Portuguese fathers to do as they will with their sons and daughters.

Don Lopez, a grandee, is insistent that his daughter, Isabella, should marry Don Guzman, whose only recommendation is wealth, and whom she detests. She tells her father that she'll die before she marries him, whereupon Don Lopez locks her in her room. To escape before the wedding-day she leaps out of the window and is caught by Colonel Britton, a Scotchman, who, having served three years in the war in Spain is visiting Lisbon on his way home, attended by his footman Gibby in Highland dress. The Colonel brings the unconscious girl in his arms to a nearby house which happens to be that of Don Pedro, another tyrannical father, who destines his daughter Violante for a nunnery. But she loves, and is loved by, Don Felix, son of Don Lopez, who has had to go into temporary hiding after fighting a duel rather than marry a girl of his father's choice, but who now has written to Violante to announce his return. As he gives the customary signal at the window Isabella drops on her knees, crying:

Oh! Violante, I conjure thee by all the love thou bear'st to Felix—By thy over generous nature—Nay more, by that unspoiled virtue thou art mistress of, do not discover to my brother I am here.

.   .   .   .   .

Vio. Depend upon my friendship, nothing shall draw the secret from these lips, not even Felix, tho' at the hazard of his love: I hear him coming, retire into that closet.

Isab. Remember, Violante, upon thy promise my very life depends.

Vio. When I betray thee, may I share thy fate.

This is the secret that gives the play its title, and for the keeping thereof Violante is at once to pay dearly. No sooner have she and Felix rushed rapturously into each others arms than the Colonel pats at the window and calls 'Donna Violante', taking this to be the name of the girl he has carried in. Felix impetuously takes this to be a signal from someone with whom Violante has an amour, and cries, 'Pray let me go, my presence is but a restraint upon you.' Bound by her secret Violante cannot reveal that it is Isabella of whom the Colonel is in quest. When Felix tries to escape by the door behind which Isabella is hiding, Violante bars the way by declaring that it leads into her father's apartment. In desperation she holds a defiant dialogue with the Colonel

which only confirms Felix in the belief that his return
has interrupted an assignation. As he hurls imprecations
at her head she vainly pleads: 'There is a cause which
I must not reveal—Oh think how honour can oblige
your sex—Then allow a woman may be bound by the
same rule to keep a secret.'

It strains probability that Isabella, having sworn
Violante to secrecy, should risk further trouble by sending a letter to the Colonel of whom she has had but a
fleeting glimpse offering to meet him veiled at five in the
morning in a street. She finds him 'a man of sense,
generosity, and good humour; in short he is every thing
I cou'd like for a husband', and she invites him to
Violante's lodgings, where the Colonel pays court to the
latter, mistaking her for the unseen Isabella. Their interview is cut short by the return of Felix, at whose approach
Violante bids the Colonel step into her bedroom. There
is a reconciliation between the lovers till Don Pedro
suddenly appears, from whom Felix escapes disguised as
an old woman, but not before his jealousy has again
been aroused by a glimpse of the Colonel behind the bedroom door. Don Pedro's announcement that the Lady
Abbess has provided everything in order for Violante's
reception into a nunnery is a warning to the lovers that
there is no time to be lost, though, like Benedick and
Beatrice, they protest while they surrender.

Fel. Well, I am convinc'd that faith is as necessary in love
as in religion; for the moment a man lets a woman know his
conquest he resigns his senses, and sees nothing but what she
would have him.

Vio. And as soon as that man finds his love return'd, she
becomes as arrant a slave as if she had already said after the
priest.

The fifth act, however, brings further complications and

misunderstandings in which Violante's pert chambermaid, Flora, and the Colonel's Highland Gibby, with
his 'heathen dialect', play their part. But through all
Violante keeps her secret till in the end the despotic
fathers are hoodwinked and the four lovers are joined
in matrimony.

The plot has its improbabilities, and the succession of
escapes into cupboards or bedrooms is more effective
on the stage than in print. But Violante's loyalty at all
costs to her promise gives something of a deep undertone
to the hilarious action, and the brilliant impersonation
of her by Mrs. Oldfield, and of Felix by Wilks and later
by Garrick, ensured the popularity of the play.

After less successful experiments in a lighter vein in
The Gotham Election and *A Wife Well Manag'd* and in a
tragedy, *The Cruel Gift*, Mrs. Centlivre displayed again
the full range of her gifts for comedy in *A Bold Stroke for
a Wife*, produced at Lincoln's Inn Fields in February
1718. As in *A Wonder* but in an even more extravagant
form the imbroglio starts from a father's exercise of his
despotic power. Colonel Fainwell while at Bath has
become enamoured of a beautiful young lady, Anne
Lovely. He learns on his return to London that her
wealthy eccentric father has left her in his will thirty
thousand pounds, provided she marries with the consent
of her guardians. To prevent this being obtained he has
chosen four men as opposite to each other as possible,
each of whom has charge of her for a quarter of a year.
One is an old beau, Sir Philip Modelove, with whom she
has been in Bath; another is Periwinkle, a silly virtuoso;
a third is Tradelove, a broker on the Exchange; and the
fourth is a canting Quaker, Obadiah Prim, into whose
charge she has just passed.

The Colonel, with the war-cry 'There is nothing

impossible to a lover', determines to deliver Anne Lovely, with the aid of his friend Freeman, a merchant, and Sackbut, a vintner, who had been in the service of the girl's father. He will begin by approaching the old beau, Modelove, dressed in a suit of velvet and gold brocade, which a French Count had left in pawn with Sackbut. He thus accosts him in the park and is taken by Sir Philip to be a fine gentleman of France, since 'this island could not produce a person of such alertness'. In a conversation, in which their tastes are found to agree, Fainwell leads up to the mention of Mistress Lovely, Modelove declares that he hates the trouble of being a guardian, and would prefer Fainwell as a husband for her to all the men he has ever seen. But the consent of the other guardians must be obtained, and he will therefore introduce him to the Quaker with whom she is now.

When they arrive Prim and his wife have been abusing Anne for the garments she has worn while in 'wicked Philip Modelove's' custody:

Mrs. Prim. Satan so fills thy heart with pride during the three months of his guardianship that thou becomest a stumbling-block to the upright.

Anne. Pray, who are they? Are the pinch'd cap and formal hood the emblems of sanctity? Does your virtue consist in your dress, Mrs. Prim?

Mrs. Prim. It doth not consist in cut hair, spotted face and bare necks—Oh, the wickedness of the generation! The primitive women knew not the abomination of hoop'd petticoats.

Obadiah echoes his wife's reproaches and vows that he will never consent to her marrying except to one of their sect, whereupon Anne counters with a charge against him of prurient desires. When Modelove brings in Fainwell in his borrowed costume Prim finds fault with his garb also as favouring too much of the vanity of the age, and Anne does not recognize him till she hears his name. When Periwinkle and Tradelove also appear, though she prays heaven to prosper Fainwell's 'contrivance', she fears that he can never redeem her.

The next phase in the contrivance is to bamboozle the virtuoso Periwinkle. In one of Mrs. Centlivre's most skilfully written scenes Fainwell, dressed as an Egyptian, including a false beard, entertains him in Sackbut's tavern with traveller's tales of the curiosities that he has gathered, culminating in a girdle, 'the wonder of the world'. 'Whenever I am girded with this, I am invisible, and by turning this little screw, can be in the Court of the Great Mogul, the Grand Signior, and King George, in as little time as your cook can poach an egg.' Even the credulous virtuoso cannot believe this, till he puts on the belt, and Fainwell and Sackbut pretend they cannot see him till he takes it off. For further proof Periwinkle asks Fainwell to put on the belt himself, and while the virtuoso and the vintner are facing east, he sinks down through a trap-door. Periwinkle's flesh creeps when he finds him gone, and when he hears his hollow voice from below declares himself satisfied. The Colonel rises again, while the pair have their backs turned.

He now declares that by the advice of a learned physiognomist in Grand Cairo he has returned to England, 'where he told me I should find a rarity in the keeping of four men which I was born to possess for the benefit of mankind, and the *first* of the *four* that gave me his consent, I should present him with this girdle'. It further transpires that the rarity is no other than Periwinkle's ward Anne Lovely, and he is about to sign a paper by which the girdle will become his, when a drawer enters and, addressing Fainwell as Colonel, brings his artful contrivance crashing down. He leaves the field to his ally Freeman, who enters to tell the enraged virtuoso that his uncle Sir Toby Periwinkle, of whom he expects to be the heir, is dying in Coventry and to urge him to hasten there at once.

It is a tribute to Mrs. Centlivre's versatile talent that she can turn easily from this episode of esoteric romancing to the realistic atmosphere of Jonathan's coffee-house in Change Alley, where brokers are shouting stock prices, while boys cry 'Fresh coffee, gentlemen', or 'Bohea tea, gentlemen'. Freeman enters with Fainwell, now impersonating a Dutch merchant, and whispers to Tradelove that he has received private information that the Spaniards have raised the siege of Cagliari, news that will make stock rise. Tradelove thereupon buys ten thousand pounds' worth of South Sea stock, and also wagers two thousand pounds with Fainwell, who talks entirely in Dutch, that the news of the raising of the siege is true. The discovery that it is false puts Tradelove into 'the damned'st passion in the world', for he cannot pay the two thousand and laments that he can never show his face on 'Change more. He grasps eagerly at Freeman's suggestion that he should consent to his ward's marriage with the Dutchman, on condition that he forgives the wager.

Meanwhile Fainwell has again had to change his disguise into that of Pillage, steward of Sir Toby Periwinkle, who brings his nephew news of his death, together with his will and a lease to be renewed. While Periwinkle is examining the pen with which he is to sign Freeman substitutes for the lease a contract that sanctions Anne's marriage. At the same time Sackbut is laying a trap for Prim. He has opened a letter addressed to the Quaker from Bristol by 'a friend in the faith',

Aminadab Holdfast, recommending to his house 'one Simon Pure, a leader of the faithful', who has arrived from the American Quaker colony of Pennsylvania. On a hint from Sackbut the Colonel decides to put on Quaker dress and pose as Simon Pure. He thus gets leave to convert Anne, to whom when left alone with her he reveals himself. Prim, listening in to their talk, is delighted.

Prim. I would gladly hear what arguments the good man useth to bend her.

Anne. Thy words give me new life, methinks.

Prim. What do I hear?

Anne. Thou best of men. Heaven meant to bless me since when first I saw thee.

Prim. He hath mollified her—O wonderful conversion!

At this point the real Simon Pure appears, to be told by Prim that Simon Pure is already here, and to be reproached by Fainwell for taking his name. While Prim is doubting which is the counterfeit, a letter is handed in, written by Freeman, warning Prim that a man passing as Simon Pure has arrived in the coach from Bristol with the design of robbing his house and cutting his throat. Anne backs this up by declaring that she remembers the face of this fellow at Bath, as a pickpocket and most notorious rogue. Fearing for his life Simon runs off to fetch proofs of his identity. Fainwell knows there is no time to be lost. He tells Prim that he sees with the eye of his inward man that Satan will buffet the maiden again, whenever he withdraws himself from her. Anne seconds him, and after an interchange on all sides of the jargon of the faithful, Prim signs a certificate of his consent to the marriage of Anne Lovely to Simon Pure. The moment afterwards the real Simon returns with the coachman who had driven him from

Bristol, but Fainwell, having gained his end, pleads guilty to having used this gentleman's name, and now gives it up to him safe and sound. When the other guardians join the company they realize that they have all been tricked. Fainwell is asked to give an account of himself. His answer is in terms that appealed to the patriotic feelings of the audience. 'I have had the honour to serve his Majesty . . . and notwithstanding the fortune this lady brings me, whenever my country wants my aid, my sword and arm are at her service.'

It needed, however, nothing but its own merits as 'good theatre' to gain for *A Bold Stroke for a Wife* its long run of popularity. In Fainwell, with his successive impersonations, a part was provided to give scope for the most quick-change of actors. And in the real Simon Pure a phrase has taken root which has been familiar to thousands who know nothing of its origin. It was not till October 1722, in the year before her death, that Mrs. Centlivre made her last bid for stage success with a comedy, *The Artifice*, which did not attract the town.

Mrs. Centlivre's was an unequal talent. She was often dependent in part for her plots on foreign models. She attempted every type of play from tragedy to farce without sufficiently realizing where her true gifts lay. But at her best she displayed remarkable ingenuity in the devising or adapting of plots. She kept the action moving with a dexterous hand. She supplied character-actors of both sexes with parts which caught the favour of the town. And in her dialogue she often throws sidelights on the social and sometimes the political conditions of the Augustan age. She can claim a distinctive rank among the comparatively small group of women who have won a place on the roll of English dramatists.

V

JOSEPH ADDISON—AMBROSE PHILIPS

OF Joseph Addison as poet, essayist, and official only slight mention need here be made. Born at Milston in Wiltshire on 1 May 1672, he was educated at Charterhouse and at Oxford, first at Queen's College and then at Magdalen, of which he became a Fellow. After a period of continental travel he began a literary and political career. He made a signal success in 1704 with his poem *The Campaign* celebrating Marlborough's victory at Blenheim. In 1706 he became an Under-Secretary of State under the Whig Government, and was thenceforward prominent in the literary and political circles of the capital. With Steele, his friend since their Charterhouse days, he initiated in *The Tatler* (12 April 1709–2 Jan. 1711) and the even more popular *Spectator* (1 March 1711–6 Dec. 1712) a new era in the periodical essay.

Like so many of his contemporaries he was also anxious to make his mark in the theatre. His first attempt, *Rosamund*, an opera intended as a counterblast to foreign domination in that sphere, was performed in 1707 but was a failure. It was not till 1713 that he again made a venture on the stage with his tragedy *Cato*, of which a considerable part had been written some time previously, and which was produced at Drury Lane on 14 April.

In founding his play on Plutarch's life of the younger Cato Addison would appear to have had two aims chiefly in view. One was to present his classical theme according to the classical model. He was thus following in the footsteps of Ben Jonson instead of adopting the irregular mould of Shakespeare's Roman plays. It is true that he succeeded in observing the unities of time and place. And the limpid purity of his style, though in a five-act play it tends to monotony in its cadence, has something of true classical quality. At times it adds an epigrammatic polish, as in the two lines spoken by Cato's son, Portius, which have become proverbial:

> 'Tis not in mortals to command success,
> But we'll do more, Sempronius, we'll deserve it.

Or when the Numidian prince Juba pays tribute, echoing Virgil, to the mission of the Roman soul:

> To civilize the rude unpolished world,
> And lay it under the restraint of laws,
> To make man mild, and sociable to man.

Or when Cato proclaims:

> A day, an hour of virtuous liberty,
> Is worth a whole eternity of bondage.

But in keeping the unities of time and place Addison transgressed the higher unity of action. Instead of concentrating the main interest on the figure of Cato he went near to making this subsidiary to the love affairs of his sons and daughter. Though Plutarch mentions only one son, Addison presents two, Portius and Marcus, both enamoured of Lucia, daughter of a Roman senator. She favours Portius, but is distressed at the thought of causing dissension between the brothers. As she tells their sister, Marcia,

> Portius himself oft falls in tears before me,
> As if he mourn'd his rival's ill success,
> Then bids me hide the motions of my heart,
> Nor show which way it turns. So much he fears
> The sad effects that it would have on Marcus.

Portius himself, when sent by the unsuspecting Marcus to plead for him, speaks to the same effect:

> O Lucia, I'm distressed. My heart bleeds for him;
> Ev'n now, while thus I stand blest in thy presence,
> A secret damp of grief comes o'er my thoughts,
> And I'm unhappy, tho' thou smilest upon me.

Not to be outdone, Lucia apprehends that if she and Portius ensure their mutual bliss by the nuptial tie, it may destroy Marcus. She therefore swears to heaven that she will never plight hands with Portius while this may happen. He denounces her as 'hard-hearted, cruel maid', whereat she swoons, but reviving bids him 'Farewell, though death is in the word, forever'.

When Marcus hears that Lucia can give him only compassion, not love, he cries that her disdain 'Has broke my heart; 'tis death must give me ease'. That ease he is soon to find in seeking to quell a mutiny by the Numidian troops, and thus Lucia is released from her vow.

To this singularly sentimental love plot Addison adds another. Marcia, Cato's daughter, is beloved by Juba, the Numidian prince. She loves him in return, but has to hide her feeling because

> While Cato lives, his daughter has no right
> To love or hate, but as his choice directs.

When Juba seeks to begin his suit for her, Cato bids him adieu:

> It is not now a time to talk of aught
> But chains or conquests, liberty or death.

Syphax, the Numidian general, offers to carry her off by his swift horsemen, but Juba indignantly replies, 'Wouldst thou degrade thy prince to be a ruffian?'

Marcia has another wooer of a baser type, the treacherous Roman senator Sempronius, who tells the double-faced Syphax:

> I long to clasp that haughty maid,
> And bend her stubborn virtue to my passion;
> When I have gone thus far I'll cast her off.

He assents eagerly when Syphax advises him to evade Marcia's guards by dressing like Juba, but the plot is foiled by the prince's own entrance, and by a duel in which Sempronius is killed. Over what she thinks is Juba's dead body Marcia gives voice to her grief:

> Alas, he knew not, hapless youth, he knew not
> Marcia's whole soul was full of love and Juba.

Juba, listening, is enraptured:

> This, this is life indeed! Life worth preserving!
> Such life as Juba never felt till now.
> *Marcia.* Believe me, prince, before I thought thee dead,
> I did not know, myself, how much I loved thee.
> *Juba.* O fortunate mistake!
> *Marcia.*   O happy Marcia.
> *Juba.* My joy! my best beloved! my only wish!
> How shall I speak the transport of my soul?

From this riot of emotion it is an abrupt transition to the steadfast figure of Cato. It has not, I think, been sufficiently noticed that Addison, in his attempt to portray the perfect exemplar of Stoic virtue, had been anticipated a century beforehand by George Chapman in the figure of Clermont d'Ambois in his play *The Revenge of Bussy d'Ambois*. With his maxims translated from the *Discourses* of Epictetus, his doctrine that the individual must act in harmony with the Universal Will, and his final suicide, Clermont is the ideal Stoic. Somewhat later Chapman, in *The Tragedy of Caesar and Pompey*, drew Cato himself, but made him the spokesman not only of the Stoic way of life but of a Christian conception of immortality.

Nor indeed has Addison's Cato drunk only from the pure milk of Stoic doctrine. The noblest spirit of the Roman Republic dwells in him. As Juba speaks of him:

> There may'st thou see to what a godlike height
> The Roman virtues lift up mortal man.
>
> .   .   .   .
>
> And when his fortune sets before him all
> The pomps and pleasures that his soul can wish,
> His rigid virtue will accept of none.

The truth of this is exemplified when Caesar's envoy Decius arrives to greet him, as from friend to friend, and as 'the second of mankind'. Cato retorts:

> I know thou look'st on me as on a wretch
> Beset with ills and covered with misfortunes;
> But by the gods I swear, millions of worlds
> Should never bring me to be like that Caesar.

But Cato's strict discipline, his 'medley of philosophy and war', provokes a mutiny in the Roman legions, which, however, his presence quells. This is followed by the revolt of the Numidian troops headed by Syphax in which Marcus loses his life. As his body is borne in Cato welcomes it.

> How beautiful is death, when earned by virtue!
> Who would not be that youth? What pity is it
> That we can die but once to serve our country.
>
> .   .   .   .
>
> Alas, my friends,
> Why mourn you thus? Let not a private loss
> Afflict your hearts. 'Tis Rome requires your tears.
>
> .   .   .   .
>
> Rome is no more.
> O liberty! O virtue! O, my country!

It is here the patriot rather than the philosopher that speaks. Even in the last act, when Cato is on the eve of suicide, it is not, as would become a Stoic, to the precepts of Epictetus that he turns for comfort but to Plato's dialogue, the *Phaedo*.

> It must be so—Plato, thou reason'st well!
> Else whence this pleasing hope, this fond desire,
> This longing after immortality?
>
> .   .   .   .
>
> 'Tis the divinity that stirs within us,
> The heaven itself, that points out an hereafter,
> And intimates eternity to man.

Thus the Cato of Addison, like the Cato of Chapman, takes refuge from a self-sought death in a vision of immortality, though this formed no part in the Stoic creed.

But such philosophical niceties were not of concern to most of the audience in Drury Lane any more than Bernard Shaw's speculations about the 'life-force' trouble many playgoers today at *Man and Superman*. It was a time of great political excitement. The Peace of Utrecht, confirming the peace policy of the Tories and bringing a halt to the military triumphs of the Whig general, Marlborough, had just been signed. The Whigs, who had partly packed the audience at the first performance, took the lead in trying to make political capital out of the play by applauding the sentiments about liberty and patriotism. They even contrived to find an analogy to Marlborough in Pope's Tory prologue describing Cato as

> A brave man struggling in the storms of fate,
> And greatly falling with a falling state.

The Tories, on the other hand, echoed back the claps

of the Whigs, and Bolingbroke sent for Booth, who acted
Cato, and presented him with fifty guineas for defending
the cause of liberty against a perpetual dictator. Besides Booth the star cast included Mills, Wilks, Cibber,
Mrs. Oldfield, and Mrs. Porter. It had a prolonged run,
excited pamphleteering criticism, and was translated
into several foreign languages.[1] It thus made its mark
not only on the English but on the European theatre. It
furnishes one of the constantly disturbing problems of
a play, formerly in high favour, now fallen into almost
complete neglect. The literary and political conditions
which gave it its *réclame* cannot be revived. But, with its
pure diction, its high purpose, and its historic tradition,
it might well be one of the stage classics to be given a
performance in a National Theatre.

With the resounding success of *Cato* Addison might
have felt tempted to make another venture in neo-classic
tragedy. But, occupied as he was in turn with political
journalism and his duties as Under-Secretary of State, his
only further contribution to the stage before his death
on 17 June 1719 was his comedy *The Drummer*. Like
Cato, it had been written some years before it was produced at Drury Lane, on 10 March 1716, on the recommendation of Steele. The action is laid in an apparently
haunted house. Sir George Truman has been falsely
reported killed in battle. His supposed widow has two
suitors, Fantome and Tinsel. The former, in order to
scare away his rival, has, with the connivance of Lady
Truman's bribed maid, Abigail, dressed himself up to
look like Sir George, of whom he is supposed to be the
ghost, beating a drum, concealed behind the wainscot.

Pat upon this, Sir George, after being 'dead' fourteen
months, turns up again, and to test his wife's loyalty,

[1] See A. Nicoll, op. cit., p. 88, note.

arranges with his steward, Vellum, to be introduced in
the guise of a conjuror, who will silence the mysterious
drummer. He provokes Tinsel by his ironical remarks
into drawing his sword, till Lady Truman cries, 'Put up
your sword, or I must never see you again!' But Tinsel
continues to press his suit in unabashed mercenary
terms till the drum is heard and Fantome appears,
whereupon Lady Truman shrieks, "'Tis Sir George, 'tis
my husband!' and faints. As Fantome advances still
drumming Tinsel falls on his knees, crying, 'By my soul,
Sir George, I was not in earnest, have compassion on
my youth', whereupon the 'ghost' points to the door,
and Tinsel only too gladly steals off.

Fantome having driven out Tinsel, it now remains
for Sir George to get rid of Fantome, a former friend.
Meanwhile, in his role of conjuror, he amazes the
servants by his knowledge of family affairs, and puzzles
Lady Truman by telling her that she will have a husband within this half-hour, and by recalling the details
of their courtship. When Fantome appears with his
drum, he bids him be off as fast as he can or 'Mr. Ghost
will have his bones broke'. Then, discarding his disguise,
he shows himself in his own habit, whereupon Fantome
decamps, leaving behind his drum for Sir George to
hang up in his hall as a trophy of victory. He has
already ordered Vellum to divulge the secret of his
return to Lady Truman, so that they now rush rapturously into each other's arms.

Lady Tru. I am now satisfied that it is not in the power
of absence to lessen your love towards me.

Sir Geo. And I am satisfied that it is not in the power of
death to destroy that love which makes me the happiest
of men.

Steele was disappointed in the reception of the play

by the Drury Lane audience. In a preface to the first printed edition (1716) he anticipated that 'the reader will see many beauties that escaped the audience; the touches being too delicate for every taste in a popular assembly'. And in the second edition (1722) he wrote in an epistle dedicatory to Congreve, 'The *Drummer* made no great figure on the stage, though exquisitely acted; but when I observe this, I say a much harder thing of the stage than of the comedy.'

Steele, in these comments, was partly swayed by his intimacy with Addison. The plot of *The Drummer*, though ingenious, might, especially at a first performance, somewhat mystify an unprepared audience. And there was not sufficient depth of attraction in the chief characters. The 'delicate touches' of which Steele spoke were to be found principally in the delineation of the household servants, especially Vellum, a sort of comic periphrastic Polonius, and in Sir George's equivocal phrases about his wife's second husband which Mrs. Abigail interprets as fitting Fantome, but which apply really to himself.

AMBROSE PHILIPS

ANOTHER figure of note in his own day among the neo-classic dramatists was Ambrose Philips. Born in 1675 he was educated at Shrewsbury School and St. John's College, Cambridge, of which he was a Fellow from 1699 to 1708. In 1709 his *Pastorals* appeared together with Pope's in a Miscellany published by Tonson. Thomas Tickell, a member of Addison's Whig circle, praised Philips's verses highly in several issues of *The Guardian*, while ignoring Pope's. Thereupon Pope in a later issue retaliated anonymously by an ironical comparison of the merits of the two *Pastorals*. The quarrel was perpetuated later in *The Dunciad*.

Philips was rewarded by his political party with official posts in England and afterwards in Ireland. During this period his chief service to literature was to bring out a collection of *Old Ballads* (1723). He also published some translations of Greek lyrics. He died in London on 18 June 1749.

In March 1712 Philips had tried his hand in tragedy by an adaptation of Racine's masterpiece, *Andromaque*, entitled *The Distrest Mother*. In the preface to the first printed edition in the same year Philips stated that he 'had the advantage to copy after a very great master, whose writings are deservedly admired in all parts of Europe', and expresses the hope that he has done him 'no prejudice in the liberties I have taken frequently to vary from so great a poet'.

In Racine's play, partly suggested by the *Andromache* of Euripides, Hector's widow, now a captive in the palace of Pyrrhus, king of Epirus, inspires passionate love in him, though he is betrothed to Hermione, daughter of Menelaus and Helen. Andromache, devoted to the memory of Hector, and concerned above all else with the fate of their child, Astyanax, is deaf to his suit. Hermione, outraged by the disloyalty of Pyrrhus, is equally irresponsive to the amorous pleas of Orestes, son of Agamemnon, who had loved her vainly in Sparta, and who has come as ambassador of the Greek princes to Pyrrhus to demand the surrender of Astyanax to them. Pyrrhus at first refuses, but finding Andromache still obdurate announces that he will marry Hermione and give up the boy. But when Andromache appears as a suppliant before him his love for her overmasters him, and he again entreats her to share his crown. The thought of wedding the son of Achilles, who slew her Hector, is still abhorrent to her, but urged by her confidant, Cephisa, and bent on saving her son, she at last gives her consent.

The infuriated Hermione summons Orestes and bids him avenge her wrongs by killing Pyrrhus in the temple where the marriage is about to take place. At first he declines to be an assassin, but when she offers to go herself and stab him at the altar and then kill herself, he yields. When, however, he brings her the news that he has been forestalled by the Greeks in his retinue, enraged by the act of Pyrrhus in crowning Andromache as his Queen and proclaiming Astyanax King of Troy, to his amazement she turns upon him with reproaches for paying heed to the frenzy of a jealous woman. Rushing forth, she meets the body of Pyrrhus borne by soldiers and stabs herself to death upon it. Hearing this from his friend Pylades, Orestes becomes distracted, and here the French play abruptly ends.

When Philips, in his preface to *The Distrest Mother*, spoke of the liberties he had so frequently taken in varying from the original, he somewhat exaggerated. Up to the close of Act IV his play was more of a translation than an adaptation of *Andromaque*.[1] But he there introduces an interview of about 150 lines in which Andromache confides to Cephisa the secret purpose of her soul.

> Andromache will not be false to Pyrrhus,
> Nor violate her sacred love to Hector.
> This hour I'll meet the king; the holy priest
> Shall join us, and confirm our mutual vows.
> This will secure a father to my child.
> This done, I have no farther use for life:

[1] This can be confirmed by a comparison of the text of Philips with that of R. B. Boswell's English version (1890).

> This pointed dagger, this determined hand,
> Shall save my virtue, and conclude my woes.

The murder of Pyrrhus saves Andromache from such martyrdom, and Philips closes the play with an addition in which she bewails the fate of Pyrrhus, bids him be buried with 'every shining mark of honour', and exclaims, in welcoming Astyanax to her arms, that

> A pleasure, which no language can express,
> An ecstasy that mothers only feel,
> Plays round my heart, and brightens up my sorrow,
> Like gleams of sunshine in a lowring sky.

This sentimental ending, with a moralizing tag appended, is out of tune with the consistently unrelieved tragic note of Racine's play. But in the main Philips's rendering of the French rhymed alexandrines into spirited English blank verse is a praiseworthy achievement, and the long declamatory speeches dear to the Gallic stage are often aptly broken up by a comment or question by a second speaker.

On its own merits *The Distrest Mother* might have been left to win popular favour, but Steele and Addison combined to 'boost' it. For *The Spectator*, no. 290, 1 February 1712, Steele described the effect on him of a reading of it by one of the actors.

> I congratulate the age that they are at last to see truth and human life represented in the incidents which concern heroes and heroines. The style of the play is such as becomes those of the first education and the sentiments worthy those of the highest figure.

For its production at Drury Lane he wrote a prologue in which he claimed for the author:

> Your treat with studied decency he serves;
> Not only rules of Time and Place preserves,

But strives to keep his characters entire
With French correctness and with British fire.

On 25 March, eight days after the *première*, in *The Spectator*, no. 335, Steele told how with Captain Sentry he had taken Sir Roger de Coverley to *The Distrest Mother*, the first play he had seen for twenty years. He reproduces some of the old knight's comments as 'a piece of natural criticism'. Thus of Andromache's obstinate refusal at first to the importunities of Pyrrhus:

These widows, sir, are the most perverse creatures in the world. But pray, says he, you that are a critic, is the play according to your dramatic rules, as you call them? Should your people in tragedy always talk to be understood? Why, there is not a single sentence in this play that I do not know the meaning of.

This is more delicate humour than the opening lines of the epilogue, spoken by Mrs. Oldfield who played Andromache. The epilogue was ascribed in the printed play to Eustace Budgell, Addison's cousin, but contemporary talk assigned it to Addison himself. One hopes that he was not guilty of the desecration of the name Astyanax.

I hope you'll own that with becoming art
I've played my game, and topp'd the widow's part.
My spouse, poor man! could not live out the play,
But dy'd commodiously on wedding day,
While I, his relict, made at one bold fling,
Myself a Princess and young Sty a King.

The ball was further kept rolling by a paper, no. 338 of *The Spectator*, on 28 March, the day of the play's publication, attacking the epilogue, and by a reply on 1 April declaring that it received unprecedented honours in the theatre.

The *réclame* thus secured for *The Distrest Mother* has overshadowed Philips's later, more original tragedies. After an interval of ten years *The Briton* was produced at Drury Lane on 19 March 1722. The plot is drawn from the same legendary British annals as *King Lear* and *Cymbeline*, but it is given a pointed contemporary political application. The Briton is Vanoc, prince of the Cornavians, one of the petty kingdoms into which the island was divided. He is thus introduced in the prologue:

> Britons, you'll see, when Vanoc comes before you,
> The love of freedom is your ancient glory.
> The Romans first this native virtue broke,
> Made us polite—and bow'd us to the yoke.
> The Saxons then, unpolish'd, greatly rude,
> Strangers to luxury—and servitude—
> Revived the British manliness of soul
> That spurns at tyranny, nor brooks control.
>
> . . . .
>
> Blest in a prince, whose high-traced lineage springs
> From the famed race of our old Saxon kings,
> Our zeal for liberty we safely own—
> He makes it the firm basis of his throne.

When the play opens the Roman Emperor Claudius has sent a new general, Didius, to avenge a defeat which the legions have suffered. Vanoc, formerly an ally of the Romans, has been turned into a foe through the action of his second wife, Cartismand, Queen of the Brigantians. She has proved false to his bed with a lover Vellocad, whom she tries to establish as ruler by force of arms. When she is defeated she seeks protection from the Roman army and thus makes the breach between them and Vanoc. Before this took place Vanoc had consented to a coming union between Gwendolen, his

daughter by his first wife, and the Roman tribune
Valens. But now she has pledged her love to his ally,
Yvor, Prince of the Silurians, whom she impatiently
welcomes after his victory over Caledonian invaders
in which he kills Vellocad. He transports her with an
ecstatic vision of their future together.

> This day the Druids join our hands—our souls
> In mutual raptures are for ever joyn'd.
> Passing from life to life, we rise in bliss—
> Age after age, till Time shall be no more.

Vanoc greets Yvor with 'a soldier's thanks, a soldier's
praise', and then bursts into a paean which recalls John
of Gaunt's deathbed rhapsody in *Richard II*:

> From the main land, why are we set apart,
> Seated amidst the waves, high-fenced by cliffs,
> And blest with a delightful, fertile soil,
> But that indulgent Nature meant the Britons,
> A chosen people, a distinguish'd race,
> A nation independent of the world,
> Whose weal, whose wisdom, it will ever be
> Neither to conquer, nor to suffer conquest—
> Nor will we suffer it.

Gwendolen, anxious for her father and her lover, urges
Vanoc to be appeased, and goes to the temple of the
goddess Adraste to give thanks for Yvor's safety. On her
way back she is seized and carried to the Roman camp,
from which Vanoc assures the anguished Yvor she will
be redeemed. Before an attack takes place Valens
appears to offer peace. Philips reaches his dramatic
peak in the dialogue that follows. Valens seeks to
mediate between Vanoc and his queen, and when
the prince angrily protests against his arbitration, the
tribune rebukes him for being a slave to passion. He

reminds him that the Romans have brought civilization to Britain:

> Far as our legions march, they carry knowledge,
> The arts, the laws, the discipline of life.

Vanoc retorts indignantly:

> Happy for us, and happy for you, spoilers,
> Had your humanity ne'er reached our world.

When Valens, still unruffled, asks him to propose his terms of peace Vanoc answers, 'Deliver up the queen; send back my daughter.' But the Romans cannot violate their pledge to Cartismand and, with rising temper, Valens accuses Vanoc of perfidy, after Gwendolen had been affianced to him, in betrothing her to Yvor. When the Briton declares, 'Were it to save her life, she should not wed a Roman', the tribune, taking him at his word, retorts, 'She shall not be a wife, but she shall be a slave.'

When, however, Valens returns to the Roman camp his love overpowers his resentment. He assures Gwendolen that her happiness will be his tenderest care, reminds her that his was the elder claim to her hand, and pours forth impassioned pleas for her favour. But she turns from him, declaring that she never loved him, or gave him hope, and that he is only trying to sever two hearts that are for ever joined. At last, stung to furious jealousy, he announces that he will avenge his torments by resigning her to Cartismand. But again his love prevails, and when Cartismand hypocritically asks that Gwendolen should be committed to her womanly care, he turns upon her with reproaches, and when she appeals to Didius, assures him that Gwendolen's life would not be safe in her charge. In the tumult of a sudden British attack the queen finds the girl momentarily un-

protected, and when she refuses to fly with her, stabs
her, crying:

> Thus, Vanoc, to thy heart
> I drive the poignard. Thus I brave thy fury.

With her dying lips Gwendolen renews her vows to
Yvor.

> *Gwen.* We are to live again. Continue mine!
> Through every life we pass, let me be yours.
> *Yvor.* O, ever—ever mine!
> *Gwen.*   Sweet, pleasing hope.
> No jealousy did ever interrupt our love,
> Nor shall it yield to death.

She dies before Vanoc comes to threaten vengeance
on the 'bloody tigress'. But with a suicidal dagger's
thrust she mocks his rage. Yvor's sword is at his own
breast when Vanoc bids him forbear:

> Our injuries, my daughter's fate, our country's cause,
> Bid us to live. We must not throw off life,
> But lay it down, when Heaven appoints us rest.

This edifying maxim does not come very aptly from the
lips of Vanoc, who has shown throughout the play an
impetuous and violent temper. Indeed one of the virtues
of this tragedy is the contrast between the more primitive emotions of the Britons and the disciplined reactions
of the Romans. Apart from either shines the figure of
Gwendolen, the embodiment of a constant spiritual love
that sets her among the radiant heroines of the Drury
Lane stage.

A year later Philips, in a tragedy *Humfrey, Duke of
Gloucester*, acted at Drury Lane from 15 to 25 February
1723, brought on the stage a less legendary vindicator
of England's liberties. In dedicating the play to the
politician, William Pulteney, Philips described this

brother of Henry V in extravagant terms as 'a man of singular goodness; a wise and upright statesman; a great opposer of the oppressive usurpations of the see of Rome . . . a most loyal subject; a learned prince, and an encourager of learning'. The last clause of this encomium is well deserved, but for the rest Philips, as he acknowledges in his address 'to the Reader', was indebted less to historical fact than to Shakespeare in Part II of *King Henry VI*. But while the Elizabethan play portrays chiefly internal dissensions, Philips converts the action mainly into a defiance of the machinations of Rome. This is set forth explicitly in some lines of the prologue spoken by Booth, who impersonated Humfrey:

> Where never-erring Rome usurps a sway,
> To go by Reason is to go a-stray.
> Freedom of thought we Britons justly prize,
> Parent of liberty and scourge of vice.
>
> .   .   .   .
>
> Our free-born bard a free-born hero draws,
> HUMPHREY, the patron of learn'd WYCLIF's cause.
> View here the force of bigotry in kings;
> View here the woes that superstition brings.
>
> .   .   .   .   .   .
>
> But, sure, destruction is the patriot's doom,
> When kings are only ministers of Rome.

Thus the chief enemy of Humfrey, Protector during his nephew's minority, and of his wife Eleanor, is Cardinal Beaufort, Humfrey's uncle. When Eleanor is sentenced to do penance for witchcraft, and Beaufort declares that this falls 'far short of her demerits', Humfrey retorts:

> Her whole demerits are that in religion
> She reasons more, perhaps, than you allow,
> Perhaps rejects, as frivolous and vain,
> What churchmen teach of witchcraft and of spells.

Together with the Queen, and her lover Suffolk, Beaufort heads a conspiracy to urge the King not only to dismiss Humfrey from his office but to arrest him on suspicion of treason. He accuses the Duke of supplanting Henry in the popular favour:

> Who has not heard the blast of vulgar breath
> Calling him Humfrey, the good Duke of Gloucester,
> Clapping their hands and crying with loud voice,
> 'Long may your Excellency live!'
> With 'Heaven preserve the good Duke Humfrey!'?
> *Suff.* No mention of the king in all their transport—
> Duke Humfrey reigns!

The King orders that the Protector be confined to his apartment. The angry protests of his supporters, the Earl of Warwick and the Duke of York, spur Beaufort to rapid action. He has also to fear the wrath of the common people who, on hearing of Humfrey's arrest, rise in insurrection and threaten to storm the royal palace. It is only when the Duke sends greetings to them that, after hearing from Warwick that he is in no danger, the tumult is appeased. But he is mistaken, Beaufort is determined that he shall die at once, and hires two ruffians who smother him in his sleep, leaving no trace of blood. As Eleanor hastes once again to his side, she is prevented by Warwick, rushing from the bedchamber and crying, 'Never more shall you behold him living.' Beaufort repudiates the charge of being his murderer, till one of the ruffians stricken by remorse confesses to Warwick's father, the Earl of Salisbury, how Gloucester has been murdered. Suffolk, who has had a lesser role than in the Elizabethan play, seeks to escape the popular rage by flight, but is killed on board a barge in the Thames. Beaufort is suddenly seized with a violent fever, and on his death-bed raves in delirium about Humfrey's murder:

> Bring me unto my trial, when you will.
> Died he not in his bed? where should he die?
> Can I make men live, whether they will or no?

These and some dozen lines that follow are lifted from *2 Henry VI*, III. iii, by Philips, who with more honesty than judgement speaks of them as not to be surpassed in beauty by any other passages in Shakespeare. In contrast with the hopeless doom of Beaufort is the final epitaph on Humfrey:

> Number'd among the best
> Gloucester partakes of everlasting rest.

Designed, as it was, to minister to popular prejudice, the play was skilfully enough planned, and, in spite of some passages of rodomontade, Philips again shows command of effective thrust and parry in dialogue.

VI

JOHN DENNIS—JAMES THOMSON

JOHN DENNIS, like Addison and Philips, was a product of public school and university education. Born in London in 1657 he was the son of Francis Dennis, a saddler in good circumstances. From Harrow as his school he proceeded to Caius College, Cambridge, where he graduated B.A. in 1679, afterwards migrating to Trinity Hall. As a zealous adherent of the Whig Party he obtained in 1705, through the patronage of the Duke of Marlborough, an official post in connexion with the port of London. But the light duties which this involved allowed him to devote much of his time to literary pursuits, and he soon tried his fortune as a writer for the theatre.

His first plays, *A Plot and No Plot*, a comedy, and *Rinaldo and Armida*, a tragedy founded on Tasso, belong to the last years of the seventeenth century. His *Iphigenia*, performed in Lincoln's Inn Fields Theatre in December 1699, was published on the first day of 1700. It was ushered in by a prologue in which the Genius of England leads in the Tragic Muse lamenting:

> 'Am I by all forsaken then?' said she.
> 'Oh, is my Britain false to this degree
> As for effeminate arts t'abandon me?
>
> . . . .
>
> Here song and dance, and every trifle reigns,
> And leaves no room for my exalted strains.'
>
> . . . .
>
> To give you wholesome, true severe delight,
> With me the tragic Muse returns to-night.
> To your soft neighbours sound and show resign,
> But listen you to her great voice and mine.

This exordium was justified in so far as Dennis adapted
from Euripides one of the great Greek legendary stage
themes. But he departed from its austere spirit by inter-
weaving with it a complicated sentimental love plot.
With Euripides, in his *Iphigenia in Tauris*, the main interest lies in the atonement of Orestes, for his killing of
his mother, Clytemnestra, by bringing to Athens from
Tauris at Apollo's command the statue of the virgin
goddess, Artemis. At her shrine his sister, Iphigenia,
supposed to have been slain at Aulis by her father,
Agamemnon, is the chief priestess who purifies before
they are sacrificed the human victims offered on the
altar. Orestes and his bosom friend Pylades, doomed
thus to suffer, are saved by Iphigenia when through her
questioning their identity has been revealed, and when
finally Athene intervenes on their behalf.

The mystical element in the Greek play was foreign
to eighteenth-century England and for it Dennis substituted a sex interest. He replaced the King in Tauris,
Thoas, by a Queen who falls in love with the noble look
and speech of Orestes and plans to make him her spouse.
Before the discovery of the relationship of Iphigenia to
Orestes, he and Pylades both become enamoured of her
but each is ready to give way to the other. In the dialogue between them Dennis is at his best, as when
Orestes declares:

> The sordid'st wretch that breathes can die for love,
> 'Tis a soft, wanton, universal flame,
> Great Nature's art to propagate mankind.
> The Gods as many lovers make as men,
> But they scarce make two friends for many ages.
> Of all the race of living men
> Fame celebrates us two alone for friendship.

Pylades incenses the Queen by telling her that Orestes

has aroused love in the heart of the priestess. She prepares a terrible revenge by telling the girl that she must
herself sacrifice him on the altar and then die by the
sacred steel;

> But know . . . that yet 'tis in thy power to save him;
> But let not pass the irrevocable moment;
> Think that the next comes hurrying on, and then,
> Unless thou first persuad'st him to abandon thee,

the doom must fall. In a somewhat too long-drawn-out
interview Iphigenia vainly begs Orestes to appease the
Queen, but as she gradually reveals that his love is
returned, he cries, 'My heart, my life, my very soul is
yours', and as she faints when guards enter to announce
the beginning of the 'dismal ceremony' he clasps her in
his arms.

Events in the last act move rapidly. Orestes, on his
way to the temple, is rescued by his Greek followers. His
place as the victim is taken voluntarily by Pylades, who
prevents Iphigenia from killing herself. As another
priestess prepares to strike Pylades Orestes enters and
intercepts the blow. He is trapped by the Queen into
an oath that, if he is freed from his passion for another
woman, he will obey her command to share her crown.
Thereupon she announces that the goddess has declared
Iphigenia her victim, and orders her to be sacrificed.
But her own subjects fear the curse that will fall on them
if they lay impious hands upon the priestess, and cry for
her to be set free. To satisfy them and the two Greeks the
Queen reveals that she is the Iphigenia whom Artemis
had doomed to die by her father's hand at Aulis, but
escaped through her mother's artifice. Thus the amazed
Orestes learns that the priestess is the sister long thought
dead. He can bestow her hand upon his 'other dearer
half', Pylades, and himself becomes the royal partner of

the Queen, who, leaving a deputy in Tauris, will sail
with him to Greece, bearing with them the statue of
Artemis, as Apollo had decreed.

Dennis certainly shows remarkable ingenuity in working up to this conclusion, and the play contains some
effective dialogue and situations. But there is an un-
wholesome element in the detailed portrayal of what
proves to be, however unconscious, an incestuous passion
between brother and sister, and the savage-tempered,
scheming Queen does not merit to become the mate of
Orestes.

After adapting *The Merry Wives of Windsor* into *The
Comical Gallant*, produced at Drury Lane in 1702, Dennis
returned to tragedy with *Liberty Asserted*, presented at
Lincoln's Inn Fields in February and March 1704. In
a dedication of the printed text to his friend, Anthony
Henley, he says that it was from him that he got 'the
happy hint upon which this poem was form'd'; and that
Henley would approve of its motive 'to open the eyes
of deluded men, to inspire them with the love of liberty,
and unite and animate them against the common foe
of Europe'. *Liberty Assured* is thus both a stage play and
a political tract, seldom a fortunate combination. Its
scene is Canada, where the English allied with the
Indian Iroquois tribes are in conflict with the French
aided by the Hurons. A Huron woman, Sakia, has been
for twelve years a captive among an Iroquois tribe, the
Angians. She had been secretly married to a French-
man, Miramont, and their son Ulamar, ignorant of his
paternity, has become General of the Iroquois and has
just gained a great victory over their enemies. Sakia is
torn between loving pride in her son and commiseration
for her Huron kindred and for the French to whom her
husband belongs.

At this point Dennis carries over from *Iphigenia* the *leit-motiv* of self-sacrificing love between two men friends. Irene, the lovely daughter of Zephario, chief of the Angians, is courted both by Ulamar and by Beaufort, General of the English. Her father has promised her hand to whichever of the pair performs the noblest deeds against their foe. Beaufort testifies that it is to Ulamar's brave example that the victory is due, and that Irene should be his. Sakia, whose husband had made her swear that she would never wed their son to an Indian maid, in vain begs Beaufort to make a prior claim. She then turns to reproach Ulamar for fighting against his own countrymen. In his reply Dennis strikes the central chord of the play:

> Every brave man's country is the Universe,
> His countrymen mankind, but chiefly those
> Who wish the happiness of all the rest,
> And who are friends to all their fellow-creatures;
> And such are all the brave Iroquian tribes,
> Such are th'unconquer'd English, free themselves,
> And loving all who actually are free
> And all who sadly sigh for liberty;
> But hating tyrants and their slaves alike,
> And equally contemning both as fallen
> Below the dignity of human nature.
>
> .   .   .   .
>
> Such are those pests of human race, the French,
> Damn'd to eternal slavery themselves,
> And therefore would like devils damn mankind.

This tribute to the English is soon confirmed by the action of Beaufort, to whom the Council of the Iroquois allots Irene. Knowing that her love is given to Ulamar he accepts the gift, merely to bestow her upon his friend. Her father assents:

> The deed is noble, for 'tis wise and just.
> The English always were a gallant nation,
> And foes to force, and friends to liberty.
> They who without the mind possess the body
> Possess by force, and ravish, not enjoy.

He promises that their hands shall be joined this very night. But before this can take place the French send envoys to offer a lasting peace. Beaufort warns that they are not to be trusted but Ulamar, under his mother's threat of suicide if the proposal is rejected, wins Zephario's assent to it. Beaufort announces that he and Ulamar must part for ever, but in love.

> *Ul.* What, must we part?
> *Beau.* Part, Ulamar? Why that's the very thing
> Thy new allies design'd:
> 'Tis by dividing old and faithful friends
> That they oft ruin both; 'tis their old cheat.

The tactics in a 'cold war' have changed little from Queen Anne's day to our own. Beaufort's suspicions are soon justified. The French, under orders from the Parisian Court, make a treacherous night attack, in which Zephario is killed, and Ulamar and Irene taken captive. In the previous battle Ulamar had spared the life of Miramont, kinsman of Frontenac, Governor of New France, who orders the General of the Iroquois to be at once executed. Miramont pleads for him, and at last Frontenac grants him life till daybreak in the hope that he may be won over to the French side. If so, he may be made commander over all the warlike Canadian tribes. Ulamar retorts by an offer in kind. If Frontenac will shake off the vile yoke of the French monarchy he will, with the help of the English and the Iroquois, be made king of Canadian France. In a long rhetorical outburst he accuses the French of having first brought 'impious war' to these 'happy groves', and he is supported by Miramont. When the time is due to expire Ulamar declares for 'liberty' and is being led off to execution, when his mother embraces him, calling on Miramont. The captain of that name answers, but she cries, 'I know thee not'; but when Frontenac appears she exclaims:

> Ha! Gods! He comes, with the same frown he comes.
> . . . .
> Com'st thou to call thy miserable wife?
> She comes, in life and death, thy own Nikaia.

Such had been her name before captivity, and the Governor, formerly Miramont, had become Frontenac by his elder brother's death. As he clasps her to him this is revealed just in time to prevent him from executing his own long-lost son.

Well may he exclaim:

> These are events surpassing all example;
> These are th' amazing miracles of fate.

To complete the reunion Beaufort returns, and saves Irene, hearing that Ulamar was dead, from suicide. He is greeted with a final panegyric on his country.

> O truly great! O truly worthy son
> Of Great Britannia, through the world renown'd
> For propping falling liberty,
> Supporting sinking nations!

To which he responds:

> Be govern'd still by reason and by law,
> And let your monarch still be Heaven's vicegerent,
> And execute his Master's will, not his.
> Thus govern'd, we are absolutely free,
> Heav'n and good kings give perfect liberty.

As in *Iphigenia* Dennis may be given credit for a certain
amount of ingenuity in plot-planning. But a number of
incidents are too fantastic, and the dialogue often too
flamboyant, for *Liberty Assured* to be of much account as
a stage play. It has, however, permanent value as an
expression of the temper of the English nation towards
the France of Louis XIV in the year of Blenheim. And
at times it is curiously relevant to some aspects of international relations in the twentieth century.

After two unsuccessful attempts in lighter vein, *Gibral-
tar* (1705) and *Orpheus and Eurydice* (1707), Dennis returned to tragedy and to a classical theme with *Appius
and Virginia*, produced at Drury Lane on 5 February
1709. Had he known the fine play on this subject some
eighty years earlier by Webster and Heywood he would
have been well advised not to seek to emulate it. But
where the Jacobean dramatists had merely the interests
of the theatre in view Dennis once more wrote with a
political aim. In dedicating the play to Godolphin, the
Lord High Treasurer, he asserts that it 'was written in
the cause of liberty', for which Godolphin and his friend,
Marlborough, had done such mighty things, between
them supporting the Queen. And the epilogue makes it
clear that it was on her account that Dennis chose this
theme of a Roman heroine:

> Virginia's death did liberty restore,
> As from Lucretia's tomb it rose before.
>
> .   .   .   .
>
> Though Rome in heroes always did abound,
> Still from her women she lost freedom found.
> So fair Britannia o'er the world is fam'd
> For men of dauntless spirits and untam'd;
> But yet when by her folly or her fate
> Her liberty was in a dangerous state,

The blessing ne'er could be secur'd by man,
But heaven reserv'd th' immortal fame for Anne.

Virginia, however, does not aspire to the role of a liberator of her country. Her betrothed lover, Icilius, tells her that she is the glorious instrument to deliver Rome from the tyrant Decemvir, Appius, who has become enamoured of her.

Think, think, that by the part which thou shalt bear
In such a glorious action, thou'lt oblige
Rome and the Gods, who have predestin'd Rome
To be the mighty mistress of the Universe.

She replies in lines which are scarcely equalled throughout the play:

The Gods of every virtue are possess'd:
'Tis the possessing all which makes them Gods.
Not so are mortals, but from Heaven derive
Those which at first the forming hand of Jove
Fitted their earthly organs to receive.
Thus Man in power and intrepidity,
And great revenge, the image is of Heaven:
Woman in soft compassion and in mercy.
The nobler virtues I admire and love,
Which shine so bright in my Icilius' soul,
But humbly am content to practise those
Which fit the softness of my sex and temper.

Icilius retorts that the creative Power gave to Roman women nobler souls than to men of other nations, and, as Appius approaches, bids her

Summon Rome's injur'd genius to thy aid.
The Gods, who gave thee all this wondrous beauty
To enslave the very soul of the proud wretch
Who thinks it great his country to enslave,
Will, if invok'd, infuse into thy breast
A spirit worthy of that matchless form.

She does indeed bravely defy the decemvir's arrogant
claim that by his boundless power he can dissolve her
contract with Icilius. And when he again asserts that he
is absolute, she rejoins that only Jove is absolute, and
that he has inspired her

> To throw my soft and tender nature off,
> And speak in his own language, speak in thunder,
> To tell thee thy dire crimes have reach'd their height.
>
> .   .   .   .
>
> Hark! how the dreadful thunder o'er thee growls,
> And is about to part with hideous roar.

It was probably as an accompaniment to these lines that
Dennis invented a new kind of stage thunder which, he
complained, after his play was withdrawn, was stolen to
be used in a production of *Macbeth*.

The tyrant, unmoved by Virginia's appeals and
threats, is panic-stricken by the discovery that the house
is occupied by a group of armed men, only awaiting
their associates, to take his life. Up to this point Dennis's
dramatization of the story has been credible but it now
becomes fantastic. Appius hypocritically pretends that
by Virginia's words, convincing him of the truth of a
dreadful night vision of Hell's torments, his soul has
been touched to repentance. Too easily deceived, she
hands him the key of a postern gate by which he escapes
just as his enemies enter to find him gone, and incredu-
lously to hear from Virginia that his penitence has saved
him.

The figure of Claudius, an uncle of Appius, who, for
the honour of the Appian house, seeks to deter his
nephew from further crimes, appears to be an invention
of Dennis. Above all he denounces the stratagem by
which Fulvius, the hireling of Appius, is to claim Virginia as his slave, and thus acquire complete rights over

her. The spectacle of tyrannic power masquerading in legal form as justice has unhappily become more familiar, and on a wider scale, to this twentieth century than it was to the early-eighteenth-century spectators of the scene in which Appius adjudges the girl to Fulvius. Another attempt by Icilius and his friends to overpower Appius in the courthouse is frustrated by a cohort which he has summoned, and in revenge he condemns them to instant execution. Icilius comforts his associates with the assurance that posterity will speak of them as deliverers of their country, and in the answer of one of them Dennis is again heard at his best:

> Then let the instruments of fate come on,
> Since 'tis as natural to die as live;
> The business is not when, but how, we die:
> Death's but a scarecrow which the Gods have plac'd
> To fright weak men from tasting immortality.

But unforeseen deliverance comes. Claudius, enraged at being dragged by the order of Appius from the court-house, prevails on the prefect of the prison, whom he had set free from slavery, to admit him and to give the prisoners arms with which they kill their warders. Appius passing the gate takes their dying groans to be those of his victims. When he makes a last appeal to Virginia's father to unite them in marriage, and Virginia answers that she is contracted to Icilius, he cries triumphantly, 'My rival's dead', and threatens Virginia with death unless she is made his. There is but one way left of saving the girl's honour. She must die.

> *Virginia.* Then strike, I am prepared.
>
> .   .   .   .
>
> And Roman law gives Roman parents power
> At pleasure to resume that life they gave.

Calling on Heaven to receive her spotless as when she first came to earth, Virginius nerves himself to deal the fatal blow before Icilius, whom he takes to be a ghost, enters with news of the safety of their friends and the liberation of Rome, only to be confronted with the sight of Virginia slain. When he vows that he alone will avenge her death, Virginius bids him strike at his heart. But Icilius refuses: 'You held the dagger, Appius struck the blow.' As Virginius distractedly rushes forth to seek suicide Appius appears and starts on seeing Icilius who points to the body of Virginia. When Appius vows to avenge her Icilius tells him that his armies have revolted and the Senate has deposed him, but that, as he has sworn that by his hand Appius must be killed, he defies him to single mortal combat. In the duel that follows Appius falls, and Icilius calls on the infernal powers to receive him.

> Attend, ye screaming ghosts of murder'd Romans!
> Behold your Judge now sentenc'd in his turn,
> And doom'd to pains at which the damn'd will tremble,
> And take their own for joys.

It is such rodomontade that Pope parodies when he tells the critics how Dennis is infuriated by their comments.

> But Appius reddens at each word you speak,
> And stares tremendous, with a threatening eye,
> Like some fierce tyrant in old tapestry.

But, as has been seen, Dennis at times can reach a higher level. Even his Appius, self-confessed victim of his infatuation for Virginia, and meeting death with dignity, is not entirely a melodramatic ogre. Claudius, the uncle, does honour to the Appian house, and is a pivot on which much of the later action of the play turns. Virginia, with her unflinching loyalty to her contracted lover, is a type of noble Roman womanhood. But the Drury Lane audience may not unreasonably have failed to find in her as a defender of liberty a prototype of Queen Anne. The play, after its first short run, does not appear to have been revived. Nor was Dennis more fortunate when a decade later he again sought in classical story (*via* Shakespeare) a parallel to events of his own day. In *The Invader of his Country: or The Fatal Resentment*, staged for three nights at Drury Lane from 11 November 1719, Coriolanus was designed to prefigure the Old Pretender of 1715.

Somewhat paradoxically it is as a critic rather than a playwright that he is now remembered. His earliest important critical treatise was *The Advancement and Reformation of Modern Poetry* (1701). This was followed in 1703 by *A Person of Quality's answer to Mr. Collier*, a defence of the stage against Collier's strictures. In 1704 appeared *An Essay on the Operas after the Italian manner*. In 1711 he crossed swords with Pope in *Reflections on a late Rhapsody called An Essay on Criticism*. In the same year he published his most important critical work, *Three Letters on the Genius and Writings of Shakespear*. This opens with memorable words: 'Shakespear was one of the greatest geniuses that the world ever saw for the tragic stage. Tho' he lay under greater disadvantages than any of his successors, yet he had greater and more genuine beauties than the best and greatest of them.' The disadvantages, in Dennis's eyes, arose from Shakespeare's ignorance of the classical 'Rules'. But these Dennis interpreted more in the spirit of Aristotle than of such theorists as Rymer, and his work in this field thus remains of value.[1]

---

[1] A complete edition of his critical works, in two volumes, has been edited by E. N. Hooker (Johns Hopkins Press, Baltimore).

His later years were shadowed by poverty and neglect, though the Earl of Pembroke and Bishop Atterbury
came to his relief, and a performance of *The Provok'd
Husband* was staged for his benefit in December 1733,
shortly before his death on 6 January 1734.

JAMES THOMSON

ANOTHER writer who, like Addison, had established his
position in another literary field, and who made a yet
more determined but less successful attempt to achieve
renown as a dramatist, was James Thomson. Born at
Ednam in Roxburghshire in September 1700, he was
educated at Southdean parish school, Jedburgh, where
his father was minister, and at Edinburgh University,
where he began to write verse. In 1725 he came to
London and in the following year began publication
with his poem *Winter*, in which his gift of natural
description was shown. It was followed by *Summer*
(1727), *Spring* (1728), and by *Autumn* which appeared
in the collected volume, *The Seasons*, in 1730.

In the previous year Thomson had made his first
dramatic venture with his tragedy *Sophonisba*, produced
at Drury Lane on 28 February 1729. He probably was
unfamiliar with Marston's play of the same title (1606),
but Lee's *Sophonisba* (1675) might have been known
to him through its revivals in 1725 and 1726 or in
one of its reprints. In any case it was the fate of this
Carthaginian heroine to have wellnigh as great attraction for dramatists as her legendary predecessor Dido
or the Egyptian Cleopatra. The prologue to Thomson's
play declared that Sophonisba had been the theme of
the Italian tragic Muse and, with Corneille, of the
Gallic.

What foreign theatres with pride have shown
Britain, by juster titles, makes her own.
When Freedom is the cause, 'tis hers to fight;
And hers, when Freedom is the theme, to write.
For this a British author bids again
The heroine rise, to grace the British scene.

It is the claim, so persistently made by these early
eighteenth-century dramatists, that in bringing on to the
stage legendary or historic champions of freedom they
are serving the cause of liberty in their own country.

With Sophonisba, daughter of Hasdrubal, her dominant passion is to prevent her native Carthage becoming
enslaved to the tyrannous power of Rome. To this she
has sacrificed her first love for Masinissa, King of
Massylia, when he had enlisted under the banner of
Scipio, the Roman General. She has given her hand in
wedlock to another royal suitor, Syphax, not through
love of him but because he was a defender of Carthage.
When the play opens news has just come of the defeat
in battle of Syphax by Masinissa and the Romans,
whereupon Sophonisba attempts to kill herself but is
restrained by her friend Phoenissa:

> Hold your rash hand,
> Nor thro' your guardian bosom stab your country.
> This is your last resort, and always sure;
> The generous gods are liberal of death:
> To that last blessing lead a thousand ways.

Syphax is led in chained, and after hurling defiance at
Masinissa bids him not touch Sophonisba, to which he
replies,

> Thy bonds divorce
> And free her from thy power. All laws in this,
> Roman and Carthaginian, all agree.

.   .   .   .

Poor Sophonisba!
She too becomes the prize of conquering Rome,
Which most her heart abhors.

When she enters, she almost echoes his words:

This, this alone I beg. Never, oh, never!
Into the cruel, proud and hated power
Of Romans let me fall.

If this be not possible, let him strike her dead and earn
her last blessing. Her tears at last prevail.

O Sophonisba, rise! while here I swear,
By the tremendous powers that rule mankind,
By heaven and earth, and hell! by love and glory,
The Romans shall not hurt you—Romans cannot,
For Rome is generous as the gods themselves,
And honours, not insults, a generous foe.

As a pledge of her safety he places his royal hand in hers.
But this cannot stifle her fury against Rome.

The Romans are the scourge
Of the vext world, destroyers of mankind.

.   .   .   .

Against her tyrant power each generous sword
Of every nation should be drawn—while Carthage
Unblemish'd rises on the base of commerce,
Founds her fair empire on the common good,
And asks of Heaven nought but the winds and tides
To carry plenty, letters, science, wealth,
Civility and grandeur, round the world.

There can be no doubt that Thomson, by the Romans,
is here referring to the French and, by Carthage, to
Britain. In dedicating his play to Queen Caroline he
speaks of her as commanding the hearts of a people
'more powerful at sea than Carthage, more flourishing

in commerce than those first merchants, more secure against conquest'.

For a time Masinissa turns indignantly from her and bids her a glad farewell. But again his passion, for whose paradoxical manifestations he pleads pardon, triumphs:

> Whose each emotion is but varied love,
> All over love, its powers, its passions, all:
> Its angers, indignation, fury—love:
> Its pride, disdain, even detestation—love:
> And when it, wild, resolves to love no more,
> This is the triumph of excessive love.

As captivity has dissolved her marriage with Syphax he urges her to bind again that very night their former broken vows, and she consents, solely for the sake of Carthage. To the bitter reproaches of Syphax for her treachery to him she retorts:

> All loves but that of Carthage I despise.
>
> .   .   .   .
>
> And if preferring
> Thousands to one, a whole collected people,
>
> .   .   .   .
>
> The liberty, the welfare of a state
> To one man's frantic happiness be shame,
> Here, Syphax, I invoke it on my head.

But now Laelius, lieutenant of the proconsul Scipio, accuses Masinissa of robbing Rome of her greatest prize, the captive Queen. And when Scipio himself follows, though a brother in arms to Masinissa, he reproaches him:

> What! perish for a woman! Ruin all,
> All the fair deeds which an admiring world
> Hopes from thy riper years, only to soothe
> A stubborn fancy, a luxurious will.

When the African pleads, 'Why should we kill the best
of passions, love?' Scipio rejoins that there is

> A virtuous, social, sympathetic love,
> That binds, supports, and sweetens human life,
> But is thy passion such?

When Masinissa further pleads his vow to save Sophonisba from the Roman power, Scipio hints darkly that
his secret thought can best inform him how to keep faith
both with her and Rome, and reminds him that

> Real glory
> Springs from the silent conquest of ourselves.
> And without that the conqueror is nought
> But the first slave.

There is only one way left to Masinissa to save her from
what she dreads. He sends her a bowl of poison, which
she drinks, and dies crying,

> O never, never, Carthage,
> Shall I behold thee more.

Over her body Laelius pronounces the epitaph which
sums up the moral of the play:

> She had a Roman soul; for every one
> Who loves, like her, his country is a Roman.
> .   .   .   .
> If generous liberty the breast inflame,
> The gloomy Lybian then deserves that name,
> And warm with freedom under frozen skies,
> In farthest Britain Romans yet may rise.

The contrast between the patriot Queen to whom her
country is all in all and the soldier King swayed by his
overpowering love for her is well conceived. But Thomson mars its effect by too long-drawn-out speeches.
Though his poetic gift shines in occasional passages he

lacks the playwright's flair for incisive interchange of dialogue which was the saving virtue of Ambrose Philips.

It was not till eight years later that Thomson again
tried his hand at tragedy in *Agamemnon*, produced at
Drury Lane on 6 April 1738. The play bears the title
of the royal leader of the Greeks who is just returning to
Mycenae after the ten years' war against Troy. But as
with *Sophonisba* it is a woman, Clytemnestra, who is the
central figure. She has sinned with Egisthus, but Thomson seeks in all ways to palliate her guilt. Agamemnon
has deserted her for ten years. On pretence of marrying
their daughter, Iphigenia, to Achilles he has sacrificed
her at Aulis to Diana, as the price of a favouring wind.
For years she had resisted her seducer, till he had banished to a desert isle Melisander, left by her husband
to guide her counsels.

When Agamemnon enters to find her not, as he had
expected, overjoyed but downcast and tearful, she gives
as excuse that the deadly scene at Aulis is still before her.
His answer might have been fitting in a council of war
but not as consolation for a bereaved mother:

> If to the mingled voice
> Of honour, duty, glory, public good,
> Of the commanding gods, I had been deaf,
> And in the feeble father poorly sunk
> The Greek, the chief, the patriot and the king,
> Greater than king, the general of the Greeks,
> Then you, yourself, my Clytemnestra's self,
> Must (let her heart avow the truth) have scorn'd me.

When Egisthus hypocritically laments that he has had
no share in the glory of the war, Agamemnon's reply is
still more closely related to the theme of 'public good',
and is probably not without a bearing on the political
situation of Thomson's day.

> Ruling a free people well in peace,
> Without or yielding or usurping power;
> Maintaining firm the honour of the laws,
> Yet sometimes softening their too rigid doom,
> As mercy may require; steering the State
> Thro' factious storms, or the more dangerous calms
> Of peace, by long continuance grown corrupt:
>
> .   .   .   .
>
> Yes, know that these are in true glory equal,
> If not superior, to deluding conquest.

It is in a less philosophic temper that the King turns upon Egisthus for defaming Melisander, whom he had by chance rescued from his banishment, and threatens to do justice between them. It is for this that Egisthus fixes Agamemnon's doom. But Clytemnestra will not go farther in guilt with him:

> Drive me no further down the gulf of woe!
> To happiness I bid a last farewell;
> I ask not happiness; no, that I leave
> To innocence and virtue: peace, alone,
> Some poor remains of peace is all I ask.

It is only when Egisthus holds before her the prospect of the captive Cassandra as Queen of Argos, while she pines in a prison, that she is roused to the thought of revenge. But when he puts his design plainly into words, 'Let Agamemnon die', she recoils in horror.

> There are degrees in guilt
> And I have still my reason left, have left
> Some resolution, some remnant of virtue.
> Yes, I dare die; and who dares die, Egisthus,
> Needs not be driven to villainous extremes.
>
> .   .   .   .
>
> And if you do not promise me, here swear,
> To drop your fell designs on Agamemnon,

To quit this palace—you may still escape—
And never see me more, I go, I go,
This moment to discover all and die.

Egisthus, after his appeals are in vain, declares:

You only court dishonour to no purpose,
For Agamemnon now cannot escape,
I am already master of this palace.

.   .   .   .

He dies—dies in the bath before the banquet.

It is left to Cassandra to prophesy the woe so soon to
come:

Short-sighted man! to dream of festal joy,
When his next banquet is perhaps with Pluto.

Almost as she speaks the voice of Agamemnon being
murdered is heard off-stage, and soon the back-scene
opens to disclose his body, with Egisthus standing
exultant beside it. Again Cassandra predicts to Egisthus
further doom. The gods will avenge Agamemnon's
death, and to confirm this the news comes that his son
Orestes has escaped, while Clytemnestra enters raving
till she faints into an attendant's arms. Well may Egisthus
cry, 'O nothing then is done!'

In this tragedy Thomson shows at times more command of the thrust and parry of dialogue than in
Sophonisba, but the action is again overweighted by long
descriptive or reflective speeches. According to the
prologue it was to teach a moral lesson:

Vice in its first approach with care to shun;
The wretch who once engages is undone.
Crimes lead to greater crimes, and link so straight,
What first was accident at last is fate.
Guilt's hopeless servant sinks into a slave,
And virtue's last sad strugglings cannot save.

The play was dedicated by Thomson to the wife of Frederick, Prince of Wales, with whose party, in opposition to Walpole and Queen Caroline, he was in sympathy. Did the Drury Lane audience, like a modern critic, find them prefigured in Egisthus and Clytemnestra? In any case it was not favourably received, and after the first performance the greater part of the epilogue, 'having been very justly disliked by the audience', was replaced.

The prologue to *Agamemnon* was written by David Mallet, and Thomson collaborated with him in a masque, *Alfred*, presented before the Prince and Princess of Wales on 1 August 1740 at Cliveden. In this presentation of the Anglo-Saxon King, rising from defeat by the Danes to victory, Thomson's political philosophy finds its voice in a hermit, who brings before Alfred and his wife Eltruda a vision of some of his greatest successors—Edward III, with Queen Philippa and the Black Prince; Elizabeth, William III, George II, and sprung from him, a Prince, Frederick, who will inherit the virtues of Alfred. It is one of the ironies of theatrical history that out of Thomson's considerable dramatic output only the ode, 'Rule, Britannia', with which *Alfred* comes to a close, survives in popular acclaim.

The Hermit's vision in *Alfred* had not included Edward I and his consort because Thomson had already, in 1739, presented them at full length in a play, *Edward and Eleanora*, which was put into rehearsal for performance at Covent Garden Theatre. It was, however, banned by the Lord Chamberlain and Thomson had to content himself with dedicating it in print, like *Agamemnon*, to the Princess of Wales. In implying a parallel between her and Eleanora he spoke of the latter's 'inviolable affection and generous tenderness for a Prince, who was

the darling of a great and free people'. The censor may
well have thought that in portraying Edward, while
still heir to the throne, as a complete paragon Thomson
was too obviously intending him to be a prototype of
Frederick.

Edward is on crusade before the walls of Jaffa, and
is debating whether to accept an offer of peace from
Sultan Selim. The Earl of Gloucester urges him to do
so and to return at once to England. Though the
crusade is a holy cause, yet it is

> A nobler office far on the firm base
> Of well-proportion'd liberty to build
> The common quiet, happiness and glory
> Of king and people, England's rising grandeur:
> To you, my prince, this task of right belongs.
> Has not the royal heir a juster claim
> To share his father's inmost heart and counsels
> Than aliens in his interest, those who make
> A property, a market of his honour?

Could anyone mistake the relevance of these lines to the
contest that was being waged round George II between
the Walpole ministry and the 'patriot prince'?

It is in a higher, pantheistic, strain that Gloucester
again pleads for a departure from Palestine.

> I venerate this land. Those sacred hills,
> Those vales, those cities trod by saints and prophets,
> By God himself, the scenes of heavenly wonders,
> Inspire me with a certain awful joy.
> But the same God, my friend, pervades, sustains,
> Surrounds and fills this universal frame:
> And every land where spreads his vital presence,
> His all-enveloping breath, to me is holy.

But before peace can be signed, a fanatic, posing as an
envoy from the Sultan, gives Edward a poisoned wound

only to be cured by someone who will incur certain
death by sucking the venom out. Thus Thomson proceeds to dramatize the traditional story that it was
Edward's wife who faced the deadly risk for his sake.
And up to a point the dramatist's treatment is effective.
When Edward first hears that his life may be saved by
another's sacrifice he protests:

> When life or death
> Becomes the question, all distinctions vanish;
> Then the first monarch and the lowest slave
> On the same level stand, in this the sons
> Of equal Nature all.

Once again Gloucester seems to be having the England
of the eighteenth rather than of the thirteenth century
in view in his appeal:

> O save our country, Edward, save a nation,
> The chosen land, the last retreat of freedom
> Amidst a world enslav'd. . . .
> On this important, this decisive, hour,
> On thee, and thee alone, our weeping country
> Turns her distressful eye; to thee she calls.

And when, to Edward's horror, Eleanora approaches as
his saviour, she too uses a similar plea.

> Let me preserve a life, in which is wrapt
> The life of thousands dearer than my own.
> Live then, and let me die for thee, my Edward.

But her appeals are all in vain. He will not submit to
what her 'horrid tenderness' proposes. Her opportunity,
however, comes when the working of the poison casts
him into a deep sleep, during which she sucks the
wound. And when she in turn feels her approaching
doom, it recalls to Thomson one of the most poignant
episodes in Greek drama, the self-sacrifice of Alcestis on
behalf of her husband Admetus. As has been pointed

out,[1] the moving description of Eleanora's farewell to
her home and household in Act III, scene iv, beginning
'Wild to her bed she rush'd', and continuing for about
forty lines, is a close paraphrase of the farewell of
Alcestis in Euripides' play.

There follows a too prolonged sentimental interchange between the dying Eleanora and her husband,
and his agonized lamentations over her which the news
that by his father's death he has become King of England only inflames. Once more Gloucester adjures him
in words with a contemporary undertone:

> Thy dejected country calls upon thee
> To save her, raise her, to restore her honour,
> To spread her sure dominion o'er the deep,
> And bid her yet arise the scourge of France.
> Angels themselves might envy thee the joy
>
> .   .   .   .
>
> Of dashing down the proud, of guarding arts,
> The sacred rights of industry and freedom,
> Of making a whole generous people happy.

And inconsistently with his former plea to Edward to
make peace and return home he now urges him to
avenge Eleanora's death by assaulting the enemy's
'guilty bowers'. So when a dervish from the Saracen
camp comes with a message of import Edward hurls the
bitterest reproaches upon him, his treacherous Prince,
and his shameless race. Unmoved the dervish answers:

> The cursed wretch who did assail thy life,
> O king of England, was indeed an envoy
> Sent by the prince of Jaffa. This we own,
> But then he was an execrable bigot.
>
> .   .   .   .

[1] By A. Hamilton Thompson, in the *Cambridge History of English
Literature*, vol. x, pp. 108–9.

For know there lives upon the craggy cliffs
Of wild Phoenician mountains a dire race
A nation of assassins. Dreadful zeal,
Fierce and intolerant of all religion
That differs from their own, is the black soul
Of that infernal state.

. . . .

Of these the villain was, these ruffian saints,
The curse of earth, the terror of mankind.

We of the mid-twentieth century have only too much
cause to recognize this as a true picture of a homicidal
fanatic. But it rouses Edward to further fury till the
dervish, throwing off his disguise, reveals himself as
Sultan Selim. Even then Edward questions his good
faith, and challenges him to a duel, but Selim retorts
that he asks him but to hear one witness—a woman.
And that woman proves to be no other than Eleanora,
saved, when in the very arms of death, by a wonderful
antidote which Selim, at the risk of his own life, has
brought. This would have been an effective *coup de
théâtre* had the play been licensed for the stage. But
viewed purely dramatically *Edward and Eleanora* is too
prolix in its later scenes; and the passionate Edward in
them, who compares unfavourably with the calm Selim,
is difficult to identify with the Prince of whom such high
hopes have been entertained. Yet as a theatrical tract
for the times, and as a plea for religious tolerance, the
play retains its interest today.

In *Tancred and Sigismunda*, produced at Drury Lane on
18 March 1745, Thomson turned to a theme which owes
its origin to Boccaccio but which had gone through
many dramatic transformations (of which Thomson
was probably unaware) at the hands of English and
continental dramatists. With Thomson the name Tan-

cred, which in the *Decameron* was that of the heroine's
father, now called Siffredi, is transferred to her lover.
This points to a change in the balance of the tragic
interest from the relation between father and daughter
to that between the lovers.

Tancred, son of a murdered noble, has been privately
reared by Siffredi, Lord High Chancellor of Sicily. On
the death of the King, Siffredi reveals to Tancred that by
his will he has been appointed heir to the throne instead
of the King's sister Constantia. Tancred accepts this
unlooked-for high destiny unless it depends on marriage
with Constantia, for his heart has been wholly given to
Siffredi's daughter Sigismunda. He greets her rapturously:

> Thou art queen of Sicily, and I
> The happiest of mankind; than monarch more
> Because with thee I can adorn my throne.

But she shrinks back at the news.

> You are my sovereign; I at humble distance.
> *Tan.* You are my queen; the sovereign of my soul.
> *Sigis.* But ah! the hearts of kings are not their own,
> There is a haughty duty that subjects them
> To chains of fate, to wed the public welfare,
> And not indulge the tender private virtues.

Thus is set forth the *leit-motiv* of the play, the contest
between the claims of public duty and of personal affection. And by an ill-considered action Tancred precipi-
tates this. He hands to Sigismunda to be given to her
father a blank paper with his signature.

> Tell him 'tis my command, it be fill'd up
> With a most strict and solemn marriage-contract.

This puts an instrument into Siffredi's hands. The late
King, as Tancred had feared, had made it a condition

in his will that his heir should wed Constantia. To avert
civil war Siffredi determines that this shall take place,
though it will mean his daughter's loss both of her lover
and a crown. Murmuring to himself that

> Necessary means
> For good and noble ends can ne'er be wrong:
> In that resistless, that peculiar case
> Deceit is truth and virtue,

he writes on the blank paper beneath Tancred's signature an absolute agreement to the terms of the will. To
the assembled Senate, with Constantia and Sigismunda
both present, Siffredi reads this aloud and Tancred, dis-
simulating his true feeling, leads off Constantia as his
consort. But when left alone with Siffredi he turns upon
the 'hoary traitor' with bitter reproach:

> Hast thou not
> Beneath thy sovereign's name basely presum'd
> To shield a lie, a lie, in public utter'd
> To all deluded Sicily?

Siffredi bids him exhaust his rage on his grey head;

> But when the storm has vented all its fury
> Thou then must hear—nay more, I know, thou wilt,
> Wilt hear the calm yet stronger voice of reason.
> Thou must reflect that a whole people's safety,
> The weal of trusted millions should bear down,
> Thyself the judge, thy fondest partial pleasure.

Similarly he pleads with Sigismunda:

> Let not thy father blush to hear it said
> His daughter was so weak, e'er to admit
> A thought so void of reason that a king
> Should to his rank, his honour, and his glory,
> The high important duties of a throne,
> Even to his throne itself, madly prefer
> A wild, romantic passion.

She sorrowfully submits to his paternal authority till he makes his last demand that she should seek shelter in the arms of a husband—Earl Osmond, the Lord High Constable. She begs that he will not thus outrage her bleeding heart. But when her confidante Laura urges that she will thus have revenge on Tancred and embitter his marriage, she gives way, though as Osmond makes his avowal of love she faints.

Too late Tancred renews to her his passionate transports and reveals her father's stratagem with the paper, only to be told that she is Osmond's wife. He declares that with his kingly power he will annul their union, and orders Osmond's arrest. Released, on parole, for the night by the governor of the castle, Osmond determines to carry off Sigismunda. But Tancred comes before him to her and hears her plea,

> Try to forget the worthless Sigismunda.
> *Tan.* Forget thee? No! thou art my soul itself,
> I have no thought, no hope, no wish but thee.
> .   .   .   .
> Ah, how forget thee? Much must be forgot
> Ere Tancred can forget his Sigismunda.

He begs her to come forth with him, but she declares that her heart cannot shake the 'unalterable dictates' within her breast.

> O leave me! fly me! were it but in pity,
> To see what once we tenderly have lov'd
> Cut off from every hope—cut off for ever!

At that moment Osmond enters, and attacking Tancred is wounded, but ere he dies stabs Sigismunda, who with her last breath appeals to her lover:

> Harbour no resentment
> Against my father: venerate his zeal

That acted from a principle of goodness,
From faithful love to thee.—Live and maintain
My innocence embalm'd, with holiest care
Preserve my spotless memory.

Siffredi himself points the moral to the parents in the audience:

Behold the fatal work of my dark hand,
That by rude force the passions would command,
That ruthless sought to root them from this breast:
They may be rul'd, but would not be opprest.

But this edifying precept comes inaptly from his lips, for throughout, even at personal cost, he has sought, however mistakenly, to subordinate a love romance to the public welfare. And it is inconsistent with the character of Tancred to lead forth Constantia, after the reading of the will, and of Sigismunda to be won over by Laura to betrothal with Osmond. Moreover, Thomson was again too prolix, especially in the later scenes, and, as he admits, the play had to be 'considerably shortened in the performance'. Yet withal it has in its own degree something of the wistful pathos of *Romeo and Juliet*—of young love crushed beneath the iron weight of an alien world. With Garrick as Tancred, Thomas Sheridan as Siffredi, and Mrs. Cibber as Sigismunda the play was well received, and enjoyed, according to Thomson, the 'protection' of the Prince of Wales, to whom he dedicated the printed text. This was later translated into French and German. It was unfortunate that Thomson closed his work for the stage with a treatment of the *Coriolanus* theme (January 1749). But the survey here made of his dramatic output may help to show that it was more worthy of the author of *The Seasons* than has been generally recognized.

VII

JOHN GAY

THE hold on the stage of the neo-classic tragedies, unrelieved by a single flash of humour, had its inevitable reaction in a series of burlesques. And in addition to the tragedies there was another species of high-flown entertainment that lent itself, partly on patriotic grounds, to parody. This was opera 'after the Italian manner', of which *Arsinoë, the Queen of Cyprus*, produced at Drury Lane in January 1705, was a herald, and *Camilla* at Drury Lane and Dorset Garden, 1706–7, a more prolonged success. With *Almahide* at the Haymarket in January 1710 and Handel's *Rinaldo* and later operas, the type was firmly established.

Amongst the wits of the Town who launched satirical shafts against the dominant theatrical fashions, John Gay, born at Barnstaple in September 1685, stands pre-eminent. Of Gay's non-dramatic works, *The Shepherd's Week* (1714), a burlesque of the pastorals of Ambrose Philips; the mock-didactic *Trivia, or the Art of Walking the Streets of London* (1716), and *The Fables*, with their blend of humour and moralizing (1727), all that need here be said is that they contain elements which reappear in his dramatic writings.

The first of these, *The Mohocks*, 'a Tragi-Comical Farce', published by Bernard Lintot in 1712, was never performed, the statement on the title-page that it 'was acted near the watch-house in Covent Garden by Her Majesty's servants' being merely an ironical description of the doings of the Mohocks, rowdy men about town who were the terror of peaceable citizens. The mocking

intention of the piece is plain from the dedication to
Mr. D[ennis].

There are several reasons which induce me to lay this
work at your feet. The subject of it is *Horrid* and *Tremendous*,
and the whole piece written according to the exactest rules
of dramatic poetry, as I have with great care collected them
from several of your elaborate dissertations. The World will
easily perceive that the plot of it is formed upon that of
Appius and Virginia, which model, indeed, I have in great
measure follow'd throughout the whole conduct of the play.

What Gay means by saying, even in jest, that the plot is
formed upon that of *Appius and Virginia* is difficult to see
except that it ends with a trial. Six Mohocks on their
knees swear fealty and allegiance to their Emperor, who
pledges them in

> Wine, potent, heavenly juice, immortal wine.
> Slothful awhile inglorious mortals lay,
> But wine to nobler action led the way:
> Wine conquers all things—all must wine obey.

Meanwhile the Watchmen are welcoming a new 'Mr.
Constable' with tales of the exploits of the Mohocks, to
which he replies that they 'are but men—and we be men
as well as they be', whereupon he is assured 'we all
stand by you with our lives and fortunes'. The Constable
then sends the greater number of them through the
streets to apprehend the Mohocks, for 'the Justices are
now sitting, and have ordered all that we shall take to be
immediately brought before them'. He asserts that there
is 'not a man among you shall step a step farther than
myself', but when the Mohocks are heard coming he
changes his note to 'let us do all things in order—Do you
advance, gentlemen, d'ye see, and while you advance
I'll lead up the rear.' But when the Mohocks enter, the

watchmen throw down their poles and fall on their knees, while the Constable trembles before the Emperor.

Up to this point the scene has some echoes of the true comedy of Dogberry and the Watch, but henceforward it sinks into pure farce. In 'a merry frolic' the Emperor changes clothes with the Constable and the Mohocks do likewise with the watchmen and take their poles and lanterns. They play these topsy-turvy roles before Gentle, a beau, and Joan, a watchman's wife, and then bring the Constable and watchmen before a bench of Justices to whom they are strangers. The Justices are neatly discriminated. Scruple wishes to search the Statute Books for guidance. Kindle asserts that 'where the Law is silent, there our Will is the Law'. Wiseman urges that they should be guided by Reason, to which Kindle retorts, 'What has Reason to do with Law?—We must judge according to the Letter of the Law', and Scruple now backs him up.

The Emperor, in his role of Constable, charges the watchmen with being Mohocks, and when they try to plead their innocence they are forced to confess to being guilty by being pricked from behind. Kindle is crying out that they must be committed, when the rest of the Watch enter with Gentle and Joan. The secret of the interchange is now out, and though the Mohocks plead that it was 'only an innocent frolic', Wiseman sternly retorts, 'Frolics for brutes and not for men', orders the watchmen to arrest them, and promises that their proceedings shall be punished with the utmost severity. Can it be that the actors rejected the piece for the stage because they thought that, ending with so rigorous a threat against fashionable rowdies, it might have riotous consequences? However this may be, *The Mohocks*, if carefully read, will be found to have more dramatic worth than critics have usually allowed.

Gay had called *The Mohocks* a 'tragi-comical farce'. Perhaps with a recollection of *The Shepherd's Week* in the previous year he gave to his next dramatic venture, staged at Drury Lane on 23 February 1715, the even more paradoxical title of *The What D' Ye Call It: A Tragi-Comi-Pastoral Farce*. This is partly justified by its being a play within a play. Members of the household of Sir Roger, a country Justice, including his son, Squire Thomas, together with some rustic neighbours, are being drilled by his Steward for the performance of a Christmas holiday play.

In this Squire Thomas is to play Thomas Filbert, the hero in love with Katherine, the Steward's daughter, as Kitty Carrot. Jonas Dock is to act Timothy Peascod, sentenced to be shot as a deserter, with a sister in the play, Dorcas, and a bastard daughter, Joyce, 'left upon the parish'. After some dressing-up problems have been settled, Sir Roger enters crying, 'I will have a ghost; nay, I will have a competence of ghosts', and is assured by the steward that he will be satisfied. When two neighbouring Justices, Sir Humphry and Justice Statute, come in, he tells them gleefully, 'We have so fitted the parts to my tenants that ev'ry man talks in his own way —and then we have made three Justices in the play, to be play'd by us three Justices of the *Quorum*.' He plumes himself upon his experience in these stage matters, he has known 'your Harts and your Bettertons'; and has heard Othello raving and roaring 'about a foolish flower'd handkerchief', and seen him 'put the light out so cleverly'.

The preparations over, the Christmas entertainment is introduced in a prologue spoken by Pinkethman, who played Peascod:

Which strives to please all palates at a time
With ghosts and men, songs, dances, prose and rhyme;
This comic story or this tragic jest
May make you laugh, or cry, as you like best.

The opening scene partakes of 'the tragic jest'. Gay
combines two aims in *The What D' Ye Call It*, theatrical
parody and indictment of the harshly administered
penal laws. Filbert, falsely accused by Dorcas that she
is with child by him, is sentenced by the Justices either
to marry her or to serve as a soldier against the French.
His cause is pleaded by Kitty, and by his grandmother
and his aunt, who pours out a list of cruel verdicts for
petty offences:

> O tyrant Justices, have you forgot
> How my poor brother was in Flanders shot?
>
> .   .   .   .
>
> What though a paltry hare he rashly kill'd
> That crossed the furrows while he plough'd the field,
> You sent him o'er the hills and far away,
> Left his old mother to the parish pay,
> With whom he shar'd his tenpence ev'ry day.
> Wat kill'd a bird, was from his farm turn'd out;
> You took the law of Thomas for a trout.

But their prayers are in vain. Filbert is dragged off by
the sergeant on the one side of the stage, and the weeping Kitty by the aunt and grandmother on the other.
The three Justices are left alone, almost at once to be
denounced by the accusing Ghosts for whom Sir Roger
had stipulated at rehearsal. But now he cowers before
them, crying,

> Why do you shake your mealy heads at me?
> You cannot say I did it—

This is, of course, a close parody of Macbeth's protest to
the Ghost of Banquo:

> Thou can'st not say I did it; never shake
> Thy gory locks at me.

The two other Justices echo, 'No, nor we', to which each
of the Ghosts answers, 'All three'; after which one of
them sings 'dismally' a song of invitation to goblins and
fairies to Sir Roger's hall, followed by a dance of all the
Ghosts round the trembling Justices.

In Act II Peascod is being led out to execution by a
firing squad as a deserter. A pitying Countryman lends
him a good book in which to pray. Peascod, weeping,
stammers out its title, '*The Pilgrim's Progress—eighth-
edi-ti-on*'. Here Gay is parodying the scene in Addison's
Cato, where the Stoic, before his suicide, ponders over
Plato's dialogue, *Phaedo*.[1] Peascod announces that five
pounds paid to the Corporal would set him free. Filbert
and other friends offer their subscriptions, but the Sergeant protests, 'No bribes.' They have a last drink together to speed him on his way, receive his parting gifts,
and bid him farewell. Then a Soldier rushes in with a
reprieve for Peascod, followed by a Constable, who gives
a topsy-turvy turn to the action by ordering the arrest of
the Sergeant, who has stolen a mare and can therefore
be hanged, though the law lets a man escape who has
stolen a horse.

Dorcas has meanwhile confessed that it is not by Filbert that she has been betrayed, and he has therefore
been released from soldiering. Kitty, however, does not
know this, and she bids farewell to fields and flocks, and
to the rake, the companion of her cares. Her laments are
echoed by a Chorus of Sighs and Groans, a burlesque of

---

[1] See p. 122, above.

the classical Chorus. But we can scarcely grudge her a
grief which finds such moving expression in the ballad
beginning,

> 'Twas when the seas were roaring
>   With hollow blasts of wind,
> A damsel lay deploring,
>   All on a rock reclin'd.

Plunging still deeper in despair she finally faints, and
has water thrown over her to revive her. Its first effect
is to send her wits astray.

> Hah! I am turn'd a stream—look all below;
> It flows, and flows, and will for ever flow.

This is like the stream in Horace's poem, *in omne volubilis
aevum*; and her invocation of

> Bagpipes in butter, flocks in fleecy fountains,
> Churns, sheep-hooks, seas of milk, and honey mountains

is a pastoral variant of Otway's distracted Belvidera's

> Murmuring streams, soft shades, and springing flowers,
> Lutes, laurels, seas of milk and ships of amber.[1]

The reappearance of Filbert, exclaiming 'Let's to church!'
at once restores her. The wedding was to have followed
in the play, but the rustic who was to have acted the
parson cannot do so because the curate (i.e. vicar) will
not lend his gown, 'for he says it is a profanation'. The
indignant Sir Roger bursts out, 'Tell him that I will not
have my play spoil'd; nay that he shall marry the couple
himself—I say he shall.' The parish-clerk then announces, 'The steward hath persuaded him to join their
hands in the parlour within', but he will not enter the
hall as it is a stage *pro tempore*. Sir Roger grudgingly
agrees to let him have his humour, but orders the doors

---

[1] See *Poetical Works of John Gay*, ed. by J. Underhill, vol. i, p. xxxiv.

to be set wide open, so that all may be seen. Gleefully he points to the details of the ceremony, 'The ring, i' faith. To have and to hold! right again—well play'd, doctor; well play'd, son Thomas.'

Then comes the astonishing *coup de théâtre*. At the rehearsal the Steward's daughter had murmured in an aside that Squire Thomas had already made love to her in earnest, as her condition showed. The Steward now greets Sir Roger:

> I wish you joy of your play, and of your daughter. I had no way but this to repair the injury your son had done my child—she shall study to deserve your favour.
>
> *Sir Roger.* Married! how married? Can the marriage of Filbert and Carrot have anything to do with my son?
>
> *Steward.* But the marriage of Thomas and Katherine may, Sir Roger.
>
> *Sir Roger.* What a plague, am I trick'd then? I must have a stage play, with a pox!

He turns angrily upon his son, 'Had you no more wit than to say the ceremony? He should only have married you in rhyme, fool.' Then Squire Thomas makes his confession, 'Look ye, father, I was under some sort of a promise too, d'ye see—so much for that. If I be a husband, I be a husband, there's an end on't.' But Sir Roger, hoist with his own petard, goes out in a passion. As in Kyd's *Spanish Tragedy* the close of the play within the play has turned out, though in happier fashion, not to be merely counterfeit. The piece had not at first an unqualified success but it won a long-term approval. It went through four editions in ten years, and it was constantly revived at different theatres during the eighteenth century. It might prove acceptable to community players today.

There is a well-supported tradition that Pope had a

hand in *What D'Ye Call It*. He collaborated with Gay
and Arbuthnot in the comedy, *Three Hours after Marriage*, produced at Drury Lane on 16 January 1717. In
spite of the distinction of the trio of authors, and of the
identification of the chief characters with well-known
contemporary figures, the piece fell flat. This may have
led Gay to turn for a time to more serious forms of
drama. The scene of *Dione, A Pastoral Tragedy* is laid in
Arcadia and the dialogue is throughout in rhymed couplets and in the conventional idyllic strain. Dione has
been brought up at Court, and it is in a love-lorn mood
that she has fled to the woods, where she thinks her
swain Evander has met a hunter's death, and where she
finds refuge from Cleanthes whom her father has ordered
her to wed. Evander, however, is not dead, and Dione
faints into the arms of her confidante Laura as she sees
him paying court, under the name of Lycidas, to the
scornful beauty Parthenia, who flies from him.

Parthenia has been adapted by Gay from Marcella in
Don Quixote for unrequited love of whom Chrysostome
dies, whose funeral the Don witnesses. In two scenes
closely modelled on the Spanish tale Menalcas, as Gay
calls him, is buried by the mourning shepherds, according to his dying wish, at the place where he had first seen
Parthenia. When she herself appears and is reproached
for murdering him she replies:

> 'Tis to his rash pursuit he owes his fate,
> I was not cruel: he was obstinate.

If they would save Lycidas from a like fate, let them
bring him to Menalcas' grave.

Laura, however, plans differently. She urges Dione to
don a shepherd's vest and, under the name of Alexis, to
seek Evander, who will turn again to her, when his

passion for the obdurate Parthenia has cooled. Posing
as his friend Dione offers to plead for him with Parthenia, but it is in vain. Evander then begs 'Alexis' to let
Parthenia know that he is no base-born swain but of
high birth and wealthy, and that it is for love of her that
he assumed a sylvan dress. 'Alexis' urges him to return
to the Court, and then he confesses his treachery there
to his former love Dione. Once more she seeks Parthenia
and tells her of the true state of 'Lycidas', only to hear
that she scorns his gifts but welcomes 'Alexis' as a friend.
Evander, overhearing them, thinks that he has been
betrayed and bitterly upbraids 'Alexis'. Dione, thus
twice wronged by him, is now to meet her more faithful,
though rejected, lover Cleanthes, who has followed her
to the forest and been attacked by brigands. In his last
moments he prays that he might see her, but before she
can reveal herself to him he dies. In self-reproach she is
about to kill herself, when Parthenia seizes the dagger
from her. But she regains it later and is again about to
strike at herself when Parthenia cries, 'Ah, hold! forbear, forbear!' Evander, thinking she is being assaulted,
snatches the dagger from Dione, and stabs her. As she
recognizes her assailant she murmurs:

> There needed not or poison, sword, or dart:
> Thy faithless vows, alas! had broke my heart.

Her last wish to Evander is for oblivion.

> Let o'er my grave the lev'ling plough-share pass.
> Mark not the spot; forget that e'er I was.
> Then may'st thou with Parthenia's love be blest,
> And not one thought on me thy joys molest.

But as Laura exclaims that he has killed his once dear
Dione he turns the dagger against himself, crying,
'Though I was false in life, in death I'm true.'

Though the Lord Chamberlain issued an order on 16 February 1720 that the play was to be acted,[1] it seems never to have been performed, but was included among Gay's *Poems on Several Occasions* (1720). The pastoral convention, with its Dresden-china swains and nymphs and its artificial types of speech, is today alien to us. The hackneyed similes from a semi-fictitious nature are distasteful, and when we weep we do not say, 'From either lid the scalding sorrows roll.' But Gay's true poetic strain is heard as follows from Dione's lips:

> When o'er the garden's knot we cast our view,
> While summer paints the ground with various hue,
> Some praise the gaudy tulip's streaky red,
> And some the silver lily's bending head;
> Some the jonquil in shining yellow drest,
> And some the fring'd carnation's varied vest.
> Some love the sober violet's purple eyes.
> Thus beauty fares in diff'rent lovers' eyes.
> But bright Parthenia like the rose appears,
> She in all eyes superior lustre bears.

And hear Parthenia herself:

> Who shall compare love's mean and gross desire
> To the chaste zeal of friendship's sacred fire?
> By whining love our weakness is confest,
> But stronger friendship shows a virtuous breast.
> In Folly's heart the short-lived blaze may glow:
> Wisdom alone can purer friendship know.
> Love is a sudden blaze which soon decays;
> Friendship is like the sun's eternal rays;
> Not daily benefits exhaust the flame,
> It still is giving, and still burns the same.

Gay must have the credit of extending the orbit of the

---

[1] See Nicoll, op. cit., p. 275.

austerely virginal maiden whom he drew from Cervantes, and of contrasting with her a paragon of self-sacrificing love.

From pastoral tragedy Gay seems to have turned to pastoral opera, for though *Acis and Galatea*, with music by Handel, was not produced at Lincoln's Inn Fields till 26 March 1731, there is ground for believing that it was written ten years before. Its plot is taken from Ovid's *Metamorphoses*, Book XIII. Acis, the handsomest Sicilian youth, and the nymph Galatea are happy in their mutual love till the Cyclops Polyphemus becomes enamoured of her and kills Acis with a rock. By her art Galatea changes him into a river. The opera is complete with a chorus of shepherds, and recitatives and airs by the principals. Two of these airs, beginning,

> Love in her eyes sits playing,
> And sheds delicious death:

and

> O ruddier than the cherry,
> O sweeter than the berry,

are still popular in the concert-room.

In 1724 Gay's theatrical bent took an unexpected turn with *The Captives*, a tragedy, produced at Drury Lane on 15 January. The captives of the title are Persian prisoners of the Medes, taken in battle, including their prince, Sophernes, whom the Median King Phraortes treats with special clemency. A conspiracy against the King, headed by Hydarnes, fails and the tyrannical minister Araxes falsely accuses and arrests Sophernes. The Queen, Astarte, a Parthian beauty raised by the infatuated Phraortes to the throne, has become enamoured of Sophernes. She offers to free him if he will fly with her to Parthia. But his love is fixed on his wife,

Cylene, missing since the battle, and he has given his *parole* not to attempt to escape. Astarte, infuriated with his cold response to her proposal, vows vengeance. At her instigation Hydarnes, on a promise of pardon, denounces Sophernes as a traitor, and he is sent back to his dungeon and to death.

A captive woman approaches the throne with a tale of how Sophernes raped her and then killed her husband. She begs that she may be allowed to give him the fatal stroke. But when she enters the dungeon she reveals herself as the lost Cylene who by her feigned tale has gained access to him. She adjures him to take her veil and escape while she will use the fatal dagger on herself. Thus when Astarte, torn with conflicting passions, comes for a last interview with Sophernes, she finds instead Cylene, who confesses who she is and what she has done. Astarte, fearing the effect on the King of a rival's beauty, urges him to have her publicly executed. But when he is proceeding to his devotions in the temple Hydarnes renews his attempt on his life, and is frustrated by Sophernes, who stabs him and begs as his reward that Cylene be spared. Hydarnes with his dying breath confesses that Astarte moved him to accuse Sophernes, and she stabs herself when reproached by the King, who gives his blessing to the reunited husband and wife.

Gay's fame in lighter dramatic fields has done prejudice to any appreciation of his only tragedy. But it was approved by the capable Princess of Wales (afterwards Queen Caroline), to whom he read and dedicated it. And it ran with applause for a week at Drury Lane, though it was not revived. Our own age has unfortunately become more familiar than that of George I with conspiracy and assassination in oriental courts. And if the conventions of heroic tragedy, to which *The Captives* reverts, are accepted, the plot and characterization are not without interest. In especial Astarte, the impersonation of the Virgilian *spretae injuria formae*, and Sophernes, a Stoic transformed into a Persian, stand out. And the blank verse dialogue, though not individualized or rising to poetic height, keeps throughout a level of lucidity.

In *The What D'Ye Call It* Gay had composed a play within a play parodying some of the features of grand opera, and containing a ballad besides other songs and dances. By October 1727 he had developed a somewhat similar scheme on a greatly extended scale. The *compère* (who is also the composer) is now not a country squire but a beggar who has invented a piece that is an opera in all its forms, except that it has no recitatives. He has often had it performed by his company of beggars in their great room at St. Giles's. He now is thanking a player for allowing it to be performed upon a professional stage. Such is the explanatory introduction to *The Beggar's Opera*. But Gay was to find the Drury Lane management less accommodating than the player in his introduction. His ballad-opera with its sixty-nine airs was rejected. He then submitted it to John Rich of the Lincoln's Inn Fields Theatre. Rich had hitherto been chiefly remarkable as a successful producer of pantomimes annually since 1717, in which he played the part of Harlequin. Though doubtful about the result, he made the venture of staging the piece at his theatre on 29 January 1728.

Swift had made the suggestion to Gay and to Pope of 'a Newgate pastoral'. There is nothing, however, of a pastoral in *The Beggar's Opera*; the atmosphere is entirely one of Newgate. The dialogue, which takes the place of recitatives, introduces Peachum, an associate of thieves and a receiver of their stolen goods, and his wife. They have social ambitions for their pretty daughter Polly which she disappoints by secretly marrying the dashing highwayman, Captain Macheath.

Mrs. Peach. Then all the hopes of our family are gone for ever and ever.

Peach. And Macheath may hang his father- and mother-in-law, in hope to get into their daughter's fortune.

Polly. I did not marry him (as 'tis the fashion) coolly and deliberately for honour or money. But I love him.

Mrs. Peach. Love him! Worse and worse! I thought the girl had been better bred.

Peachum calms his angry wife, and asks Polly has she thought of a jointure and being a widow?

Polly. But I love him, sir; how then could I have thought of parting with him?

Peach. Parting with him? Why, that is the whole scheme and intention of all marriage articles. The comfortable estate of widowhood is the only hope that keeps up a wife's spirits. . . . Secure what he hath got, have him peached the next sessions and then at once you are made a rich widow.

. . . .

Mrs. Peach. Away, hussy! Hang your husband, and be dutiful.

Polly warns Macheath to escape, but before he goes he visits his gang and a set of women of the town, two of whom give him away to Peachum for arrest. Lockit, the chief turnkey, welcomes him back to Newgate. So, after another fashion, does his daughter Lucy, whom he had seduced under a promise of marriage, and who now accuses him of being the husband of Polly, which he denies. Meanwhile Peachum and Lockit are at loggerheads over their gains from thieves and informers, till Lucy comes in tears to her father, and the scene between Peachum and Polly is repeated.

Lucy. One can't help love; one can't cure it. 'Tis not in my power to obey you, and hate him.

Lock. Learn to bear your husband's death like a reasonable woman. . . . No woman would ever marry, if she had not the chance of mortality for a release. Act like a woman of spirit, hussy, and thank your father for what he is doing. . . . Consider, girl, you can't have the man and the money too—so make yourself as easy as you can by getting all you can from him.

With Polly coming to the prison to stay with her dear husband till death, there follows the duel between the two women, each claiming him as her own, till Peachum pulls Polly away and Macheath persuades Lucy to give him the means of escape, though she fears he will return to Polly, whom she vainly tries to poison when she revisits Newgate. Here also Macheath comes back, once more betrayed by a woman, and is sentenced to instant execution.

As he goes out guarded, to the tolling of a bell, the player who has given leave for the performance suddenly intervenes:

But, honest friend, I hope you don't intend that Macheath shall be really executed.

Beggar. Most certainly, sir. To make the piece perfect, I was for doing strict poetical justice. Macheath is to be hanged; and for the other personages of the drama, the audience must have supposed they were all either hanged or transported.

Player. Why then, friend, this is a downright deep tragedy. The catastrophe is manifestly wrong, for an opera must end happily.

This is not an argument that would hold water today but it impresses the beggar, who admits that the objection is 'very just, and is easily removed, for you must allow that in this kind of drama 'tis no matter how absurdly things are brought about'. So he bids the rabble cry a reprieve, though it spoils the moral the piece was intended to show, that 'the lower sort of people have their vices in a degree as well as the rich, and that they are punished for them'.

So Macheath re-enters and declares that the day is to be celebrated by a dance, in which he will take Polly as his partner, as also for life—'for we were really married'. So the truth is out at last.

From this outline of the plot of *The Beggar's Opera* it is evident that even when stripped of its musical setting the piece has its own interest. It is a keenly observed presentation of the rogues' gallery of its day. And the struggle between the two girls for the love and the hand of the fascinating highwayman appeals to the emotions. The only feature that seems out of key is Lucy's attempt to poison Polly. One source of attraction to the contemporary audience has passed. Among hits at the Whig government by the Tory Gay was the quarrel scene between Peachum and Lockit, here standing for Walpole and Townshend. Sir Robert, who was among the very distinguished first-night audience, had the tact to applaud it.

But what turned the scale, for a time doubtful, in the opera's favour were the airs, which, with the exception of a march from Handel's *Rinaldo*, were set to traditional English and Scottish tunes.[1] It was Polly's singing of Air XII,

---

[1] On these see the notes by G. H. Macleod to his edition of the opera, published by the De La More Press (1905).

> O ponder well! be not severe:
> So save a wretched wife.
> For on the rope that hangs my dear
> Depends poor Polly's life.

that first roused the audience to enthusiasm. Among
others of special note that followed were the duet between her and Macheath, beginning, 'Were I laid on
Greenland's coast' and ending 'Over the hills and far
away'; Macheath's song, 'If the heart of a man is deprest
with cares', and, most moving of all, as he stands between Polly and Lucy,

> How happy could I be with either,
> Were t'other dear charmer away.

The final result was a triumph. The piece had an unprecedented run of sixty-three days and was revived
year after year in different theatres. It made its way to
the chief English provincial towns, to Wales, Scotland,
and Ireland, and even to Minorca. Seven editions were
published by 1745. Out of the theatrical proceeds the
usually impecunious Gay got about £800 and Rich
£4,000, and Lavinia Fenton, who played Polly, became
the Duchess of Bolton. How their ghosts must have
rejoiced in the success of the play when, nearly two
centuries after its *première*, it was revived by Sir Nigel
Playfair at the Lyric Theatre, Hammersmith.

It was natural that Gay should seek to exploit the
triumph of the *Beggar's Opera* by providing it with a
sequel, but it is astonishing that he made such a mess
of this with *Polly*. It would have been well had he taken
as a warning the words that he had put into the mouth
of the poet addressing a player in the introduction to
Polly, 'A sequel to a play is like more last words. 'Tis
a kind of absurdity: and really, sir, you have prevail'd

upon me to pursue this subject against my judgment.'
In *The Beggar's Opera* Gay had combined the realism
due to his intimacy with London low life with something
of an operatic *bravura* atmosphere. He now transported
(in more senses than one) several of its characters to the
West Indies, of which he knew nothing. Macheath, returning to his evil courses, has been banished there and
is living as a husband with Jenny Diver, one of the
women who had betrayed him to Peachum. He has
dyed himself black and under the name of Morano is
acting as negro chief of a band of pirates. Polly, now an
orphan, has come in search of him. Robbed on shipboard
of her money she falls into the hands of Mrs. Trapes,
a former associate of Macheath, now a bawd in the
Indies, who sells her to a wealthy planter, Ducat. From
his attempt to ravish her she escapes, with the connivance of his wife, in the dress of a youth, and is taken
by the pirates. In a skirmish between them and the
Indians, who are allied with the planters, she is made
a prisoner together with the Indian prince Cawwawkee.
She is attracted by his simplicity and virtue, and by
bribing their guards they escape to the Indian camp.

Fortified by the return of their prince the Indians
attack and are now victorious. As a planter Ducat
should have taken part in the fight, but he prefers, in
less entertaining fashion, to emulate Falstaff on the field
of Shrewsbury.

A slight wound now would have been a good certificate;
but who dares contradict a soldier? 'Tis your common
soldiers who must content themselves with mere fighting:
but 'tis we officers that run away with the most fame as well
as pay. Of all fools the foolhardy are the greatest, for they
are not even to be trusted with themselves. Why should we
provoke men to turn again upon us, after they are run

away? For my own part, I think it wiser to talk of fighting than only to be talk'd of. The fame of a talking hero will satisfy me.

Still more pointed is the satire in the dialogue between Pohetohee, the Indian King, and 'Morano', when taken captive.

> *Poh.* Have ye notions of property?
>
> *Mor.* Of my own.
>
> *Poh.* Would not your honest industry have been sufficient to have supported you?
>
> *Mor.* Honest industry! I have heard talk of it indeed among the common people, but all great geniuses are above it.
>
> *Poh.* Have you no respect for virtue?
>
> *Mor.* As a good phrase, sir. But the practicers of it are so insignificant and poor that they are seldom found in the best company.
>
> *Poh.* Is not wisdom esteem'd among you?
>
> *Mor.* Yes, sir. But only as a step to riches and power: a step that raises ourselves, and trips up our neighbours.
>
> *Poh.* Honour and honesty; are not these distinguish'd?
>
> *Mor.* As incapacities and follies. How ignorant are these Indians!

Morano's attitude so repels Pohetohee that he orders him to be instantly executed. Jenny Diver, pleading for his life, calls him by his true name, Macheath, whereupon Polly, who has revealed her sex, cries, 'Spare him, save him. I ask no other reward.' But the reprieve here comes too late. None of the players intervenes, as in *The Beggar's Opera*, to avert tragedy. Yet there is the promise of a brighter future for Polly. The Indian prince declares his love for her, and after she has given 'a decent time' to her sorrows it is clear that she will accept his hand. His father gives his consent, a readier form of recognizing a union between a coloured potentate and an Englishwoman than southern Africa has provided in our own day.

Gay had arranged with Rich for the play to be put into rehearsal when an order came from the Lord Chamberlain, the Duke of Grafton, that it was first to be submitted to him. Gay, accordingly, left a copy with him on 7 December 1728 and on 12 December received it back, with a ban upon its performance. No reasons were given, but it has been believed that the Lord Chamberlain acted at Walpole's instigation. There are no such signs in *Polly* as in *The Beggar's Opera* of personal caricature. But the whole tone of the piece, contrasting with an imaginary Indian golden age of innocence and virtue a thoroughly corrupt European civilization, in which every moral principle was violated in the struggle for power and place, might well give offence to the Government. Even Polly, in one of her airs, draws a cynical comparison between sportsmen and politicians.

> The sportsmen keep hawks, and their quarry they gain.
> Thus the woodcock, the partridge, the pheasant is slain.
> What care and expense for their hounds are employ'd!
> Thus the fox and the hare and the stag are destroy'd.
> The spaniel they cherish whose flattering way
> Can as well as their masters cringe, fawn, and betray.
> Thus staunch politicians, look all the world round,
> Love the men who can serve, as hawk, spaniel or hound.

The words of the airs are, as a rule, on a lower level than in *The Beggar's Opera* and they are set to less popular tunes. *Polly* had to wait for half a century, till 19 June 1777, to be staged at the Haymarket, and it has never won a place in theatrical repertory. But paradoxically the Lord Chamberlain's ban proved very advantageous to Gay financially. It excited public curiosity, and printed copies of the play were widely sold at high prices.

In a few years, however, he was again impecunious, and was trying in 1732 to raise his finances 'by doing something for the stage'. This appears to refer to the last of his operas, *Achilles*. But as with *Polly* Gay made an ill-considered theatrical venture by turning to a debased use one of the stories from the Greek heroic age. Thetis, the mother of Achilles, to prevent him joining the expedition against Troy, made him dress like a woman and placed him, under the name of Pyrrha, in the care of King Lycomedes. Gay represents Lycomedes, mistaking his sex, as falling in love with him, and seeking to force him to his desires, till he is unexpectedly overpowered by his superior strength. His Queen, Theaspe, stung to jealousy, seeks to make a match between 'Pyrrha' and her nephew Periphas. Though he cares nothing for her, he is challenged to a duel by Ajax who has also become enamoured of the supposed girl, till they are put under arrest. The secret of the sex of Achilles is known only to the princess Deidamia, who is with child by him, and whose condition provokes the spiteful comments of her sisters, Lesbia and Philoe.

All of this, based upon the stage confusion of sex, leaves an unpleasant taste. But with the entrance of the Greek warriors, Ulysses, Diomedes, and Agyrtes, disguised as merchants, the tone of the piece, though cynical, becomes more legitimately entertaining. Their mission is to find and recruit Achilles. They begin by asking the princesses if they may show them their wares, and are told by a lady-in-waiting, 'Unless you have anything that is absolutely new and very uncommon, you will give us and yourselves, gentlemen, but unnecessary trouble.'

Ulyss. To produce any thing that had ever been seen before wou'd be a downright insult upon the genius of a lady of quality.

Diom. Novelty is the very spirit of dress.

Lesb. Let me die, if the fellows don't talk charmingly.

Phil. Sensibly, sister.

But when the so-called merchants display the contents of their packets the princesses show themselves petulantly fastidious.

Diom. Now, ladies, here is all that art can show you.

Lesb. This very individual pattern, in a blue pink, had been infinitely charming.

Ulyss. Look upon it again, madam—Never was so delightful a mixture.

Diom. So soft, so mellow!

Ulyss. So advantageous for the complexion!

Lesb. I can't bear it, man: the colour is frightful.

Phil. I hate our own tame home-bred fancy—I own I like the design—but take it away, man.

Another packet is then opened, and a suit of armour appears. The merchants are profuse in their apologies for the mistake, and open yet another packet. While the ladies are examining the new stuffs, Achilles is handling the armour. 'This very sword seems fitted to my hand. The shield too is so little cumbersome: so very easy!' Ulysses watching him knows their stratagem has succeeded. 'That intrepid air! that godlike look! It must be he. His nature, his disposition shows him through the disguise.' He accosts him as son of Thetis, and declares, 'Greece demands thee and now, Achilles, the House of Priam shakes.' Ulysses reveals himself, and Achilles is about to follow him, when Deidamia pleads with him to stay. 'Think of my condition. Save my honour', to which Ulysses retorts, 'Think of the honour of Greece.' Achilles satisfies both by going through a ceremony of marriage with Deidamia before leaving for the war. Ulysses points the moral, 'We may for a while put on a feign'd character, but Nature is so often unguarded that it will show itself—'Tis to the armour we owe Achilles.'

Gay, dying on 4 December 1732, was not fated to see *Achilles* on the stage, where it did not appear till 10 February 1733 at Covent Garden, where it had a fair run and short revivals in 1734 and 1737. It was not helped by some of its airs, the words of which met with contemporary ridicule. Nor did two other posthumous pieces, a comedy, *The Distress'd Wife*, produced at Covent Garden for four performances in March 1734, and *The Rehearsal at Goatham*, a farce based on a tale by Cervantes, never performed but printed in 1754, help to enhance Gay's reputation. It is doubtful if his versatility as a dramatist has received due recognition, but it would have been well if he had ceased work for the stage after the triumph of *The Beggar's Opera*. He had thereby achieved the distinction of initiating a novel theatrical type, the ballad-opera. He might have boasted with Falstaff, 'I am not only witty myself, but the cause that wit is in other men.' Where he had blazed the trail, many others were to follow. To some of these we now turn.

VIII

HENRY CAREY

ONE of the first to pay the flattery of imitation to *The Beggar's Opera* was Henry Carey. The date of his birth and his paternity are uncertain, but he was believed to be the illegitimate son of George Savile, Marquis of Halifax. He began his literary career with a volume of poems in 1713. In 1715 his farce, *The Contrivances*, had been produced at Drury Lane. After the resounding success of Gay's piece Carey converted *The Contrivances* into a ballad-opera with a series of airs, including several duets. The plot is on conventional lines. A despotic and miserly father, aptly called Argus, forbids the marriage of his daughter Arethusa with Rovewell, a Captain in the army, apparently without means. He is determined to wed her on the next day to a country squire, Cuckoo, whose sister is hourly expected. To baffle Argus Rovewell impersonates this sister, with his servant Robin as her clownish man. It is Robin with his country dialect that is the most entertaining character. When Argus asks naturally, 'Where's the Squire?' he has his answer.

Why one cannot find a mon out in this same Londonshire, there are so many taveruns and chocklen-housen;[1] you may as well seek a needle in a hay-fardel, as they say'n i' the country . . . we had much ado to find out your worship's house . . . and it were not for an honest fellow that know'd your worship and set us i' the right way.

Meanwhile the supposed sister is 'so main bashful' that

---

[1] Chocolate houses.

she only curtsies to Argus, but when left with Arethusa
Rovewell finds his tongue and urges her to fly with him.
But Argus overhears them, puts Arethusa under
lock and key, and turns away all the servants except a
cook-maid and a boy. The latter, however, betrays him
by lending Rovewell the keys of the room. The versatile
Robin now plays the part of a lawyer and knocks up
Argus at night with a profitable money proposal. While
he is giving ear to this several soldiers (it is to be supposed
from Rovewell's regiment, off duty) rush in, blindfold
and gag Argus, while the Captain carries off Arethusa.
Neighbours, aroused by his cries, are of little help till
Robin appears now in the guise of a Constable. One of
the neighbours addresses the King's Officer in an obsequious corruption of the King's English.

An't please your noble worship's honour and glory, we
are his Majesty's liege subjects, and were terrified out of our
habitations and dwelling-places by a cry from abroad, which
your noble worship must understand was occasionable by
the gentleman of this house, who was so unfortunable as to
be killed by thieves who are now in his house to the number
of above forty . . . we thought 'twas best your honour shou'd
come and terrify these rogues away with your noble
authority.

Robin commands them in the King's name to aid and
assist him, but they hang back till they hear that all the
thieves are gone. Then Argus recognizes Robin as the
Constable, but the stratagem has given time for Rovewell and Arethusa to be married off-stage. Then appears
an unexpected *deus ex machina*. Hearty, who has been a
companion for a short time to Rovewell, reveals himself
as his father, and an old friend of Argus. He had been
in the Indies for twenty years, taken another name, and
amassed a large fortune which he will bestow on Rove-

well, to match which Argus will let his daughter have his every penny.

This unconvincing close is scarcely worthy of the more skilful passages of the dialogue or the words of the airs which keep a generally even level. They rise above this in Arethusa's description of her ideal lover, beginning,

> Genteel in personage,
> Conduct, and equipage,
> Noble by heritage,
> Generous and free:

and the duet at Arethusa's window, when Rovewell serenades her,

> Make haste, and away, my only dear,
> Make haste, and away, away!
> For all at the gate
> Your true lover doth wait,
> And I prithee make no delay.[1]

Carey was less well advised when in *Amelia*, an 'English opera after the Italian manner', produced at the Haymarket on 13 March 1732, he turned to a serious theme, of which the dialogue, apart from the airs, is in blank verse. Amelia is the wife of Casimir, General of the Hungarian army, who is defeated and made prisoner by Osmyn, Commander of the Turks. To rescue him his friend Rodulpho disguises himself as a Turk, and, with Amelia as his pretended captive, enters Osmyn's tent. Inflamed by her beauty Osmyn promises her whatever she may wish, and at her entreaty sets Casimir free. But his sister Augusta, in love with Rodulpho, is stirred to frantic jealousy, and when Casimir returns to the

---

[1] The full text of these and most of the other songs mentioned in this chapter will be found in my *Songs and Lyrics from the English Masques and Light Operas* (Harrap, 1949).

Hungarian camp accuses Amelia and Rodulpho of playing false with him. Thus, when they make their escape, he condemns them to execution, from which, having learnt the truth, he rescues them at the last moment, and even, to reward Rodulpho, gives him Augusta as his bride!

In 1734 Carey turned for a time from opera to burlesque. On 22 February there was produced at the Haymarket *Chrononhotonthologos*. This is the ludicrously cumbrous name of the King of Queerummania. He is angry with the God of sleep for tormenting him and decrees:

> Henceforth let no man sleep, on pain of death:
> Instead of sleep let pompous pageantry
> Keep all mankind eternally awake.
> Bid Harlequino decorate the stage
> With all magnificence of decoration.

A grand pantomime is performed before him, in the midst of which a captain of the guard enters, crying, 'To arms, to arms!'

> Th' Antipodean powers, from realms below,
> Have burst the solid entrails of the earth.
>
> . . . .
>
> Armies on armies march in forms stupendous,
> Not like our earthly regions, rank by rank,
> But tier o'er tier, high pil'd from earth to heaven.

The King orders his General, Bombardinian, to draw forth his legions, and, in anticipation of victory, the priests to prepare their temples

> For rites of triumph. Let the singing sisters
> With vocal voices, most vociferous
> In sweet vociferation out-vociferize
> Ev'n sound itself. So be it as we have order'd.

It is by this verbal piling of Pelion upon Ossa that Carey
parodies the rhetorical flights of heroic tragedy. But
Chrononhotonthologos at any rate prophesies truly.
The Antipodeans are routed, leaving as a prisoner their
King, with whom the Queen of Queerummania, Fad-
ladinida, instantly falls in love. While her confidante
Tatlanthe urges her to swell the triumph of her hero
husband, her only thought is for 'the topsy-turvy King,
the gentleman that carries his head where his heels
should be'.

> In what a charming attitude he stands;
> How prettily he foots it with his hands!
> Well, to his arms, no, to his legs I fly,
> For I must have him, if I live or die.

But as she cannot understand his gestures or his roaring
noise she invokes Venus and Cupid, who both appear,
and the latter tells her that before night she will be a
widow and then share two jolly young husbands. The
prophecy is fulfilled. Bombardinian, at a banquet in his
tent, drinks in Falernian wine the health of his King,
who retorts that it is fitting 'with so much wine to eat
a little bit'.

> *Bomb.* Traverse from Pole to Pole: sail round the Globe,
> Bring every eatable that can be eat;
> The King shall eat, tho' all mankind be starv'd.
> *Cook.* I am afraid his Majesty will be starv'd before I can
> run round the world for a dinner; besides, where's the money?
> *King.* Ha! dost thou prattle, contumacious slave?

He thereupon kills him and, when the General makes
further excuses, strikes him.

> *Bomb.* A blow! shall Bombardinian take a blow?
> Blush, blush, thou sun! Start back, thou rapid ocean!
> Hills, vales, seas, mountains, all commixing crumble,
> And into chaos pulverize the world!

It is a capital skit upon the idea that the smallest breach of social order has its reverberations throughout the Cosmos. He draws against the King and in the fight kills him, whereupon he goes mad.

> Ha! what have I done?
> Go, call a coach, and let a coach be call'd,
> And let the man that calls it be the caller,
> And in his calling let him nothing call,
> But coach, coach, coach! O! for a coach, ye Gods!

Is this not a burlesque echo of Richard III's 'A horse, a horse! my kingdom for a horse!' mixed with the frantic Ophelia's 'Come, my coach'? When a doctor declares that the King is 'beyond the power of physic', Bombardinian kills him and then turns his sword against himself. Over such a pile of corpses the spectators may all give 'a tragedy groan'. But there is light for the future. When two courtiers are at odds as to which will be the Queen's future husband, she settles the matter (forgetting the Antipodean King) by saying that she will have them both. It is a fitting close to a display of some first-class fooling.

With his next piece, *The Honest Yorkshireman*, which Carey called a ballad farce, he had at first bad luck. The Drury Lane manager, after keeping the manuscript for nine months till the end of the season, returned it to him. After it had been accepted by Giffard and produced successfully in the summer of 1735 at the Haymarket and in the following winter at Goodman's Fields, Carey had another grievance because a piratical publisher anticipated him by issuing a highly priced spurious edition. The prologue makes an unusually strong claim, for so light a piece, of its moral intention:

It has a double aim,
To honour wedlock and put fools to shame.

.   .   .   .

Our author does in virtue's cause engage,
In hopes to make her shine upon the stage.

The plot is a variation upon that of *The Contrivances*.
Sir Penurious Muckworm, uncle and guardian of Ara-
bella, has arranged for his own financial profit for her
to marry a rich Yorkshire squire, Sapscull. But she is in
love with a young barrister, Gaylove, who is now suing
Sapscull's father for property of which he has been de-
frauded. To defeat Muckworm's plan Gaylove's servant,
Slango, proposes that he shall impersonate Arabella,
with Gaylove as Muckworm, and thus impose upon
Sapscull, who has just arrived with his clownish servant
Blunder. London amazes them, as they stare about and
Sapscull exclaims, 'What a mortal big place this same
London is! ye mun ne'er see end on't, for sure—Housen
upon housen, folk upon folk! One would admire where
they did grow all of 'em.' And he breaks into one of
Carey's most attractive ditties, beginning,

O London is a dainty place,
A great and gallant city.

He is further surprised when he is greeted by name by
Gaylove, posing as Muckworm, who asks for his creden-
tials, and is handed all his documents. He is then advised to attire himself in the tiptop of the mode, and
Gaylove thus gets hold of Sapscull's country clothes in
which, now posing as the squire, he interviews Muckworm, and sings another of Carey's pleasing airs,

I am in truth
A country youth,
Unused to London fashions.

This is addressed to Arabella, who does not see through his disguise till, as he goes out, he drops a letter disclosing it. Sapscull and Blunder, in their elegant London attire, are fooled by Slango impersonating Arabella, who goes through a mock marriage with the squire. Meanwhile Gaylove and Arabella, eluding Muckworm, are joined in matrimony by a clerical friend of the lovers, and Muckworm learns this from an air sung by Arabella's maid. His threat to provide Gaylove with 'a wedding suit, a fine long Chancery suit' before he can touch a penny of her fortune is countered by Gaylove who, as a barrister, dares him to embezzle a farthing of it. And when Sapscull, finding out the trick practised on him, exclaims, 'Where's my writings? I'll ha' you all hang'd for cheats', Gaylove retorts, 'You had better hang yourself for a fool . . . as for the writings, they happen to be mine, and kept fraudulently from me by your father, to whom they were mortgag'd by my late brother. The estate has been clear these three years.' But he adds that he has no quarrel with Sapscull himself, who is free to use his house. Whereupon the squire wishes him joy and declares that, seeing Gaylove so happy in a wife, he'll not be long without one. And the edifying moral of the piece is pressed home in a final chorus,

> Come, learn by this ye bachelors
> Who lead unsettled lives,
> When once ye come to serious thought,
> There's nothing like good wives.

The music to this air, as to most others in *The Honest Yorkshireman*, was provided by Carey himself, but for one he was indebted to a Signior Porpora, for another to Handel, and for a song to Worsdale's *Cure for a Scold*. The success of the piece must have consoled Carey for its rejection by Drury Lane.

With *The Dragon of Wantley*, a burlesque opera, 'moderniz'd from the old ballad after the Italian manner by Sigr. Carini' the versatile Carey transferred his scene to Yorkshire itself. A dragon is making widespread havoc. Gaffer Gubbins and his daughter Margery take counsel together how to defeat him.

> *Gub.* This dragon very modish, sure, and nice is:
> What shall we do in this disastrous crisis?
> *Marg.* A thought to quell him comes into my head;
> No way more proper than to kill him dead.
> *Gub.* O miracle of wisdom! rare suggestion!
> But how, or who to do it, that's the question.

Margery suggests a nearby valiant knight, Moore of Moore Hall.

> He has done deeds St. George himself might brag on.
> This very man is he shall kill the dragon.

This facility for double-rhyming is shared by Moore, who is found drinking with companions and declaring

> Zeno, Plato, Aristotle,
> All were lovers of the bottle.

He at once assents to Margery's plea, asking only the reward of a kiss. He thereby awakes the jealousy of a previous flame, Mauxalinda, who attacks Margery with a bodkin, till Moore seizes it:

> *Moore.* Why, what the devil is the woman doing?
> *Maux.* To put an end to all your worship's wooing.
> *Moore.* 'Tis well I came before the whim went further;
> Had I stay'd longer, here had sure been murther.

Gubbins now cries that the dragon is coming, and Moore, after taking refuge in a well, meets and kills him. The burlesque ends with a chorus which is a *tour de force* of triple rhyming:

Sing, sing, and rorio
An oratorio
To gallant Morio
    Of Moore Hall.
To Margereenia
Of Roth'ram Greenia,
Beauty's bright queenia,
    Bellow and bawl.

Produced at Covent Garden on 26 October 1737 with the music by J. F. Lampe, the piece met with great favour, and went rapidly through many editions in print. Carey would have done better to leave well alone but he chose to write a sequel to *The Dragon* called *The Dragoness*. As such Margery, now Lady Moore, shows herself, even on her wedding-day. When her husband regrets the absence from the nuptial feast of Mauxalinda, Gubbins explains that she has packed up in a hurry, 'and went away this morning by the carrier'. Whereupon, not very tactfully, Moore comments, 'She's a smart girl; some Londoner may marry her.' Instead of admiring her husband's gift of double rhyming (in which Carey again proves himself an expert) she becomes furious.

I might be Marg'ry Gubbins heretofore,
But now I'll make you know, I'm Lady Moore.

The former conqueror is cowed.

Alas! what mighty deeds have I to brag on?
I'm more afraid of her than of the dragon.

He flies to the desert whither Mauxalinda has also betaken herself instead of to London, and he finds consolation in her arms. Lady Moore pursues them with a body of constables, orders Mauxalinda to be arrested, and prevents Moore from following her. She even pursues her rival to prison, and after taunting her,

> So, madam, how d'ye like your stately lodging?
> Is not this better than in deserts dodging?

she draws a dagger to kill her, when Gubbins enters with her discharge from a justice of the peace. He then surprises her by asking her to be his wife, to which she consents out of spite.

> And when I'm Madam Marg'ry's mother-in-law,
> By Jove, I'll keep her Ladyship in awe.

The rivals prepare to fight each other, when Gubbins intervenes, and tells his daughter that it is by gentle means that she must engage her knight. She confesses her fault, and asks forgiveness of Mauxalinda, who embraces her as no more a rival but a daughter dear: Moore is less easily pacified:

> Like Bajazet, I'll keep her in a cage,
> While I, like Tamerlane, but mock her rage.

One would like to think that he had been reading Marlowe, but it is probably a reminiscence of Rowe.[1] Yet when Gubbins leads her in, and she kneels and asks for pardon, as a converted and obedient wife, Moore takes her to his arms. Even if we make allowance for what Carey himself calls 'the custom of all operas, no matter how improbable, absurd or ridiculous', his talent would have been better employed than in such a sequel, which was produced at Drury Lane on 9 December 1738, again with music by Lampe, but was a failure.

He returned nearer to reality next year in what he called an Interlude, corresponding to the Italian *Intermezzo*. *Nancy; or The Parting Lovers* was founded on an

---

[1] See p. 8, above.

incident he had seen when a young fellow was hurried away by a press-gang from his weeping sweetheart. True-Blue and Nancy are courting when Dreadnought, a Lieutenant, with his gang presses him for the King's service. In vain she cries,

> Oh, where will you hurry my dearest,
>   Say, say to what clime, on what shore?

The Lieutenant answers:

> Honour calls, he must obey;
> Love to glory must give way.

And True-Blue hearkens to the call:

> Yes, I must leave my Nancy,
>   To humble haughty Spain,

and in a parting duet each leaves the other to Heaven's protection. Nancy's father pulls her from him, declaring,

> Love and courtship are but stupid,
>   Glory has superior charms;
> Mars should triumph over Cupid,
>   When Bellona calls to arms.

When he takes her away True-Blue gives the Lieutenant his hand as a pledge of his resolution.

> Death or victory now must determinate
>   All disputes with haughty Spain.
> That proud race we'll entirely exterminate,
>   Or be masters of the main.

It is another *feu de joie* of triple rhyme. In 1755 the piece was revived at Covent Garden, renamed *The Press-Gang, or Love in Low Life*. Owing to the change in the political situation France now took the place of Spain as the enemy, and a Boatswain opens the Interlude with a new song in honour of the brave Tars of old England.

Since again bold defiance appears in proud France,
Ye staunch British Tars, let us boldly advance,
And now in our turns let us teach them to dance.

And at the conclusion a new personage, the Commodore, at the head of the boat's crew sings 'a grand ode in honour of Great Britain'—none other than Thomson's 'Rule, Britannia', here introduced without acknowledgement. But for this Carey is not responsible, as he had died on 4 October 1743. His judgement, as has been seen, was at times at fault, but in his inventive versatility and command of verbal technique he may be said to run second to Gay.

IX

WILLIAM RUFUS CHETWOOD
CHARLES JOHNSON
CHARLES COFFEY

WILLIAM RUFUS CHETWOOD, after a short period as a publisher, was prompter at Drury Lane from 1722 to 1740. In the preface to his first theatrical venture, *The Lover's Opera*, he paid a tribute to Gay by stating that it was 'begun soon after the run of the celebrated *Beggar's Opera*, to mention which gives me some confusion, while I am speaking of my own weak endeavours'. It was produced at Drury Lane on 14 May 1729 and its reception exceeded Chetwood's modest expectations. It is another variation on the standard theme of the ballad-operas, young lovers outwitting the matrimonial designs for them of tyrannical or avaricious parents or guardians.

Justice Dalton has chosen for his daughters Clara and Flora, well dowered by a legacy from an uncle, a trio of potential husbands, from whom they may select two, from each of whom he is to receive £2,000. The girls, however, have fixed their affections on two swains, Clara on Edgar and Flora on Moody. To learn their secrets Dalton bribes their maid Lucy, who sees the opportunity of playing a double game, and carries messages of her own devising from one side to the other.

The first of Dalton's chosen wooers, Aminadab Prim, addresses Clara in Quakerish jargon, 'Thou art a lovely creature surely: thy comeliness doth move the Spirit, which is the inward Light, towards thee: nor is the out-

ward man unmov'd, but yearneth, and doth pant, as it
were, to embrace thee.' Next the French Beau, Varole,
makes his appeal.

> I'm of de Nation
> Do teach de fashion . . .
> Beside me love you,
> And to improve you,
> Me come from France.

Squire Clotpole dismisses them both as 'poor insignifi-
cant wretches'. He is a man of war. 'I have been Captain of the Militia several years, and have behav'd with
courage and conduct in the greatest dangers.' The two
girls turn a deaf ear to their wooing, while Lucy assures
each in turn that he is the favoured one. And by further
somewhat obscure manœuvres she tricks, while masked,
Prim into a marriage with her and Clotpole into a
mock one with Varole dressed as a woman. Meanwhile
the true lovers are joined in matrimony, and 'to make
Mr. Prim easy and satisfied with his wife', Edgar and
Moody offer each to advance £500 to Lucy. Prim accepts this on condition she will turn unto the Light, and
Lucy replies in suitable terms, 'I thank thee lovingly'.
It is as a skit on the Quakers that *The Lover's Opera* is
chiefly of interest today.

On the other hand, in his next piece, *The Generous
Free-mason*, Chetwood, himself a mason, glorified the
Brotherhood to whose Grand Master and the other
members he dedicated this 'tragi-comi-farcical ballad-
opera', first produced in August 1730 in a booth at
Bartholomew Fair and later at the Haymarket. It has
the peculiarity of two plots entirely unrelated, except
that one deals seriously with Freemasonry and the other
farcically.

In the serious plot, with dialogue in blank verse or

couplets, Sebastian, to save his beloved Maria from a hateful marriage, persuades her to fly with him to Spain where his uncle is British Consul.

> But yet one pang I feel thro' all my joy
> That from my noble Brethren I must part,
> Those men whose lustre spreads from pole to pole,
> Possessing every virtue of the soul.

On their voyage their ship is captured by Mirza, high admiral of the King of Tunis, by whom they are imprisoned. But the King falls in love with Maria and the Queen with Sebastian, and complications follow. Mirza sees Sebastian making a Masonic sign and hails him as a Brother. He tells an amazing tale. Born in Britain his father, who was Consul in Tunis, brought him there in infancy and soon afterwards died. Though he clung, in spite of pressure, to his Christian faith he gained the favour of the King and was raised to his high office. But he never forgot his countrymen some of whom, when resident in Tunis, had made him 'a Mason in most perfect form'. In this capacity he considers it his duty to enact a pious fraud by which the King and Queen, thinking to satisfy their novel passions, are lured in the dark into each other's arms. Meanwhile Mirza assists the captives to escape with him on shipboard, and leaves a letter for the King from his 'faithful slave', begging him to 'pardon the deceit I have been guilty of; I had no other motive than to assist the virtuous'. Only in a ballad-opera could a deceived monarch at once assent:

> Such generous sentiments I must approve,
> Tho' I am lost for ever to my love.

Only there, too, could Neptune, attended by Tritons, rise to a symphony of soft music and bid the lowering tempests cease to roar till the voyagers reach Albion. And still more surprisingly does the sea-god voice a final eulogy on the Masonic Brotherhood:

> Great, generous, virtuous, good, and brave,
>   Are titles they may justly claim;
> Their deeds shall live beyond the grave,
>   And every age their fame proclaim.

It is of interest that the setting to this air as well as to an earlier one was provided by Henry Carey.

Running side by side with these scenes in the grand manner are others in prose on a strangely different level. Sir Jasper Moody (no relation of his namesake in *The Lover's Opera*) is bent on marrying his daughter Caelia to the boorish Squire Noodle. But she is in love with Cleremont who seeks the help of her maid Lettice, akin to Lucy in *The Lover's Opera*, with her quick wit. When Cleremont offers her as reward the Indies, she retorts,

The Indies! Lard, lard! Lovers and poets in their plays are plaguey generous; they'll give a woman a fortune of fifty thousand pound, tho' they can't pay their tailor. I'd advise you to keep the Indies to yourself. . . . No, no, Tickledown farm will content me at the skirt of your estate in the country.

He promises her this, and Caelia backs him up with the offer of a hundred pounds to his man Davy to stock it.

Noodle, accompanied by his man Doodle, addresses Caelia with some absurd verses of his own making, and then flings some taunts at Cleremont who retaliates with throwing snuff in his face, while Davy similarly blinds Doodle. But when Moody announces that the marriage with Noodle must take place immediately, it is Lettice who saves the situation. She tells Noodle that Caelia has vowed she will never marry a man who is not a

Freemason, and that he must be made one at once. He is put through a roughly farcical ceremony in which his face is blackened, his purse and rings stolen, and he is tied up in a sack from which Doodle releases him. When he sends for a doctor, Cleremont plays the part in disguise and fools him into sending for a parson so that he may frustrate his rival by marrying the lady. But Lettice so manœuvres that he takes as his bride her masked sister, Jenny, while Cleremont and Caelia are joined off-stage. Moody makes the best of the business by giving his blessing, Lettice takes Davy as a tenant for life, and Noodle is handed back his money and rings. If the piece was intended to attract Freemasons it failed, for it had a short run, but it is of historical interest as the only piece of its kind concerned both eulogistically and farcically with the Brotherhood.

In 1749 Chetwood published a *General History of the Stage*, which was too ambitious in scope, but which contains some valuable details about actors who were his contemporaries. But his later years were overshadowed by imprisonments for debt in London and Dublin, and he died in poverty on 3 March 1766.

CHARLES JOHNSON

CHARLES JOHNSON (1679–1748), of the Middle Temple, who had been a prolific writer of comedies, especially the two not entirely original Drury Lane plays *The Wife's Relief* (November 1711) and *The Country Lasses* (February 1715), and a few tragedies, was stimulated by Gay's triumph to the single venture of *The Village Opera*. Produced at Drury Lane on 6 February 1729, its somewhat short run was not proportionate to its merits, where the hand of the practised playwright lent vitality to some of the stock characters in ballad-opera and added others. The words of the airs also were as a whole above the general level.

Freeman, son of Sir William Freeman, is designed by Sir Nicholas Wiseacre to be the husband of his daughter Rosella, though the pair have never met and she has given her heart to Freeman's friend, Heartwell. Freeman, a truant from his father's house, has fallen in love with Betty, whom he had accidentally met in a stage-coach, and who is now filling the part of maid to Rosella. To be near her, under the name of Colin, he is serving as under-gardener to Sir Nicholas. The head gardener, Lucas, warns him in horticultural phrase against his musing over Betty:

Luc. You can think of no other part of Nature.
Col. She is a fine flower. I am curious.
Luc. Young man, young man, she is too much known and admired to fall to thy share; thou wo't never transplant her, I warrant. . . . She has been raised in a hot bed; she is delicate and tender, not fit for thee.

Lucas has a poor opinion of his employer. 'He thinks, forsooth, because he hath money, that he is ignorant of nothing; and he will be directing me every now and then, when he does not know the vine of a melon from that of a cucumber.' When Sir Nicholas enters with his wife, he justifies the gardener's estimate. He is not only the conventional despotic father but is insufferably conceited and testy, and a bully to his meek wife. When she agrees, as to his plan for the marriage, that 'it wou'd be right', he interrupts 'How do you know it wou'd be right? How shou'd a woman know any thing that is right? 'Tis fifty to one, wife, that you are never in the right.' To which she dutifully replies, 'That may be,

Sir Nicholas, for I always agree with you in everything.'
When Betty tells him that it is not a happy mating for
Rosella, as she does not know whether she is to marry
a man or a monster, and 'it is hard never to have seen
the person she is to be married to', he blusters, 'Hard!
why I have never seen him, nor her mother; why is it
harder on her than on us?'

None the less he is perturbed by the non-appearance
of either the bridegroom or his father, as the wedding has
been fixed for noon that day. Meanwhile the *soi-disant*
Colin has arranged with a footman, Brush, to have
ready a coach and six, and the other apparatus for a
midnight elopement, by which Rosella is to be met by
Heartwell (who never appears on the stage) at the gate,
and which will give himself an opportunity of being near
Betty, who is to accompany her. Rosella is overjoyed at
the prospect.

> At twelve of the night,
> When the moon shines bright,
> With my lover I shall be a gadder.
> I'll steal from the house
> To the arms of my spouse,
> Tho' my father grows madder and madder.

But things take an unexpected turn. Another footman
appears, File, with a message from Sir William Freeman, who has been laid up with gout, to say that he
does not know the whereabouts of his son. Brush reveals
that he is here in the disguise of a gardener, and that
Sir Nicholas does not know him. The precious pair
thereupon concoct a plot by which Brush is to pass himself off as Freeman, with File as his attendant, in order
to win the hand and fortune of Rosella. Meanwhile
Colin, in happy expectation, sings of Adam's bliss when
he first saw Eve.

Our parent thus in Paradise
    Beheld the virgin fair,
And trembling with ecstatic joys
    Confess'd his heav'n was there.

As he sees Rosella and Betty coming he pretends to be
asleep and hears them talking of their lovers till Rosella
bends down and unties a bracelet on his arm containing
a picture of Betty, revealing that he wears her image in
his heart. He throws himself at her feet, declaring that
this accounts for his transformation, and that his purpose
is 'to admire, to serve, to love, to make it the whole
business of my life to adore'—when Sir Nicholas de-
scends upon them with 'Hey-day! what worshipping of
graven images', and bids Colin get back to his business.
He then receives Brush, attended by File, in his impersonation of Freeman, paying fulsome compliments
to Lady Wiseacre, while File urges that Sir William is
anxious for the matter to be consummated immediately.
Rosella is in despair till Betty seeks out Colin, and begs
him to be a knight-errant and deliver Rosella from the
monster, the husband who has come and who is called
Freeman. He assures her that the fellow is an impostor
and that he will send for Freeman himself, who is now
in this village. Betty hastens to Sir Nicholas with the
news, but even when Colin appears in his proper costume as Freeman, Brush and File brazenly keep up the
deception, and the irascible Sir Nicholas bids three of
his servants 'just toss this fellow into the horsepond
without any regard to his lac'd clothes, or his counterfeit squireship'. Rosella begs him to consider before
coming to these extremities. His wife pleads 'I think it
might be right'—to which he retorts, 'First, wife, you do
not think; and, secondly, if you did think, it could not
be right.' Betty is more imperious: 'I do not intreat, but

command you in the name of Venus, Cupid, and all the Graces, to give this lover his liberty.'

It is all in vain, but at this moment Sir William Freeman, at the cost of some pain, arrives and greets his son as 'my boy, Billy'. To the discomfiture of Sir Nicholas the whole trickery is exposed, and after a laboured apology by Brush the rogues are too easily forgiven. And now it is Sir William's turn to be astonished. He is all agog for Freeman to marry Rosella at once, but instead he brings forward Betty as his heart's choice. For the moment Sir William is as outraged as Sir Nicholas, 'What, my boy, marry a chambermaid! . . . What, bring a beggar into the family!' But Betty then confesses that she too has been playing a part. She is the daughter of Sir William's neighbour, Mr. Bloom, and has run away to escape marriage with a detestable Squire Guzzle and taken service with Rosella who had treated her as a friend. It is an artificial close to an otherwise skilfully managed action, but it more than satisfies Sir William, who advises Sir Nicholas to have Rosella's marriage-articles drawn over again, with Heartwell's name in the place of Freeman's, for 'if you don't give her the man she likes, she will certainly take him'. And all ends happily in pastoral fashion with a sheep-shearing ballad and country dances.

CHARLES COFFEY

CHARLES COFFEY was another of the dramatists born in Ireland at an uncertain date. He acted at the Smock Alley Theatre in Dublin, especially in parts which suited his deformed figure. His first piece, *The Beggar's Wedding; A new Opera* (a title evidently modelled on Gay's precedent), was first staged in the Smock Alley Theatre on 24 March

1729. But here the beggar (or rather beggars) is not the presenter of the opera but a personage in it. And the trade of begging is allied with that of thieving, with something of the glamour of Macheath's exploits. The place of Peachum as the receiver of stolen goods is here taken by Alderman Quorum who, though a justice of the peace, is in league with the beggars. And as Polly, in defiance of her parents, made a match with Macheath, Quorum's daughter, Phebe, is in love with Hunter, son of the Beggar King, whom her father first approved, but has now rejected for a wealthier suitor.

Coffey presents the beggars attractively when their king, Chaunter, holds a grand Council of State, and, after business is over, proclaims a general suspension of all counterfeited pains or aches whatever. 'Let false blindness and lameness be now far from you . . . throw away rags and crutches, whilst nothing but mirth and glee go round.' Grigg, who is a sort of prime minister to the fraternity, leads off with a song,

> While discord and envy in mighty kingdoms dwell,
> The beggar lives at ease within his humble cell.

It is Grigg who brings Hunter a letter from Phebe begging him to come at once, as her father will be out of the way till dinner, and he has forbidden her to see him any more. Quorum none the less is ready for his own ends to receive Chaunter, who discourses to him of the golden age.

> How happy was the primitive world, when there were no other laws to govern by than those of Nature; when men enjoy'd every thing in common, and no such crimes were heard of as robbery or petty larceny; when if a poor man wish'd any thing his rich neighbour possess'd he might take it without farther ceremony, and be in no danger of a gaol.

Quorum affects to agree, but is sure that neither he nor Chaunter will ever see a reformation in the world as it is. After a quarrel, when Chaunter tells the Alderman some home truths, and a reconciliation over a bottle of Burgundy, the Beggar King departs. His place is taken by Grigg in disguise, with a cock and bull story of how in the service of the great Cham of Tartary he had taken prisoner a rebel prince, who has been given to him as a servant, and whom he wishes to exhibit publicly, if Quorum will grant a licence. The Alderman is all agog to see him, but when he is brought in, and gabbles in a strange lingo, Quorum is scared of this man-monster, and is glad to be called away to magisterial functions by his clerk. Grigg's captive is then revealed as Hunter, who carries off Phebe with her maid Tibbet. The King invites all the beggars to the grandeur of a wedding between Grigg and Tib Tatter, 'the celebration of which we intend to honour with the nuptials' of his son and Quorum's daughter. But before this can take place the Alderman appears with constables, arrests Grigg, whom he recognizes as having tricked him, and finds on him a letter from Hunter asking a clergyman to come at once and marry him. Quorum forces Grigg to lead him to Hunter, who now with Phebe has come to see the beggar's wedding. The Alderman tries to seize his daughter, but the beggars worst the constables, and Grigg, turning the tables, arrests him in King Chaunter's name.

Then comes one of those unexpected recognitions which are a usual but unsatisfactory feature of these ballad-operas. Chaunter's wife discloses that she is a long-lost sister of Quorum, and Hunter his only son carried off in infancy by a gang of gipsies. Chaunter explains that he has married the sister and has brought

up the son like a gentleman. This blasts Phebe's hopes
for she cannot marry a brother. But now Quorum makes
a further revelation that Phebe is not his daughter, but
an orphan left in his care, whose estate he has increased.
So, with no obstacle to their nuptials, they are witnesses
of the beggar's wedding with its peculiar ritual. One of
the crew, Cant, acts as priest and puts Grigg and Tib
Tatter through a catechism as to their qualifications for
the solemnity. This satisfactorily answered, they go
through the ceremony of the crutches under which, held
by a pair of arms, she passes, and over which he thrice
leaps to show his superiority. After an ironical blessing
all the men kiss the bride and the women the man.
Quorum is now so delighted that he asks Chaunter to
share his house, but he declares:

I would not change my condition with the greatest prince
in Europe; for there is not one of 'em all but envies the
freedom of us beggars. . . . As for our dirt and uncleanness
they are without us, and signify nothing at all to true
happiness; and for our rags 'tis to them we chiefly owe our
felicity.

The Beggar's Wedding proved extremely popular and
held the stage in its original form for a considerable time
both in London and Dublin. But it was even more
attractive when cut down to one act under the title
Phebe. As this indicated, the love-plot was now given the
chief prominence. But the compression was skilfully
done. Nothing essential to the action was omitted. The
two episodes that were left out were a drinking bout of
Mrs. Chaunter with half a dozen of her female boon
companions, which was no great loss; and the amusing
but extravagant scene in which Grigg befools Quorum
with his traveller's tales and brings in Hunter in the
disguise of a man-monster.

It is somewhat surprising that after the success of *The Beggar's Wedding* Coffey, instead of relying on his own invention, should have fallen back on turning into a full-dress opera, with the help of another playwright, John Mottley, a Restoration piece by Thomas Jevon, *The Devil of a Wife, or a Comical Transformation*, produced at Dorset Garden in April 1686. This Restoration comedy proved very popular, and went through numerous editions before Coffey made it the basis of his *The Devil to Pay, or The Wives Metamorphosed*, produced at Drury Lane. The only acknowledgement of his debt to Jevon is in the prologue:

A merry wag, to mend vexatious brides,
These scenes begun, which shak'd your fathers' sides;
And we obsequious to your taste prolong
Your mirth by courting the supplies of song.

This scarcely suggests that Coffey plagiarized Jevon's dialogue wholesale. He changed the names of some of the chief characters and introduced a large number of airs, though *The Devil of a Wife* was not without some good songs. The plot is thus of Restoration origin and type and does not call for detailed notice here. The proud, shrewish wife of a kindly country squire, and the gentle young wife of a bullying cobbler, are transformed by a travelling doctor-conjuror into the semblance and character of each other, with astonishing consequences and the final reformation of the lady and the cobbler.

Coffey struck a more original vein in *The Boarding-School, or The Sham Captain*, though this ballad-opera, produced at Drury Lane on 29 January 1733, also harks back to the temper of the Restoration stage. Ned Brag, whom his father Zachary, an old Grenadier, had apprenticed to a blacksmith, is posing as Captain Bouncer, and is being kept by Lady Termagant, who despises and bullies as 'a little fribling cit' her second husband, Alderman Nincompoop. His daughter Molly and Lady Termagant's daughter Jenny are at the same boarding-school, where Molly has fallen in love with her singing-master Warble, and Jenny with her dancing-master Coupee. The two masters have planned an elopement with their 'golden prizes', though Warble knows that he has a rival for Molly in the Captain, 'who has an hawk's eye upon her fortune of six thousand pound'.

The parents, with the Captain, attend a display of dancing at the school, where Termagant rhapsodizes over her daughter:

Ay, now the guitars are come, pray observe Jenny—there's an air, there's a shape, there's an ingenious look—Fogh! T'other awkward romp makes me sick (*They dance ridiculously to guitars out of tune.*) Very fine upon my honour, these guitars agree with the dance admirably.

The festivity is interrupted by the entrance of Zachary Brag, denouncing the Captain as his son, till Ned whispers to him that he is courting a young lady with six thousand pounds, and that his father shall have half of it, if he will own himself to be Colonel Brag 'an acquaintance of mine at the siege of Buda'. But in an amusing scene at a nearby tavern, Coupee puts the pair through an inquisition about the siege which leads Zachary to 'give the show away'. He tells Ned, who had thought 'I had cram'd a dozen or two of lies in the hinder part of my jaw . . . I'd have you know I was of too honest a principle.' The Captain is thus exposed, and his Lady's *envoi* is 'Bid somebody give the blacksmith here a tester.' But he might well complain that Coffey uses him hardly in comparison with the two intriguing masters, who successfully manage for their love-sick pupils to elope with them to Coupee's house, and go through a form of marriage. As Jenny tells her mother, 'The man ask'd Mr. Coupee a question, and he said "Ay"; and then he ask'd me a question, and I said "Ay"; and then we both join'd hands together, kiss'd, and were marry'd as fast as any thing.' Molly chimes in, 'So was I, and I like it very well.' Whether 'the man' was qualified to join persons in holy matrimony is not disclosed, but the parents accept the situation with surprising equanimity.

> *Lady Term.* Well, since it can't be otherwise, live and be happy.
> *Ninc.* Ay, ay, bless ye all together, seriously.

It is the *reductio ad absurdum* of the reconciliation with which this type of comedy usually ends. But the glimpse that it gives of a Georgian boarding-school for girls in their bib and apron, and of a headmistress with a great rod, is something out of the common. And of the lusty airs which enliven the piece none is more outstanding than the concluding quartet sung by the newly wed couples, beginning, 'The world's like a Boarding-school, common to all, And so ev'n let it pass', and ending, 'O rare work for the stage'.

After the success of *The Boarding School*, Coffey would have done better not to turn back to *The Devil to Pay* by providing a sequel, *The Merry Cobbler*.

In dedicating it to Lady Walpole, who had patronized the earlier piece, he urged that, though wanting 'the force of magic', it rested its claim on its native simplicity and 'its great affinity to true nature'. But this is scarcely made good in the play. The characters are all to some degree haunted by memories of the consequences of the previous transformation. The squire, Sir John Loverule, dressing up as the conjurer, attempts to gain the favour of the cobbler's wife, Nell, and the cobbler himself, Jobson, in disguise, similarly seeks the love of Lady Loverule, who pretends to encourage him. Sir John gets a drubbing, and Jobson has to make a humiliating retreat under a table. But in the end no virtue is lost and there is general reconciliation. The chief attraction of the piece, apart from some of the airs, are the laments of Tony, Jobson's famished apprentice, contrasted with the cobbler's tippling carousals with his boon companions, the tinker, smith, and tailor.

X

HENRY FIELDING

IN just under three weeks after the triumph of *The
Beggar's Opera* on 29 January 1728 a man of genius
began his career as a dramatist, though it was in another field that he was fated to win the highest laurels.
Henry Fielding, born at Sharpham Park near Glaston-
bury on 22 April 1707, was the son of Edmund Fielding,
who was of aristocratic connexion. Henry was educated
at Eton and later, from March 1728 for about two years,
at the University of Leyden. Already on 16 February
1728 he had made his first theatrical venture at Drury
Lane with a comedy, *Love in Several Masques*. Its main
plot deals with the attempt of Sir Positive and Lady
Trap to force their niece and ward, Helena, into a
match with the wealthy Sir Apish Simple while her
heart is set on the less-well-endowed Merital, whom she
finally secures. Sir Positive is of note as Fielding's first
anticipation of the Squire Western type, the proud,
ignorant country gentleman, who thinks his coat of arms
far superior to a coronet. He asserts that 'an old English
baronet is above a lord. A title of yesterday! An innovation! Who were lords, I wonder, in the time of Julius
Caesar? And it is plain he was a baronet by his being
called by his Christian name.'

Fielding's second comedy, *The Temple Beau*, was produced at Goodman's Fields, after his return from Leyden, on 26 January 1730. The title part is that of young
Wilding (akin to Ovid in Ben Jonson's *Poetaster*), who
has been six years at the Temple, but who tells the fair
Bellaria, 'I cannot think you believe that I ever studied

law: dress and the ladies have employed my time.' When his father visits his chambers and asks to see 'his library, his study, his books', he can only find Rochester's poems and plays. Wilding's foil is Pedant, to whom books are 'as much preferable to women as the Greek language to the French'; and who, when left by his father to make love to Bellaria, tells her that 'matrimony is a subject I have very little revolved in my thoughts, but obedience to a parent is most undoubtedly due'. Both these juvenile plays showed that the new recruit to the theatre had powers of dialogue and characterization, but they were in the decadent artificial comedy tradition.

It was almost by accident that Fielding found where his more original dramatic power lay. The closing of Goodman's Fields Theatre in April 1730 brought him into touch with the Little Theatre in the Haymarket, where a nonsensical piece, *Hurlothrumbo, or the Supernatural*, by Samuel Johnson, a Cheshire dancing-master, had been a great success. For the Haymarket audience burlesque was in demand, and to meet this Fielding wrote *The Author's Farce. With a Puppet-Show, called The Pleasures of the Town*, produced on 30 March 1730 as by 'Scriblerus Secundus'. The chief figure is Luckless, a penniless dramatist, who, like Lyrick in Farquhar's *Love and a Bottle*,[1] is a forerunner of Tom Wrench in Pinero's *Trelawny of the Wells*. He is in difficulties with his landlady, Mrs. Moneywood, who is dunning him: 'Never tell me, Mr. Luckless, of your play, and your play. I tell you, I must be paid.' As he is in love with her daughter Harriot, his plight is even worse when Mrs. Moneywood murmurs, 'If thou can'st not pay me in money, let me have it in love.' When in desperation Luckless asks the publisher, Mr. Bookweight, to advance

[1] See pp. 33–34, above.

50 guineas on the play he refuses to give even 50 far-
things, and he draws a shrewd distinction. 'Your acting
play is entirely supported by the merit of the actor, in
which case it signifies very little whether there be any
sense in it or no. Now your reading play is of a different
stamp and must have wit and meaning in it.' How many
histrionic reputations have been since then built up on
'acting plays'!

Luckless next submits his tragedy to the actor-
manager Marplay, who claims all the merit of a success
for the producer. 'When a play is brought us, we consider it as a tailor does his coat; we cut it, sir, we cut
it; and let me tell you, we have the exact measure of the
town.' When Luckless reads passages from his tragedy
Marplay suggests emendations and at last declines to
have anything to do with it. So Luckless throws up
tragedy and offers a puppet-show which is accepted. It
has a remarkable peculiarity in that the scene lies on the
other side of the river Styx, and all the people in the play
are dead. Here Fielding makes an innovation in English
theatrical history by following *The Frogs* of Aristophanes
and Lucian's *Dialogues of the Dead.* In the underworld
Don Tragedio, Sir Farcical Comic, Signior Opera, and
others plead before the throne of Nonsense for a chaplet
which she is to bestow upon the one most distinguished
for foolishness. Finally Opera wins the award, and thus
Fielding continues the crusade against Handel and
foreign singers which Addison had carried on in *The
Spectator.*

On 25 April *The Author's Farce* was supplemented by
an afterpiece, also by 'Scriblerus Secundus', *The Tragedy
of Tragedies, or The Life and Death of Tom Thumb the Great.*
On the second night the Prince of Wales was present,
together with a crowd of persons of quality. Later Field-

ing added a prologue and epilogue, and in March 1731
expanded the original two acts to three. It thus became
a full-dress burlesque of heroic tragedy. Fielding had
read the chap-book beginning,

> In Arthur's Court Tom Thumb did live,
> A man of mickle might.
>
> .   .   .   .
>
> His stature but an inch in height,
> A quarter of a span:
> Then think you not this little knight
> Was prov'd a valiant man?

This suggested to him the happy idea that the lofty sentiments and rodomontade of plays from Dryden and Lee
to Philips and Thomson could be effectively ridiculed
by being put into the mouth of a hero of diminutive
size. He could not foresee that today, with associations
in our minds from Malory, Tennyson, and Wagner, it
seems almost a desecration to make Arthur's Court the
scene of this masquerade. In honour of the advent of Tom
Thumb, the conqueror of giants, the King proclaims:

> Let nothing but a face of joy appear.
> The man who frowns to-day shall lose his head,
> That he may have no face to frown withal.

When Thumb enters Arthur effusively welcomes him,
and Queen Dollallolla falls in love with him at first
sight. When asked what he has done with the giants,
Thumb explains that the castle-gates were too low to
admit them, except their Queen, Glumdulca, with
whom Arthur is at once enraptured:

> But ha! what form majestic strikes our eyes!
> So perfect that it seems to have been drawn
> By all the Gods in council: so fair she is
> That surely at her birth the Council paus'd,
> And then at length cry'd out, 'This is a woman'.

Here Fielding is parodying Lee in *Lucius Junius Brutus*:

> At his birth the heavenly Council paus'd,
> And then at last cry'd out, 'This is a man'.

Thumb retorts to Arthur,

> Then were the Gods mistaken—she is not
> A woman but a giantess.

Glumdulca now laments:

> We yesterday were both a queen and wife,
> One hundred thousand giants own'd our sway,
> Twenty whereof were married to ourself.

Such a polygamous Paradise excites the envy of Dollallolla, now enamoured of Tom Thumb.

> O happy state of giantise—where husbands
> Like mushrooms grow, whilst hapless we are forc'd
> To be content, nay, happy thought, with one.

But she sighs in vain. Thumb asks as his only reward the hand of the Princess Huncamunca which Arthur, to her joy, bestows upon him. But Thumb has a rival in Lord Grizzle, whom she also favours and to whom she makes an unusual offer:

> My ample heart for more than one has room.
> A maid like me Heav'n form'd at least for two;
> I married him, and now I'll marry you.

But Grizzle declines half-shares in a bride, and goes off muttering vengeance on Thumb. Then an unexpected character appears. Fielding, ignoring the succession of ghosts in Elizabethan tragedy, notes that 'there is one respect in which the modern stage falls short of the ancient, its great scarcity of Ghosts'. To remedy this he introduces the ghost of Tom Thumb's father, who warns Arthur that Grizzle is leading an armed mob against his

palace. They are defeated by Thumb, who kills Grizzle
and bears off his head in triumph. The Royalties are
awaiting his victorious entrance, when a courtier arrives
with terrible news:

> I saw Tom Thumb attended by the mob—
>
> .   .   .   .
>
> Aloft he bore the grizly head of Grizzle;
> When of a sudden thro' the streets there came
> A cow of larger than the usual size,
> And in a moment—guess! oh, guess the rest,
> And in a moment swallowed up Tom Thumb.

In the ballad his cries from inside the cow lead to his
restoration, but in the play it is the end of him. And after
his death there is a general slaughter among the characters, ending with the King's suicide, so that we can echo
Horatio's words at the close of *Hamlet*, 'This quarry
cries on havoc.' Of this scene Fielding declared that
none received greater honours. 'It was applauded by
several Encores, a word very rare in tragedy. And it
was very difficult for the actors to escape without a
second slaughter.' Though this may have been said in
jest, *Tom Thumb* in truth proved even more popular
than *The Author's Farce*. In May 1733 it was turned into
The Opera of Operas by Mrs. Haywood and William
Hatchett, with music by J. F. Lampe and T. A. Arne.
Another musical adaptation was produced by Kane
O'Hara at Covent Garden in October 1780. Nearly all
the hits at Restoration and later plays, of which it has
been estimated that there are forty-two, have now lost
their point except for specialist students. But that the
wit and verbal dexterity of *Tom Thumb the Great* can still
exercise their attraction was amply proved when the
play, slightly revised, was one of the chief successes of
the Malvern Dramatic Festival in the summer of 1932.

Fielding's next important venture was *The Welsh Opera, or The Grey Mare the Better Horse*, later known as *The Grub Street Opera*, produced at the Haymarket on 22 April 1731. It was a ballad-opera, after the style of Gay, but more pointedly satiric of the Court and Walpole. The easy-going Welsh squire, Ap-Skinke, with his wife, 'Gouvernante to her husband', are the King and his dominating Queen Caroline, both speaking English with a foreign accent. Their mischievous son Owen is Frederick, Prince of Wales, at enmity with his father. The thieving butler, Robin, is Walpole, and Sweetissa, the waiting-woman, his sweetheart, is Miss Skerrett, his mistress. William, the coachman, who quarrels with Robin, is Pulteney, head of the discontented Whigs. All this is now only of historical interest, but what keeps this opera alive is the rollicking song:

When mighty roast beef was the Englishman's food,
It ennobled our hearts and enriched our blood:
Our soldiers were brave, and our courtiers were good.
   Oh, the roast beef of Old England,
   And Old England's roast beef!

Fielding's next ballad-opera, *The Lottery*, produced at Drury Lane on New Year 1732, has no political edge but satirizes the gambling spirit. Stocks, by running a lottery and fooling his dupes, has made a fortune. One of his brothers, who runs a hostel, writes to him that a young lady who has come to lodge there wants to know how to dispose of £10,000 to the best advantage. Another brother, Jack, who is down and out, comes to borrow 'a brace of hundreds' from him. Stocks refuses but asks, 'What say you to £10,000 and a wife?' He tells him to assume the title of a lord and the laced coat left by him in pawn, and lay siege to the wealthy lady.

The girl, Chloe by name, has been wooed in the country by Lovemore, whom she favours. But attracted by the lure of London she has taken flight there. She has taken a ticket in the lottery for a £10,000 prize which she reckons on winning. As she assures her maid, 'It is not only from what the fortune-teller told me, but I saw it in a coffee-dish, and I have dreamt of it every night these three weeks. Indeed I am so sure of it that I think of nothing but how I shall lay it out.' And she at once plunges into extravagance. When Jack Stocks appears as a suitor she is captivated by his bogus title and fine costume, and goes through what she thinks is a form of marriage with him. But when the news comes that she has drawn a blank, and that her fortune is a myth, Jack turns upon her with coarse abuse. It is left to the faithful Lovemore, who has followed her to London, to come to the rescue, and to take her off his hands. But it is an excess of generosity when he offers him, on resigning all pretensions to the lady, a thousand pounds on the instant—not in a lottery. The piece, as a whole, is below Fielding's general dramatic level, but it proved popular at Drury Lane and later at Covent Garden. It probably had interest for an audience which included the counterpart of those attracted by football pools today. And it has a permanent lesson in the air with which it ends:

> That the world is a lottery what man can doubt,
> When born we're *put in*, when dead, we're *drawn out*;
> And tho' *tickets* are bought by the fool and the wise,
> Yet 't is plain there are more than ten *blanks* to a *prize*.

Much shorter shrift was given to *The Covent Garden Tragedy*, produced at Drury Lane on 6 June 1732, which was a coarse burlesque of Ambrose Philips's *The Distrest Mother*. Later in the same month Fielding made a 'box office' hit with *The Mock Doctor, or The Dumb Lady Cur'd*, an adaptation of Molière's *Le Médecin Malgré Lui*, in ballad-opera form. This was followed with similar success in February 1733 by *The Miser* from Molière's *L'Avare*, retaining its five-act comedy design but with changes and additions. Another well-received adaptation from the French was a farce, *The Intriguing Chambermaid*, from J. F. Regnard's *Retour Imprévu*, produced at Drury Lane 15 January 1734.

Spain provided Fielding with material for more original dramatic development than France in *Don Quixote in England*. This comedy had been begun by him at Leyden in 1728 but laid aside. In 1734 it was completed with additional scenes of political application, and produced at the Little Theatre in the Haymarket in April. The Don arrives with Sancho Panza at an inn, which he takes to be a castle besieged by a giant at the head of an army. Sancho tells him that he is mistaken.

Why, sir, this giant that your worship talks of is a country gentleman who is going a-courting, and his army is neither more nor less than his kennel of foxhounds. . . . Sir, your true English squire and his hounds are as inseparable as the Spaniard and his Toledo. He eats with his hounds, drinks with his hounds, and lies with his hounds.

This truly describes Squire Badger, another forerunner of Squire Western, who is a wealthy suitor for Dorothea, daughter of Sir Thomas Loveland, though he has not yet set eyes upon her. She has made an assignation at the inn with her lover Fairlove. The Don takes her to be an imprisoned princess, and infuriates the innkeeper by breaking some of the windows to set her free. He also makes trouble by opposing the entrance of the stage-coach into the inn yard.

It is an abrupt change when the Mayor of the town waits upon Quixote to ask him to stand for Parliament against Loveland, the knight of the long purse.

Mayor. I suppose, sir, it may be in your power to do some services to the town.

Quix. Be assured it does. I will, for your sake, preserve it ever from any insults. No armies shall ever do you any harm.

Mayor. I assure you, sir, this will recommend you very much . . . but I hope your honour will consider that the town is very poor, sir. . . . I believe you guess already that he who spends most would not have the least chance.

Quix. Ha! caitiff, does thou think I would condescend to be the patron of a place so mercenary? . . . Hence from my sight!

Writs for the elections to a new Parliament had just been issued and Fielding was here attacking the bribery in country elections.

There is a shift again to romance when the Don invokes the presence of his divine Dulcinea whom Sancho pretends that he has brought from Spain in the person of Jezebel, Dorothea's waiting-woman, and whose pre-eminence over all other ladies he proclaims. His idealism is more happily employed in intervening on behalf of Fairlove against Badger. He rebukes Loveland for his mercenary spirit.

Do you marry your daughter for her sake or your own? If for hers, sure it is something whimsical to make her miserable in order to make her happy. Money is a thing well worth considering in these affairs, but parents always regard it too much and lovers too little. No match can be happy which love and fortune do not conspire to make so.

In that speech alone there would be sufficient justification for Fielding bringing Don Quixote to England, though neither after its production at an uncertain date (about April 1734 at the Haymarket Little Theatre) nor in print does the comedy seem to have met with much appreciation.

Much more of a welcome was given by the town to a more conventional operatic farce, *An Old Man Taught Wisdom, or The Virgin Unmask'd*, produced at Drury Lane on 23 June 1732.

A rich father, Goodwill, is anxious to settle his sixteen-year old daughter Lucy in marriage, but when he asks her if she would like to have a husband she only wants to know if she will have a coach. She has been told that she would have a coach when she married. When he further asks her whom she would like best for a husband of all the men she ever saw, she answers 'I like Mr. Thomas, my Lord Bounce's footman, the best, a hundred thousand times.' But Goodwill has sent for several relatives among whom he wishes her to make her choice. First comes Blister, the apothecary, who inquires about her health, sleep, and appetite. He is followed by Coupee, a dancing-master, who tells her that not learning to dance is ruin to a young lady. Then comes Quaver, a singing-master, who declares that 'a voice is the greatest gift nature can bestow'. All other perfections, without a voice, 'are nothing to it'. Lucy promises herself to all three and goes out. Last of all appears Wormwood, a lawyer, who thinks he has been summoned in a family lawsuit. But when Goodwill insists that the finally favoured suitor must give up his employment each of them declines. This does not matter, for Lucy reappears married (incredibly quickly) to Thomas. The footman assures Goodwill that he is 'a man of some learning, and one who has seen a little of the world, and who by his love to her, and obedience to you, will try to deserve

your favours'. Goodwill declares that he will suspend
judgement, and thinks little of one of the 'booby relatives' when Wormwood asks 6s. 8d. for his journey.

In March 1736 Fielding reverted in *Pasquin, a
Dramatic Satire on the Times,* to a mixture of burlesque
and political irony. There was a tradition that in Rome
there had been two statues, Pasquin and Marforio, on
which epigrams were fastened, the former bringing the
charge and the other the reply. The scene is in a playhouse where Trapwit is rehearsing his comedy, 'The
Election', and Fustian his tragedy, 'The Life and Death
of Common Sense', with Sneerwell, a critic, looking on.
In the comedy Lord Place and Colonel Promise are
seeking election for Walpole's Court party, and Sir
Hardy Fox-Chace and Squire Tankard for Bolingbroke
and Pulteney's country party. Lord Place addresses the
Corporation and says, in an aside to the Mayor, 'Give
me leave to squeeze you by the hand in assurance of my
sincerity.' Trapwit criticizes the actor, 'You, Mr., that
act my lord, bribe a little more openly, if you please, or
the audience will lose the joke, and it is one of the
strongest in my whole play.' The country party candidates' bribery is more indirect but equally acceptable,
though the Mayor proclaims,

The world should not bribe me to vote against my
conscience.

Trap. Do you take the joke, sir?

Fust. No, faith, sir.

Trap. Why how can a man vote against his conscience,
who has no conscience at all?

After Trapwit has assured Fustian that he will comply
with the laws of comedy by having a marriage, but that
he defies him to guess the couple till the thing is done,

Fielding makes mock of the poet laureate, Colley
Cibber's, odes. Lord Place promises a voter that he shall
be made poet laureate.

Voter. Poet! my lord, I am no poet. I can't make verses.
Place. No matter for that—You'll be able to make odes.
Voter. Odes, my lord? What are those?
Place. Faith, sir, I can't tell what they are. But I know
you may be qualified for the place without being a poet.

The country party gets most votes, but the Mayoress,
typifying Queen Caroline's petticoat government, persuades her husband to declare Place and Promise duly
elected. Promise, who has hitherto been dumb, proposes
to the Mayor's daughter, and asks her to forgive his ill-
usage which (as Trapwit explains to Fustian) has taken
place entirely behind the scenes. With their wedding,
also behind the scenes, the play ends.

After the rehearsal of Trapwit's comedy comes that
of Fustian's tragedy. It is a burlesque in verse of the same
general type as *Tom Thumb*. But it lacks the genial
absurdity of that play, and its satire is more involved.

Firebrand (priest of the Sun), Law, and Physic are
rebelling against Queen Common Sense, and preparing
to join with Queen Ignorance, who has just landed

> With a vast power from Italy and France
> Of singers, fiddlers, tumblers and rope-dancers.

Queen Common Sense declares that she will head an
army against them. Sneerwell is therefore naturally surprised to find her in the next scene asleep on a couch.
Fustian explains:

You do not understand the practical rules of writing as
well as I do; the first and greatest of which is protraction or
the art of spinning, without which the matter of a play would
lose the chief property of all other matter, namely extension,
and no play, sir, could possibly last longer than half an hour.

The Ghost of Tragedy is then called, but before he can begin to tell a thousand things, the cock crows and he has to descend. But the Ghost of Comedy is supposed not to have heard the cock, and bids Common Sense awake, for while she reigns,

> Play-houses cannot flourish, while they dare
> To Nonsense give an entertainment's name.
> Shakespeare and Jonson, Dryden, Lee and Rowe,
> Thou wilt not bear to yield to Sadler's Wells.

Queen Ignorance appears with her motley following, and Harlequin arrives as an ambassador from the two theatres (Drury Lane and Covent Garden) with absurd hostages of whom he recites a catalogue. The Queen sends back the hostages and instead instructs them to act a play which she hands over, and which has neither head nor tail. A parley takes place between the two Queens, followed by a fight between their armies, of which Fustian declares, 'I never saw a worse battle in all my life upon the stage', till he bids some of them go over to the other side, and fight as if they were in earnest. In any case stage-battles are superior to the pantomimical farces called Entertainments.

What these Entertainments are, I need not inform you, who have seen 'em. But I have often wondered how it was possible for any creature of human understanding, after having been diverted for three hours with the productions of a great genius, to sit for three hours more, and see a set of people running about the stage after one another, without speaking one syllable, and playing several juggling tricks.

Here Fielding makes his most direct attack upon the popular pantomimes and similar shows, and Sneerwell adds, 'It's very true, and I have heard a hundred say the same thing, who never fail'd being present at them.'

To bring the play to an end Firebrand stabs Queen Common Sense to death, but her ghost appears, and puts Ignorance and her host to flight:

Sneer. I am glad you make Common Sense get the better at last; I was under terrible apprehensions for your moral.

Fust. Faith, sir, this is almost the only play where she has got the better lately.

It is a neat final hit.

In March 1737 Fielding produced at the Haymarket Little Theatre the sharpest of his satirical dramas, and one that had momentous consequences. For some time there had appeared annually a summary of the events of the previous twelvemonth with the title 'The Historical Register, Containing an Impartial Relation of all Transactions, Foreign and Domestic'. Fielding presents the rehearsal of a three-act farce, *The Historical Register* by Mr. Medley, and implies that in it will be found the events of real importance during 1736. 'My Register', says Medley, 'is not to be filled like those of vulgar newswriters with trash for want of news.' The play begins with a nonsensical Ode to the New Year, parodying Colley Cibber's effusions:

> This is a day in days of yore
> Our fathers never saw before.
> This is a day, 'tis one to ten,
> Our sons will never see again.
> > Then sing the day,
> > And sing the day,
> > And thus be merry
> > All day long.

There is also later some capital banter of Cibber's attempt to rewrite Shakespeare's *King John* for production at Drury Lane. But it is the political satire that is predominant in the play. Never before had Fielding attacked Walpole's government so boldly. He lays the scene in Corsica, but it is a transparent veil. Five politicians, the ablest heads in the government, are consulting round a table:

5th Pol. Hang foreign affairs; let us apply ourselves to money.

All. Ay, ay, ay.

2nd Pol. All we have to consider relating to money is how we shall get it.

3rd Pol. I think we ought first to consider whether there is any to be got, which, if there be, I do readily agree that the next question is how to come at it.

.   .   .   .

2nd Pol. I have considered the matter and I find it must be by a tax.

3rd Pol. I have thought of that, and was considering what was not tax'd already.

Up to this point the dialogue is even more applicable to a Cabinet meeting today than to a council of ministers under George II. But a modern Chancellor of the Exchequer would find some other expedient than the second politician's suggestion of a tax on learning, to which the third politician moves, so to speak, an amendment.

Learning, it is true, is a useless commodity, but I think we had better lay it on Ignorance; for Learning, being the property but of a very few, and those poor ones too, I am afraid we can get little among them; whereas Ignorance will take in most of the great fortunes in the kingdom.

All assent, and they leave the stage. To an inquirer who asks what has become of them, Medley, the author, explains:

They are gone, sir, they're gone; they have finish'd the business they set about which was to agree on a tax; that being done, they are gone to raise it. And this, sir, is the full account of the whole history of Europe, as far as we know of it, compris'd in one scene.

Fielding's point here is that Walpole's government could do nothing but impose taxes and collect them. In a later scene Sir Robert, under a thin disguise, appears as using the money thus amassed to bribe his opponents over to his side. He had hitherto shown remarkable tolerance of the succession of attacks on him by dramatists whose sympathies were with the opposition. But *The Historical Register* proved the last straw. Walpole struck back by getting Parliament to pass the Licensing Act in June 1737, which closed all theatres except Drury Lane and Covent Garden, and brought plays under the censorship of an official in the Lord Chamberlain's department. With this Fielding's occupation as a dramatist was virtually gone. The only other piece of any significance which reached the stage was *Miss Lucy in Town*, a sequel to *The Virgin Unmask'd*, a farce with songs, produced at Drury Lane on 6 May 1742. Fielding was thus tempted to exploit the enduring success of the earlier play. But he now drew too heavily on the credulity of his audience. Lucy coming, within a few weeks of their marriage, with her husband, to London lodges with Mrs. Haycock who keeps a bawdy-house. While Thomas goes out to find a tailor, Haycock's maid gives her lessons in how to become a fine lady, which is her one ambition now.

Fine ladies do everything because it's the fashion. . . . They lose their money at whist without understanding the game; they go to auctions without intending to buy; they go to operas without any ear; and slight their husbands without disliking them; and all—because it is the fashion.

She is enraptured by the maid's description of the town beaux, and nearly becomes the victim of the rich Jew Zorobabel, and of the rake, Lord Bawble. In her silly innocence she confides to him, 'I am married to an odious footman, and can never be my Lady Bawble. . . . But I assure you, if I had not been married already, I should have married you of all the beaus and fine gentlemen in this world.'

When Tom returns, Lord Bawble (whom Lucy had called Bounce in *The Virgin Unmask'd*) recognizes him as his former footman, and asks him what property he has in the lady.

> *Thom.* The property of an English husband, my Lord.
> *Lord B.* How, madam, are you married to this man?
> *Lucy.* I married to him! I never saw the fellow before.
>
> . . . .
>
> *Lord B.* Come, Tom, resign the girl by fair means, or worse will follow.
> *Thom.* How, my Lord, resign my wife! Fortune, which made me poor, made me a servant, but Nature, which made me an Englishman, preserv'd me from being a slave. I have as good a right to the little I claim as the proudest Peer hath to his great possessions; and whilst I am able, I will defend it.

They both draw their weapons, but Goodwill, who has also come to Town, intervenes, and Bawble goes out. Even then Lucy refuses to accompany her husband, till he sternly asserts his authority. Then at last she begs him to forgive her, and promises never to attempt to be more than a plain gentlewoman in the country. Thus Fielding ends with an edifying moral, but Lucy's conduct has been so extravagantly fatuous that it undermines the play.

In February of the same year, 1742, *The History of the Adventures of Joseph Andrews* appeared. Here Fielding had found the vocation in which he was to prove himself a master in the first rank. It was inevitable that under his resounding fame as a novelist his dramatic achievement should suffer eclipse. But it was in his long apprenticeship to the stage that he gave an edge to the tools that he was to employ with such consummate effect in *Joseph Andrews* and *Tom Jones*. And, though 'Time with his cold wing' has withered the topical elements in Fielding's literary and political burlesques, there is enough in them of permanent interest to entitle them to a secure place in the chronicle of the British stage.

XI

GEORGE LILLO—EDWARD MOORE

T HE reaction against the high-flown action and speech of heroic or pseudo-classical tragedy took two chief forms. One was burlesque, in which Gay and Fielding, in different ways, were pre-eminent. The other was *bourgeois* domestic tragedy, wherein George Lillo was the most conspicuous figure. Born in 1693, Lillo appears from his name to have been of Flemish descent. Son of a jeweller in the city of London, he was brought up to his father's trade. He did not make his first theatrical venture till November 1730, when, following the fashion set by Gay, he composed a ballad-opera, *Silvia, or The Country Burial*, which was produced at Lincoln's Inn Fields, but did not find favour.

He then decided to experiment in a different type. That he was not ignorant that domestic tragedy had its place in the Tudor and Stuart theatre is proved by his adaptation later of *Arden of Feversham*, but his aim was to connect it more closely with everyday London commercial life, and to stress the lesson to be drawn from it. He makes this clear in the prologue to *The London Merchant, or The History of George Barnwell*:

> The tragic muse, sublime, delights to show
> Princes distressed, and scenes of royal woe;
> In awful pomp, majestic to relate
> The fall of nations or some hero's fate,
> That sceptred chiefs may by example know
> The strange vicissitude of things below.
>
> .   .   .   .
>
> Forgive us, then, if we attempt to show
> In artless strains a tale of private woe.

A London prentice ruined is our theme
Drawn from the famed old song that bears his name.
We hope your taste is not so high to scorn
A moral tale esteemed e'er you were born.

The 'famed old song' is 'the Ballad of George Barnwell',
which told the tale of the downfall of this young apprentice, but from which, as will be seen, Lillo made important variations. The ballad gives no date for the story
but Lillo puts it just before the sailing of the Armada.
The upright merchant, Thorowgood, is an exception to
the general run of despotic fathers in the plays. He tells
his daughter Maria that she is his only heir, and that he
is 'daily solicited by men of the greatest rank and merit
for leave to address you', but that he hopes to 'learn
which way your inclination bends'. Maria, of whom the
ballad knows nothing, declares that 'high birth and titles
don't recommend the man who owns them to my affections'. Her secret preference is for the apprentice Barnwell. Chance has thrown him in the way of the harlot,
Millwood, who is bent on avenging on some innocent
young man the wrongs inflicted by men generally on her
sex. She entices him to her house, by her arts persuades
him that she loves him, and makes him for the first time
neglect his service to his master.

When he returns next day to Thorowgood's house his
fellow apprentice and best friend Trueman (also not in
the ballad) is taken aback by his coldness and silence,
and asks if their friendship is to continue. Barnwell
makes the condition 'Never hereafter, though you should
wonder at my conduct, desire to know more than I am
willing to reveal.' Their master so generously forgives
his lapse that Barnwell determines to renounce Millwood. But at that moment she arrives with her maid
Lucy, who tells a cock-and-bull story of how her guar-

dian, jealous of Barnwell, vows her ruin unless she grants him similar favours. She has but an hour to decide, and has come to take her farewell. Agonized by this prospect he takes money of his master's and gives it to her to purchase her deliverance. He knows that the fraud will be revealed when his accounts are examined, but to forestall this discloses it in a letter to Trueman, which announces that he will never return. Trueman gives the letter to Maria and together they lament over the 'lost' Barnwell:

Trueman. Never had youth a higher sense of virtue. Justly he thought, and, as he thought he practised; never was life more regular than his. . . .
Maria. This and much more you might have said with truth.—He was the delight of every eye and joy of every heart that knew him.

To prevent her father from knowing his crime she offers to make good out of her own fortune the missing sum.

But Barnwell's infatuation is driving him farther on the downward path. In the ballad it is he who plans the murder of his wealthy uncle. In the play it is Millwood who proposes it to him and he cannot endure life without her:

Aye, there's the cause of all my sin and sorrow. 'Tis more than love; 'tis the fever of the soul and madness of desire. In vain does nature, reason, conscience all oppose it; the impetuous passion bears down all before it, and drives me on to lust, to theft, and murder.

He does the fell deed, only to hear his uncle, with dying lips, invoke blessings on him, forgiveness for his murderer, and endless mercy for his own soul. And when he returns conscience-stricken to Millwood, without anything of value to show, she repels him, and to save herself denounces him to the authorities as a murderer. But she is herself betrayed by the repentant Lucy, on whom she brazenly tries to fasten the guilt when Thorowgood accuses her. In a loftier strain before her arrest she indicts as the cause of her fall the social and religious order of things.

> I hate you all, I know you, and expect no mercy; nay, I ask for none; I have done nothing that I am sorry for; I followed my inclinations and that the best of you does every day. All actions are alike natural and indifferent to man and beast. . . . I am not fool enough to be an atheist, though I have known enough of men's hypocrisy to make a thousand simple women so. Whatever religion is in itself, as practised by mankind, it has caused the evils you say it was designed to cure . . . as if the only way to honour heaven were to turn the present world into hell.

Barnwell, on the other hand, has learnt in prison from a clergyman sent by Thorowgood the infinite extent of heavenly mercy and is truly repentant. He is visited by Trueman, with whom he is reconciled, and by Maria, who comes to partake of his misery, and vows never to forget him, and who, as the bell tolls for his execution, hears his cry, 'Pray for the peace of my departing soul.'

The play was produced at Drury Lane on 22 June 1731. In anticipation of the performance the ballad had been extensively reprinted, and it has been told how many spectators, who brought copies with them to the theatre to make a ridiculous comparison between it and the play, before the end threw these away and took out their handkerchiefs. And Lillo certainly had in many ways improved upon the ballad. He had, as has been shown, introduced several new characters and fitted them skilfully into a plot which moves inexorably to its tragic climax. Its close, in particular, is far more apt than that of the ballad, wherein Barnwell goes off to sea, and thence writes to the Lord Mayor disclosing his and Sarah's (as she is there called) guilt, for which she is hanged at Ludlow, while he meets the same fate later for a murder in Polonia.

Of the characters taken from the ballad the merchant is more individualized. Like Shakespeare's Antonio in Venice he gives the title to the play, though he is not the chief figure. He is not only benevolent and honourable, but is a student of the 'science' of merchandise, 'founded in reason and the nature of things', and 'by mutual benefits diffusing mutual love from pole to pole'. The history of trade between nations brings into question so rose-coloured a view. Millwood also, though totally devoid of fascinating charm, gains in stature in Lillo's hands in that her wickedness is not merely wanton but springs from an inflexible resolve to avenge the wrongs done to herself and her sex. Barnwell himself remains too much of an easily swayed nincompoop for us to appreciate the warmth of feeling that he excites in Trueman and Maria.

But where Lillo, judged by later standards, conspicuously failed, was in his use of prose instead of verse for tragedy. He evidently thought that this was fitting from the lips of the everyday persons in his drama. And this might have been well had they spoken in accents akin to those in use in their normal intercourse. But instead he made them one and all discourse in an artificial, stilted phraseology unsuited to their commonplace surroundings. Thus Barnwell when first returning from Millwood compares himself to Lucifer: 'Such, such was the condition of the grand apostate when first he lost his purity; like me disconsolate he wandered, and while yet in heaven bore all his future hell about him.'

And here is how Lucy, a maid, describes Barnwell when Millwood had proposed the murder of his uncle:

Speechless he stood; but on his face you might have read that various passions tore his very soul. Oft he in anguish threw his eyes towards heaven, and then as often bent their beams on her . . . at length with horror not to be expressed he cried, 'Thou cursed fair, have I not given dreadful proofs of love?'

It is to be feared that if *The London Merchant* were revived in a National Theatre handkerchiefs would only be used to choke laughter at it as a burlesque. But it was otherwise in 1731, even with such an auditor as Pope. The play was immediately successful, had a run at Drury Lane, and was put on later at other theatres. It also rapidly went through a number of printed editions. It thus had a greater influence on continental than on English drama. It was translated into French by Pierre Clément in 1748, and thus became known to Diderot, whose *Le Fils Naturel* (1757) and *Le Père de Famille* (1758) were in the type of Lillo's domestic tragedy, to which Diderot paid tribute. In Germany similar tribute was paid by Lessing, whose earliest play, *Miss Sara Sampson*, was indebted to Lillo's example.[1]

It is surprising that after the success of *The London Merchant* Lillo, instead of continuing in the same vein, should have next turned to an entirely different dramatic type, both in style and subject. The Albanian fifteenth-century patriotic leader against the Turks had already figured in two English plays, *Scanderbeg*, by William Havard (March 1733), and *Scanderbeg, or Love and Liberty*, by Thomas Whincop, not published till 1747. Lillo

---

[1] For further illustration of Lillo's continental influence see Sir A. W. Ward's Introduction to *The London Merchant* and *Fatal Curiosity* (Belles Lettres Series, 1906).

now presented him at Drury Lane in January 1735 as
The Christian Hero. The writer of the preface to the posthumous edition of Whincop's play accused Lillo of
having plagiarized from it. The author of *Biographica
Dramatica* did not think this accusation 'perfectly authen-
ticated', and a comparison of the two plays lends little
support to it. Nowhere has Lillo drawn upon Whincop's
dialogue, and except for Scanderbeg and the Sultan
Amurath the characters are varied or bear different
names. The background of fierce hostility between
Christians and Turks is necessarily the same, but the
action is in important respects varied. Whincop makes
more of the original friendly relation between Amurath
and Scanderbeg when as a youth he was sent as a
hostage to the Turkish quarters. And in his play Seli-
mana, wife of the Sultan, falls in love with the Christian
captive. With Lillo it is Amurath's daughter, Hellena,
who becomes enamoured of him and who in the opening
scene protests to her waiting-woman Cleora:

> Love busies not
> Himself with reconciling creeds, nor heeds
> The jarring of contentious priests: from courts
> To shades, from shades to courts he flies,
> To conquer hearts, and overthrow distinctions,
> Treating alike the monarch and the slave.

This spotlight thrown at once upon Hellena's hopeless
passion diverts to some degree the interest of an audience
in Scanderbeg's faithful love for his Althea (Arianissa
in Whincop's play), who through treachery has fallen
into the hands of the Turks. Even to rescue her he cannot accept the conditions which in a parley during a
truce Amurath offers:

> Renounce the errors of the Christian sect,
> And be instructed in the law profest

> By Ishmael's holy race; that light divine,
> That darts from Mecca's ever sacred fame,
> T'illuminate the darken'd souls of men.

But the struggle is almost too much for him.

> No, nature unassisted cannot do it.
> To thee I bow me then, fountain of life,
> Of wisdom and of power . . .
> Give me to know, and to discharge my duty,
> And leave th'event to thee.

His worst fears are almost realized when, assuming his disguise, the Sultan's son, Mahomet, all but succeeds in a rape of Althea. Yet it is from another of Amurath's kin that a warning of danger to Scanderbeg's life is to come. Hellena, ordered by her father to love the hated apostate, Amaric, who has plotted to kill Scanderbeg, sets forth with Cleora, both in men's attire, to bid the Christian leader be on his guard. Mistaken when near his camp for Turkish spies they are surrounded, and an officer misunderstanding (not unnaturally) Hellena's cry, 'Scanderbeg must die', retorts, 'Not by thy hand', and wounds her. The commander, still ignorant of her sex, listens to her appeal to bring her at once to Scanderbeg, in whose tent Cleora reveals to him who she is.

> *Scan.* Why would'st thou give thy life to ransom mine?
> Would I had died, or yet could die, to save thee!
> *Hel.* I'd not exchange my death, lamented thus,
> And in your arms for any other's life—
> Unless Althea's.
> *Scan.*   Were Althea here,
> She would forget her own severe distress,
> And only weep for yours.
> *Hel.*   May she be happy!
> Yet had you never seen her, who can tell,
> You sometimes might perhaps have thought of me.

This is a truly moving scene, and it is a high tribute to
Lillo to claim that Hellena is here of the same sister-
hood as Beaumont and Fletcher's equally ill-fated Aspa-
tia in *The Maid's Tragedy*. Her flight enrages the Sultan,
and he orders Althea and her father Aranthes to be at
once put to death, the girl to suffer first. The reluctant
official in charge of the executioners can offer only one
favour:

> The sad choice of dying by the bow-string,
> The fatal poniard, or this pois'nous draught.

As Althea chooses the last, and raises the bowl to her
lips, Scanderbeg, now victorious, rushes in and saves
her. Amurath is brought in prisoner but Scanderbeg
orders him to be set at liberty. He earns thereby no
gratitude.

> *Am.* Can this be true? Am I cast down from that
> Majestic height where, like an earthly god,
> For more than half an age I sat enthron'd,
> To the abhorr'd condition of a slave?
> A pardon'd slave!

Blaspheming against his prophet, and looking forward
to revenge by his son, he dies. Yet the sway of his powerful personality lingers on. Over his body his Vizier
laments:

> Eclips'd and in a storm our sun is set. . . .
> This was his fate:
> 'Tis ours to be left without a guide,
> Disperse, wander away; our shepherd's lost.

With the desolate state in which Amurath leaves his
subjects is now contrasted the happiness of those under
Scanderbeg's rule. As one of his officers declares,

> To say each subject loves you as himself
> Is less than truth: we love you as we ought,

As a free people should a patriot king.
Scan. This is to reign; this is to be a king.

.   .   .   .

For this alone was government ordain'd;
And kings are gods on earth, but while, like gods,
They do no ill, but reign to bless mankind.

Thus is the moral drawn, with probably an implicit contrast between Britain and less happy lands. *The Christian
Hero* has certainly features of interest, but the abrupt
change from the prose of *The London Merchant* to a blank-
verse tragedy on Albanians and Turks was too much for
the Drury Lane audience and the play fell flat.

In the following year Lillo returned to *bourgeois*
tragedy in *Fatal Curiosity, A True Tragedy of three Acts*,
produced at the Haymarket on 27 May 1736. He again
based his play upon a popular publication, *Newes from
Perin in Cornwall of a most Bloody and unexampled Murther
very lately committed*, &c., first published in 1618. And, as
in *The London Merchant*, he varied in important respects
from his original, and added new characters. In style,
however, he made a fundamental change. Instead of the
prose of the earlier citizen-play he continued the blank-
verse dialogue of *The Christian Hero*.

In both *The London Merchant* and *Fatal Curiosity* the
dramatic problem is, at bottom, the same—how to make
plausible the murder of an innocent victim by a man
who is not by nature a criminal. No less a person than
Fielding provided the prologue.

No fustian hero rages here to-night,
No armies fall, to fix a tyrant's right.
From lower life we draw our scene's distress,
Let not your equals move your pity less.

Old Wilmot, fallen from prosperity into a 'hell of
poverty' by what his wife calls his 'wasteful riots', is

embittered against the world. He is giving his cynical counsel to Randal, the only one of his servants who has remained faithful to him.

> Quit books and the unprofitable search
> Of wisdom there, and study human kind.
> No science will avail thee without that;
> But, that obtain'd, thou need'st not any other.
> This will instruct thee to conceal thy views,
> And wear the face of probity and honour,
> Till thou hast gain'd thy end, which must be ever
> Thine own advantage, at that man's expense
> Who shall be weak enough to think thee honest.

His conduct has driven into exile his son, who for many years has gone through adventures and privations in foreign lands. Now, returning from the Indies with a friend Eustace, they have been the sole survivors of a wreck on the Cornish coast. To his joy he finds that his beloved Charlot (a creation by Lillo) has remained constant to him. In his strange costume and looking 'more like a sun-burnt Indian than a Briton', she does not recognize him till he reveals who he is. So, too, when he meets the old servant Randal. Hence springs the momentous idea,

> Why may I not
> Indulge my curiosity, and try
> If it be possible, by seeing first
> My parents as a stranger, to improve
> Their pleasure by surprise?

The first instance of a curiosity so well intentioned, with such dire results!

The entrance of this stranger into their impoverished house reawakens in Old Wilmot and his wife Agnes the grief at the loss of their son. So overcome is he by their misery that he almost betrays himself. But he asks leave to repose, and entrusts Agnes (whom Lillo makes his mother, not his stepmother) with a casket, whose contents are of value. He thus gives the opportunity for another exercise of curiosity which is to prove fatal. Agnes opens the casket:

> My eyes are dazzled, and my ravished heart
> Leaps at the glorious sight. How bright's the lustre,
> How immense the worth of these fair jewels!
> Ay, such a treasure would expel for ever
> Base poverty and all its abject train.

The thought thus comes that instead of suicide, which Old Wilmot has counselled, murder may be their refuge. In a dialogue which is singularly reminiscent of that between Macbeth and his lady she works up her reluctant husband to a pitch where he agrees to do their sleeping guest to death. She even goes into young Wilmot's room to fetch the dagger which he had laid aside, and when her trembling husband lets it fall, she is ready to do the deed herself. But at last he strikes, as his son cries, 'O father! father!' When Charlot, Randal, and Eustace enter to join in the joy of the reunion, and to witness the parents' transports at their son's return, they only hear his dying groans. In agony at the awful revelation of what they have done Old Wilmot first stabs his wife and then himself to death. Only one plea he makes:

> You'll do but justice to inform the world,
> This horrid deed, that punishes itself,
> Was not intended as he was our son;
> For that we knew not till it was too late.
> Proud and impatient under our afflictions,
> While Heaven was labouring to make us happy,
> We brought this dreadful ruin on ourselves.

And Randal draws the appropriate lesson that men should be resigned to Heaven's mysterious ways.

Fatal Curiosity had neither the popular success nor the widespread influence of *The London Merchant*. But it is the better play. The stages of the plot are skilfully developed to give plausibility to its paradoxically sinister close. The blank verse of the dialogue, without being in any high degree melodious, is in the main lucid and appropriate to the theme. It is one of the plays which might be revived in a National Theatre.

As after *The London Merchant* Lillo had turned to a foreign historical theme in *The Christian Hero*, so, except for an adaptation of *Pericles*, he followed *The Fatal Curiosity* with another more exotic historical drama, *Elmerick, or Justice Triumphant*, produced at Drury Lane on 23 February 1740.

Andrew II, King of Hungary, is about to proceed on a crusade. He appoints as Regent during his absence the high-souled Elmerick, with the injunction,

> Take the sword
> And bear it not in vain. Should any dare,
> Presuming on their birth or place for safety,
> Disturb my subjects' peace with bold injustice,
> Let no consideration hold your hand,
> As you shall answer it to me and Heav'n.

Queen Matilda resents her husband's departure, though, as she confesses to Elmerick's adoring wife, Ismena, she has no love for him. What she does not confess to her is that she has conceived a passion for Elmerick himself. A similar passion for Ismena had inflamed Matilda's brother Conrade, Prince of Moravia, on a previous visit to the Buda Court. It now brings him back to try his fate with her once more, and in this the Queen sees a means of furthering her own amorous design on Elmerick.

She appeals to the amazed Regent for a return of her
love for him, and cries 'Shame and ruin!' when he
replies:

> Almighty power! Shall I, who bear the sword
> To punish bold offenders, break the laws
> Your providence has call'd me to defend?
> Doth the least subject look to me for justice,
> And shall the King, my ever-gracious master,
> In recompense for his unbounded favour,
> Receive the highest, most opprobrious wrong
> A king or man can suffer?

As Conrade, who has already found his suit scorned by
Ismena, enters, the Queen exclaims:

> That wretch, presuming on his boundless power,
> Has talk'd to me of love.

A duel follows in which Elmerick disarms Conrade but
grants him life—which only wakens in him a thirst for
revenge, to which Matilda ministers by luring Ismena
into his power. He takes possession of her by violence,
after which she is so shamed and agonized that when
Elmerick seeks to embrace her she starts back, exclaiming, 'Thou hast no wife. . . . Avoid me, fly, and think
of me no more.' She then tells how her honour has been
wronged, to which he answers, 'Thou art innocent, thy
mind unstain'd', and he promises vengeance.

> I'll weigh it as the action of my life
> That must give name and value to the whole;
> And raise a monument to thee and justice
> Shall strike exalted wickedness with terror.

The Queen, to forestall him, has already sent Conrade
with letters of accusation against the Regent, to over-
take the King. Relying thereon she brazenly confronts
Elmerick:

You refus'd my love,
And, in my turn, I have undone Ismena.
Elm. You do confess it, then?
Queen.   I glory in it.
To wound you where I knew you most secure,
To taint your Heav'n, to curse you in Ismena,
Was my contrivance: Conrade's desperate passion,
Subservient to my vengeance, wrought her ruin.

Thus dared, Elmerick hastens to offer up this 'high
delinquent' to 'inexorably firm, eternal justice' and to
Ismena. He calls in executioners, who pull the Queen
into the recess in the back scene and strangle her.
Thereafter the King returns with Conrade, to find his
wife dead and to threaten Elmerick with dire destruction. Composedly he answers the charge:

You may remember, Sir,
When you appointed me your substitute,
You did pronounce, in presence of your states,
The worst abuse of law and all just power,
Is when the great offend and pass unpunish'd.
This you enjoin'd me strongly not to suffer,
Nor bear the sword in vain. You've been obey'd—
The Queen transgress'd—and I have done my duty.

Unwillingly the King is convinced that Elmerick speaks
truth by his report of the Queen's confession and by the
written testimony of two of her servants. He declares
that he will comfort Ismena's sorrows, but when Elmerick questions a messenger, 'Be brief, how fares my
wife?' the answer, is 'As angels fare, with whom she now
inhabits'. As Conrade, now repentant of his foul deed,
hears this he knows that he has murdered her, and in
atonement stabs himself to death, with 'Ismena' on his
dying lips. Elmerick draws the same moral as Randal at

the close of *The Fatal Curiosity*, and this must be Lillo's
own religious conviction:

> Unerring power! whose deep and secret counsels
> No finite mind can fathom and explore;
> It must be just to leave your creatures free,
> And wise to suffer what you most abhor;
> Supreme and absolute of these your ways
> You render no account—we ask for none.
> For mercy, truth and righteous retribution
> Attend at length your high and awful throne.

All his plays, however different otherwise, carry with
them a deeply felt moral implication. And in *Elmerick*
this stands the acid, almost paradoxical, test of a
sovereign's recognition of the justice of the extreme
penalty exacted by his representative on his Queen and
his wife.

Lillo had died on 3 September 1739, about six months
before the play was performed, but so great was his
admiration for Frederick, Prince of Wales, that he had
adjured his friend John Gray to dedicate the play when
printed to this 'most illustrious patron of justice, heroic
virtue and the rights of mankind'. The same year, 1740,
saw also the posthumous publication of a masque,
Britannia and Batavia, which Lillo had written in celebration of the marriage, in 1734, of the Princess Royal and
William, Prince of Orange. It pays tribute to the alliance
as a bulwark against tyranny and superstition in their
two countries, and ends with the marriage procession
'as near as possible with the same magnificence, as it was
really performed'. Lillo's dramatization of the *Arden of
Feversham* murder was left imperfect when he died and
was finished by John Hoadly. It had to wait until July
1759 for a performance at Drury Lane, and for publication till 1762. His versatile and enduring dramatic

achievement is all the more remarkable because as a member of a dissenting family and a jeweller by trade he was by birth and vocation outside of theatrical and literary circles.

EDWARD MOORE

THE career of Edward Moore was in various ways akin to that of Lillo. Born on 22 March in 1712, he was the son of a dissenting minister in Abingdon. His earliest vocation was in trade as a linendraper, and thus like Lillo he was of mature age before he made his first literary venture in 1744 with *Fables for the Female Sex*, partly after the manner of Gay. Four years later, on 13 February 1748, his first play, *The Foundling*, was produced at Drury Lane. For the most part it follows conventional lines. Colonel Raymond, son of the royalist Sir Charles, is in love with Rosetta, the sister of his friend, young Belmont, a good-hearted rake. In a midnight adventure the latter has rescued from an attempted rape a lady of unknown origin, Fidelia, whom he gives out to be the daughter of a dead college friend bequeathed to his guardianship. The girls have become bosom friends, though opposite in temper. Rosetta, a gay coquette, holds, as she declares, the mighty Colonel in chains, while Fidelia's concealed feeling for Belmont makes her afraid of herself. To tease the Colonel Rosetta pretends to encourage the advances of a ridiculous fop, Faddle, who writes to her: 'Dear creature, since I saw you yesterday, time has hung upon me like a winter in the country; and unless you appear at the rehearsal of the new opera this morning, my sun will be in total eclipse for two hours. . . . Madam, most unspeakably yours.'

In a design upon Fidelia's virtue, and to estrange her from Rosetta, Belmont bribes Faddle to write to his sister anonymously, accusing Fidelia of being a woman of the town. Fidelia, in her distress, seeks help from Sir Charles Raymond, and Faddle, eavesdropping, twists this into an assignation, till Sir Charles forces him to confess that he wrote the vile letter, and thus he gives Belmont away. There is further entanglement when Villiard enters, claiming to be Fidelia's lawful guardian and insisting on her being returned to him. Fidelia protests, 'He bought me for the worst of purposes; he bought me of the worst of women', and tells how it was from his assault that Belmont saved her. When Villiard goes out, threatening to seek justice in a court of law, Belmont, repentant, asks for Fidelia's hand.

Then follows an electrifying *coup de théâtre*. Sir Charles runs to Fidelia, crying, 'My daughter! my daughter!' and tells a strange tale. When exiled under the Commonwealth, he had left the infant child with her *gouvernante* who told her she was a foundling, wrote to him that she was dead, and sold her when she was twelve to Villiard. Fallen ill, she had sent for Villiard, and, after hearing from him, she had sought out Sir Charles and unburdened herself to him. It is one of the most involved and unsatisfactory of the 'recognition' instances with which the dramatists helped themselves out of complications. Little sympathy, too, can be felt with Belmont who, after rescuing Fidelia from a ravisher, is intent, till a too-long-delayed repentance, to dishonour her himself. But Moore showed some true dramatic insight in the character-contrast of Rosetta and Fidelia, and in the selfless loyalty of Sir Charles and the Colonel.

His next play, *Gil Blas*, produced at Drury Lane on 2 February 1751, was based on the story of Aurora in the fourth book of Le Sage's novel. Having fallen in love with Don Lewis Pacheco, whom she has seen from her window in Madrid, she follows him to Salamanca in masculine disguise with her maid Laura as her page. She passes herself off as her twin brother, Don Felix de Mendoza, and in this Moore improves upon Le Sage who had made them only cousins. The earlier scenes of the comedy, with Aurora playing the two parts, in different lodgings, of herself and her brother, are well managed. And the scene between Aurora and Gil Blas in which the servant, like Malvolio with Olivia, thinks that his mistress is in love with him when she is leading up to a confession of her passion for Don Lewis, is skilfully handled. As Gil Blas gave the name to the play, and as the part was acted by Garrick, it was natural that he should throughout be given greater prominence than in this section of the French novel. But Moore unduly complicates the action by an elaborate underplot in which Don Gabriel, the supposed friend of Don Lewis, seduces his mistress, Isabella, with a resulting quarrel ending with an attempt of Don Gabriel to assassinate Don Lewis. His life is saved by the real Don Felix who does not appear in the novel, but who in the play comes unexpectedly to Salamanca. It is only when Don Lewis is confronted by Don Felix in double form that Aurora is compelled to reveal her true sex, and to bring her love-affair to a happy close. Incidentally, the servant of Don Lewis, in speaking of a visit to England, tells that play (gambling) 'is the key to every great man's door in England. . . . Do but play deep and you rank with the best of 'em.' Moore's thoughts must already have been running on the theme of his next play.

It was with *The Gamester*, produced at Drury Lane on 7 February 1753, that Moore won a popular success akin to that of Lillo with *The London Merchant*. As Lillo had depicted the tragic downfall of a man not naturally

evil through a sensual infatuation, so Moore pointed
the moral of a similar collapse through an equally
powerful infatuation with the prevalent vice of gambling.
Moore, too, followed Lillo in using prose as the vehicle
of tragedy, but his dialogue is in the main simpler, without echoes of blank-verse rhythm.

When the play opens Beverley has already had to sell
his house and furniture, though Lewson, in love with the
Gamester's sister Charlotte, has redeemed some of the
pieces specially valued by his devoted wife. Lewson also
alone justly suspects Beverley's false friend, Stukeley,
whom he ironically congratulates upon his late successes
at play. 'Poor Beverley!—But you are his friend; and
there's a comfort in having successful friends.' Stukeley's
treachery to Beverley is rendered plausible by the fact
that he was a disappointed rival for the hand of Mrs.
Beverley, and hopes by her husband's ruin to get her
into his power. He beguiles Beverley into the belief that
he too has been undone, and suggests that in the hope
of better fortune at the gaming-table, Beverley should
sell his wife's jewels. After a first refusal he assents. 'She
shall yield up all—My friend demands it. . . . The jewels
that she values are truth and innocence. These will
adorn her ever; and for the rest, she wore them for a
husband's pride, and to his wants will give them.'

To fortify Beverley's resolution Stukeley writes to say
that sooner than face prison in England he will leave the
country, whereupon Beverley cries that he must relieve
or follow him. His wife at once offers her jewels, 'trifles,
not worth speaking of, if weighed against a husband's
peace'.

Beverley, playing against loaded dice again, loses all
and pledges his credit. Stukeley tries in vain to wake his
wife's jealousy by accusing him of having a mistress, and

is scornfully repulsed when he pays court to her. Lewson, having won a promise from Charlotte that their
union will take place at once, tells that her brother has
lost her fortune which she had entrusted to him. He then
seeks out Stukeley, denounces him as 'a little, paltry
villain', and draws his sword, from which Stukeley
shrinks, calling upon the protection of the laws. In the
passage that follows lies the very kernel of the play's
motif.

Lew. Laws! Dar'st thou seek shelter from the laws—those
laws which thou and thy infernal crew live in the constant
violation of?

Stuke. Ay, rail at gaming, 'tis a rich topic and affords
noble declamation. Go, preach against it in the city—you'll
find a congregation in every tavern. If they should laugh at
you, fly to my lord, and sermonize it there; he'll thank you
and reform.

Lew. And will example sanctify a vice? No, wretch; the
custom of my lord or of the cit that apes him cannot excuse
a breach of law, or make the gamester's calling reputable.

Stukeley, in alarm, suborns his confederate Bates to
waylay Lewson by night and kill him, and by involving
him in a quarrel with Beverley plans to lay the guilt
of the murder upon him. He has him arrested and
lodged in prison as a debtor. Comfort comes to his distracted wife and sister with the news of the death of his
uncle, who has left him his whole estate. They rush to the
prison with the news, only to hear from Beverley that on
the previous night, tempted by Stukeley, he had sold the
reversion of the estate for a scanty sum and lost it at the
tables.

They are followed by Stukeley with his accusation of
murder against Beverley, but the plotter is confounded
when the supposed victim, Lewson, enters. Bates,

appalled at the idea of murder, had played Stukeley false, and turns, so to speak, King's evidence against him. Lewson charges Stukeley with a thousand frauds and with ruining Beverley by sharpers and false dice. When Beverley moans that the room turns round, Lewson thinks that it is the villain's presence that disturbs him and bids Stukeley be removed under guard. But Beverley's attack in head and heart has a deeper source. In an agony of shame and despair he has swallowed poison and now goes to his account. With a prayer to Heaven for mercy, and a cry of remorse for the miseries of which he has been the cause, he dies. Lewson pronounces his epitaph and points the moral. 'Save but one error, and this last fatal deed, thy life was lovely. Let frailer minds take warning; and from example learn that want of prudence is want of virtue.'

The difficulty that the play presents to the reader of today is the realization that Beverley's life ever had been 'lovely'. His state of innocence was already behind him when he first appears on the stage, with his house and its contents sacrificed to his ruling passion, for which 'one error' is too mild a term. And, like Barnwell, he is so fatuously persistent in his vicious course that his tragic fate evokes little sympathy. His wife is too much of the passively all-enduring Chaucerian Griselda type to be much more than a lay figure. Lewson and Charlotte, and the faithful old retainer, Jarvis, have in them more of flesh and blood. Stukeley is the stock villain of melodrama, but the retribution for his crimes is left tantalizingly vague.

XII

JOHN HOME

JOHN HOME was born at Leith on 22 September 1722, a son of the town clerk. He was educated at the local grammar school and the University of Edinburgh, where he followed the curriculum suitable to a student preparing to become a minister in the Church of Scotland. He was licensed to preach on 4 April 1745, but in the same year enlisted as a volunteer in the loyalist ranks against the Jacobite rebels. He was taken prisoner at the battle of Falkirk, but later made his escape and returned to his clerical vocation. As Gibbon's service in the Hampshire militia fifteen years later gave him fuller insight into the movements of the Roman legionaries, so Home's regimental experience during 'the '45' helped to account for the warlike background of both his earliest plays, *Agis* and *Douglas*.[1]

As a student he had not confined his reading to theological works. He was deeply interested in the biographies of notable Greeks and Romans, especially as related by Plutarch. He was thus moved to compose a tragedy upon the fate of Agis IV, a king of Sparta, which was completed in 1746. The idealist bent of Home's nature was attracted to the subject of this patriot king who was murdered while seeking to promote the welfare of all his subjects. He was opposed, in the strange Spartan double monarchy, by the other reigning king, Leonidas, who stood for the privileges of the oligarchy. Among the supporters of Agis was Lysander

[1] The section of this chapter dealing with these two plays is mainly reprinted from my article in *The Fortnightly Review*, November 1950.

(not to be confused with his earlier more renowned namesake); and as Home's younger contemporary, Henry Mackenzie, later told the Royal Society of Edinburgh, fearing that his subject 'was too barren of incident and passion to suit the prevailing dramatic tastes', he introduced a sub-plot of the love between Lysander and an Athenian maiden, Euanthe. But, as no less a person than the elder Pitt was to point out, their amorous passion was too loosely related to the main plot and divided the interest.

Euanthe has another lover in Amphares, whom Home develops from slighter mention by Plutarch. A double-faced schemer, he plays the role of a partisan of Leonidas, but his aim is to become himself a king of Sparta, with Euanthe seized, if need be by force, as his queen. Instigator of the murder of Agis, whom his mother mourns, he meets his own doom from the avenging steel of Lysander.

Home had high hopes that Garrick would produce his tragedy at Drury Lane in 1747. Nor was he without some justification. The play had some striking situations, and the dialogue, especially in reflective passages, had a beauty of rhythm and imagery. Thus Lysander in Act II declares:

> Let never man
> Say in the morning that the day's his own:
> Things past belong to memory alone;
> Things future are the property of hope.
> The narrow line, the isthmus of the seas,
> The instant scarce divisible, is all
> These mortals have to stand on.

In Act IV he makes this appeal:

> Ye mighty minds of sages and of heroes!
> Epaminondas, Plato, great Lycurgus!

Who once with such transcendent glory shone,
Brighter than all the stars that deck the heavens;
Is your celestial fire for ever quench'd,
And nought but ashes left, the sport of chance,
Which veering winds still blow about the world?

Agis, echoing closely the words of Plutarch, bids his
executioner

                    Weep not for me!
O thou, whose nature suits not thy employment,
Weep not for me! I would not change conditions
With these bad men.

His mother, Agesistrata, over his body, gives poignant
voice to her lonely anguish:

                    Alas! alas! my son!
O son of Jove, great author of our race,
Sustain my soul! For he who was my stay,
My comfort and my strength is now no more.
Yet in the path his generous spirit chose
He fell, and conscious virtue crown'd his fall.

Is there not here a foreshadowing of the parting between
Lady Randolph and Douglas? Home's disappointment
at Garrick's unexpected rejection found singular vent.
He wrote with a pencil on Shakespeare's monument in
Westminster Abbey (what were the custodians doing?)
lines of bitter lament:

            Image of Shakespeare! To this place I come
            To ease my bursting bosom at thy tomb;
            For neither Greek nor Roman poet fired
            My fancy first, thee chiefly I admired:
            And day and night revolving still thy page,
            I hoped, like thee, to shake the British stage;
            But cold neglect is now my only mead (*sic*),
            And heavy falls it on so proud a head.

It is evident that Home had taken Shakespeare's
Roman-history plays as his model, and had anticipated
similar success. But, apart from any question of their
authors' relative dramatic powers, he ignored one predominant factor in the comparison of *Agis* with *Julius
Caesar* and *Antony and Cleopatra*. Shakespeare there
brought on the stage personalities and events of world-
wide import and repute, familiar to men in general.
Even his genius achieved less with the more local issues
in *Coriolanus*. Garrick therefore had good grounds for
believing that a Drury Lane audience would find little
of interest in the obscure and confusing rivalries of
Spartan kings and their respective factions.

After his disappointment over *Agis* Home turned to
a very different source for his next venture as a tragic
dramatist. This was the old Scottish ballad called in
different versions 'Child Maurice' or 'Gil Morice', as it
appears in Bishop Percy's *Reliques of Ancient English
Poetry*. The ballad in Scottish vernacular tells how Gil
Morice, 'an erle's son', sent 'boy Willie', an unwilling
messenger, to Lord Barnard's hall, to bid his lady meet
him in 'the gude grene wode' alone. Willie delivers his
message as Lord Barnard and his wife sit at meat, and
the enraged 'bauld baron' cries,

> I'll gae to the gude green woode
> And speik with zour lemman.[1]

Then the ballad describes Gil Morice in his youthful
beauty singing in the woods and wondering,

> O what mean a' the folk coming?
> My mother tarries lang.

In this naïve fashion the secret of how Gil Morice is
related to the lady is revealed before the tragic sequel,

[1] Your lover. Throughout the ballad 'z' takes the place of 'y'.

The baron came to the green wode,
　Wi' mickle dule[1] and care.
And there he first spied Gil Morice
　Kameing his zellow hair
That sweetly wav'd around his face,
　That face beyond compare:
He sang sae sweet it might dispel
　A' rage but fell despair.

But the youth's attractions serve only to inflame Lord
Barnard's jealousy. He draws his sword,

　　And thro Gil Morice' fair body
　　He's gar[2] cauld iron gae.

He cuts off his head and has it borne on a spear to his
castle. At the sight his lady exclaims:

　　Far better I lo'e that bluidy head,
　　　Both and that zellow hair
　　Than Lord Barnard, and a' his lands,
　　　As they lig here and thair.

And movingly she makes her confession:

　　I got ze in my father's house
　　　Wi' mickle sin and shame;
　　I brocht thee up in gude grene wode,
　　　Under the heavy rain.
　　Oft have I by thy cradle sitten,
　　　And fondly seen thee sleip;
　　But now I gae about thy grave,
　　　The saut tears for to weip.

She begs Barnard to kill her with the spear that slew her
son, but he declares:

　　Enouch of blood by me's bin spilt,
　　　Seek not your death frae me.
　　I rather lourd[3] it had been mysel
　　　Than eather him or thee.

[1] grief.　　　[2] caused.　　　[3] liefer.

It will be seen that to lay undue stress on Home's debt to 'Gil Morice' does not do justice to his power of dramatic invention. It is true that the ballad furnished him with the fundamental concept of his play, the murder of a woman's son by her husband who believes that she is making an assignation with him as her lover. But the details are changed almost out of recognition. Lady Barnard had borne her boy in her father's house, 'wi' mickle sin and shame', no doubt illegitimately. Home substituted a far more honourable cause for the secrecy attending the child's birth. Her brother had saved in battle the life of Douglas, the hereditary foe of her house. The pair had sworn eternal friendship, and Douglas in a borrowed name had visited her home, won her love, and married her in the authorizing presence of her brother. When questioned by her stern sire, Sir Malcolm, she had taken an equivocal oath that she would never wed one of the Douglas name. Within three short weeks her husband and brother were both slain in the same battle, and she was now wedded to Lord Randolph for whom she has esteem but not love. As she avows in her opening speech:

> O Douglas, Douglas . . .
>   Though I am call'd
> Another's now, my heart is wholly thine.
> Incapable of change, affection lies
> Buried, my Douglas, in thy bloody grave.

But her mourning is not only for him but for the son born of their wedlock who, she believes, has been drowned in his infancy, but who has been saved by a shepherd who has reared him as his own child, under the name of Norval (earlier Forman), among his flocks on the Grampian hills. Here Home may have had in mind the story of Perdita in *The Winter's Tale* similarly thought to be lost, and brought up as a shepherd's child. But the youth's inborn ambition to win glory on the field of battle is a reflex of Home's own experience as a soldier.

It is this that moves Norval to leave his supposed father's house on the report that the King has summoned the Scottish peers to lead their warriors against the invading Danes. On his way he rescues Lord Randolph from an attack by assassins hired by the villain of the play, Glenalvon, who is Randolph's heir. As the elder Pitt had criticized in *Agis* the Lysander-Euanthe plot, so another celebrity, David Hume, a kinsman of Home, objected to Glenalvon's character as 'too abandoned'. But he is necessary to the working out of the tragedy. I think it has not previously been noted that in his character and in the part that he plays Glenalvon is a magnified facsimile of Amphares in *Agis*. Like him he is double-faced. As described by Lady Randolph,

> Subtle and shrewd, he offers to mankind
> An artificial image of himself;
> And he with ease can vary to the taste
> Of different men its features.

And as Amphares by lawless means sought the possession of Euanthe and of the Spartan crown, so Glenalvon was determined to do away with Randolph that he might enjoy his lands and wealth, and force his wife to yield to his overmastering passion which he has 'madly blabb'd' to her.

Lord Randolph's praise of his rescuer fires his Lady's imagination:

> I thought that, had the son of Douglas lived,
> He might have been like this young gallant stranger.
> While thus I mused, a spark from fancy fell
> On my sad heart, and kindled up a fondness

For this young stranger, wand'ring from his home,
And like an orphan cast upon my care.
I'll be the artist of young Norval's fortune.

Then follows the discovery, in the central scene of the
play, that Norval is in truth her son Douglas, and her
appointment with him, evidently suggested by Gil
Morice's message in the ballad, for a meeting by night
in the neighbouring wood. Randolph's jealousy, fanned
by Glenalvon, of the favour shown by his wife to this
'acquaintance of a day' is inflamed to fury by the news,
betrayed to him, of this 'assignation'. He seeks, like Lord
Barnard in the ballad, to take the life of the 'lover', but
in Douglas he finds more than his match. It is the
treacherous blow of Glenalvon from behind that is fatal,
though, like Amphares, the double-dealing villain meets
his own doom.

In the last farewell between mother and son Home
reaches the height of his dramatic achievement:

> *Lady Rand.* And we must part: the hand of death is on
> thee.
> O my beloved child! O Douglas! Douglas!
> *Doug.* Too soon we part. I have not long been Douglas.
>
> .   .   .   .
>
> O had I fall'n as my brave fathers fell,
> Turning with great effort the tide of battle,
> Like them I should have smiled and welcomed death.
> But thus to perish by a villain's hand,
> Cut off from nature's and from glory's course,
> Which never mortal was so fond to run.
> *Lady Rand.* Hear, justice, hear! stretch thy avenging
> arm!
> *Doug.* Unknown I die; no tongue shall speak of me.
>
> .   .   .   .
>
> But who shall comfort thee?
> *Lady Rand.*   Despair, despair!

Doug. O had it pleased high heaven to let me live
A little while—My eyes that gaze on thee
Grow dim apace. My mother, oh, my mother!

As he dies there is nothing left for her but to follow him by leaping into the void.

Once again Home rode with his play to London to have it rejected by Garrick as 'totally unfit for the stage'. But his Scottish friends rallied to his support and planned for its production at an Edinburgh theatre. Henry Mackenzie has recorded the excitement thus aroused. 'The men talked of the rehearsals, the ladies repeated what they had heard of the story; some had procured, as a great favour, copies of the most striking passages, which they recited at the earnest request of the company.' Its performance at the Canongate Theatre on 14 December 1756, with West Digges as Douglas and Mrs. Ward as Lady Randolph, was a triumph. 'The town', as a contemporary has recorded, 'was in an uproar of exultation that a Scotchman did write a tragedy of the first rate and that its merits were submitted to them.' But the cry of one enthusiast: 'Whaur's yer Wully Shakespeare noo?' suggests a comment not intended by him. This patriot spoke in the Scottish vernacular, and of this there is no trace in *Douglas*. Even its scenic background, in spite of the mention of the Grampian Hills, the Carron Water, and the Teviot, does not bear the impress of 'Caledonia stern and wild'.

Home's *Douglas* was completely anglicized in diction and technique. While this may lessen its interest today for Scottish literary antiquaries, it has accounted for its long stage career. Its success in Edinburgh was followed by its production at Covent Garden in 1757 with Spranger Barry as Douglas and Peg Woffington as Lady Randolph. Garrick was thus induced at the second time of asking to put on *Agis* at Drury Lane in 1758, with himself as Lysander and Mrs. Cibber as Euanthe; and *Douglas* in 1769, with Brereton in the titular part and Mrs. Barry as Lady Randolph. Edmund Kean as Douglas and Mrs. Siddons as Lady Randolph continued the high tradition, sustained by Dame Sybil Thorndike in our own day acting the heroine in the grand manner in Edinburgh. Throughout these impersonations it has not been local colour or association but the universal twin tragedies of frustrated mother-love and youthful idealism (both foreshadowed in *Agis*) that have given *Douglas* an enduring appeal.

The resounding success of *Douglas* naturally encouraged Home to further dramatic efforts, but it is surprising that after his initial disappointment with *Agis* he should have again turned to a classical theme in *The Siege of Aquileia*. This belonged, however, not to early Greek history but to the period when the Roman empire was disintegrating before the attacks of barbarian invaders. Aquileia was a key fortress-town near the head of the Adriatic. In Home's play it is being besieged by the savage Dalmatian chief Maximin, and defended by the Roman consul, Aemilius, with his two sons Paulus and Titus, watched by his wife Cornelia. And though time and place and surroundings are so different, the basic interest of *The Siege of Aquileia*, produced at Drury Lane on 21 February 1760, is akin to that of *Douglas*—the too-early death of a heroic youth and a mother's anguish.

Titus, the younger of the two brothers, is aflame to win martial glory by leading the attack on a tower built by the enemy. He pleads to his father, 'Let me go forth: be this my first exploit.' He has scarcely gone when news comes that a relief force will arrive in three days, and

Paulus rides after him to prevent his sally. But he is too
late and both brothers are taken prisoner. An officer
comes with terms from Maximin, who will execute the
two captives unless their father 'Before the sun shall set,
give up the city'. Aemilius scornfully rejects the offer,
whereupon a priest suggests that without breach of
honour he

> May stipulate with Maximin, to yield
> The city on the fourth returning day
> If not relieved.

Cornelia urges this upon her husband:

> If thou reject'st this counsel, I will say,
> Not Maximin the tyrant slew my children,
> But their own cruel father. . . . Oh, Aemilius!
> Alike the father and the mother bear
> The name of parent; but a parent's love
> Lives only in the tender mother's heart.

The last line is significant of much in Home's outlook.
The relief force arrives sooner than expected, and Maximin, feeling he has been tricked, orders gallows, which
can be seen from the Roman walls, to be erected for the
execution. Cornelia beholds her sons in chains ready for
sacrifice, and entreats her husband to follow her thither
that he may relent.

> *Aemil.* Relent, Cornelia! O, eternal powers,
> That see the anguish of my tortured soul,
> Sustain me still! let not my duty yield
> To the strong yearning of a father's heart.

Then enters an officer with the surprising news that

> Titus comes to end the war,
> And to compassion move his father's mind.

The word 'compassion' enrages Aemilius, and when

Titus enters, dear to his mother still, he turns from
him:

> Art thou my Titus? Thou that fear'st to die,
> And comes a servile suppliant for life,
> With coward prayers to seduce the Consul.
> No! thou art not my son.

Then follows a highly effective *coup de théâtre*. Titus has
not come to be a counsellor of shame.

> The cause of honour, of my father's honour,
> The cause of Rome against myself I plead,
> And in my voice the noble Paulus speaks.
> Let no man pity us; aloft we stand
> On a high theatre, objects, I think,
> Of admiration and of envy rather.

His repentant father clasps him in his arms. A Roman-
born officer, Varus, leader of the British bands in
Maximin's heterogeneous army, who has acted as a go-
between to the tyrant and the Consul, promises that he
will lend aid. As Titus bids farewell, his mother sobs:

> Thou goest to die, and say'st thou but 'farewell'?
> It were too little, if from Rome thou went'st
> A sportful journey to the Baian shore.
> But thou art going, never to return,
> To the dark region.
> *Titus.*   Where all men have gone:
> Where all must go: but glorious is the path
> Thy offspring tread. An honourable death
> Is the sole gift which fate cannot resume.

Maximin detects the design of Varus against him and
puts him to death, but his legions rise to avenge him,
and in the struggle that follows Titus kills Maximin.
But he is fatally wounded, and when he is borne in by
Paulus, Cornelia cries, 'O, my Titus dies!'

Titus. I stood the chance of war. Do not bewail
A fate so far above my highest hope
When last we parted. Men are born to die.
Cor. But not like thee, in youth untimely slain.
Titus. This active day has been an age of life.

As with Douglas a mother mourns the loss too soon of a
gallant son, but here he can leave a brother to soothe her
grief, and she can bear to gaze on his face that in death
wears a look of triumph. His is a finely conceived character, and Home shows true dramatic skill in the contrast
between Aemilius, torn between parental feeling and
patriotic duty, and Cornelia, wholly dominated by
mother-love.

Garrick evidently hoped that 'the just portrait of
a Roman youth' would appeal to the emotions of an
English audience lamenting the casualties in the Seven
Years War, for the prologue which he spoke thus ended:

> Perhaps your hearts may own the pictured woe,
> And from a fonder source your sorrows flow:
> Whilst warm remembrance aids the poet's strain,
> And England weeps for English heroes slain.

But the subject of the play was too remote in its interest
for a Drury Lane crowd, and it had a short run.

Meanwhile Home's career had taken a sharp turn.
The spectacle of a minister of the Kirk coming out with
Douglas as an applauded playwright had outraged many
of his brethren. They retaliated with a series of pamphlets, in one of which it was proclaimed that *Douglas*
ought to be publicly burnt at the hands of the hangman,
and in another it was called the thrice accursed tragedy.
Home's friends rallied to his defence, but he found it
advisable to resign his ministerial charge on 7 June 1757
and to migrate to London. He there became private

secretary to Lord Bute, through whom he was appointed tutor to the Prince of Wales. The Prince accepted the dedication of a volume containing Home's first three tragedies in 1760, and when later in the year he became king, as George III, he granted him a sinecure office and a pension of £300 a year.

Thus almost a decade elapsed before Home entered upon his second dramatic period with *The Fatal Discovery*, produced at Drury Lane on 23 February 1769. He had met James Macpherson in 1759, and the play is conceived in the spirit of Ossianic legend. Rivine, daughter of Kathul, King of the Isles, is betrothed to Ronan, Prince of Morven. There is a rival for her hand in Durstan, King of the Picts. During a visit of Ronan to Erin Durstan spreads a false report through an agent Valma that Ronan has wedded the beautiful Queen of Erin. In the shock of what she believes to be this betrayal Rivine is persuaded by her father to marry his ally Durstan, though her whole love is given to Ronan. Her brother, Connan, the bosom friend of Ronan, had fled distracted from his father's hall. But now he returns to tell his sister that

> Ronan is innocent; he loves thee still;
> He never ceased to love thee.
> *Riv.*   I believe it.
> He never ceased to love, who never loved.

But Connan relates how by chance he had heard from the dying lips of Valma the confession of his treacherous falsehood. He bids her renounce Durstan, but with a broken heart she cries farewell to her native land. When, however, Durstan returns to take his bride away she sees Ronan's sword in the hand of one of his bodyguard and claims it. Durstan tells how it was the one relic found

after a shipwreck in which all, including Ronan, had
perished.

> *Riv.* In those wild waves the chief of warriors died:
> To me he hasten'd through the seas and storms;
> Unknowing of his wrongs for me he died.
>
> .   .   .   .
>
> For ever I renounce thee, Durstan!
> To Ronan's memory I devote my days.

But Ronan alone has escaped from the shipwreck, and
has been given shelter in the cave of the hermit Orellan.
Here for her safety Connan lodges Rivine and the lovers
come face to face, only for Ronan to hear from Orellan
that Rivine has been betrayed into marriage with his
foe, the Pictish King. Kneeling before Ronan she
protests:

> I never ceased to love thee. My fond heart,
> Even when I thought thee false, and strove to hate thee,
> Even then my tortured heart was full of thee:
> 'Tis this that sends me to an early grave;
> I could not bear to be and not be thine.

As he declares his love for her, and bids her not speak
of death, Calmar enters with the news that his master,
Connan, is threatened by a Pictish horde, and Ronan
rushes to his aid. Then follows a too-long-drawn-out
scene, in which Ronan and Durstan defy each other and
engage in combat, till Kathul intervenes, and they part
after fixing a duel for the morrow. Before then, by an
artifice, Durstan lures Ronan and Connan at midnight
into a wood where, in the darkness, they nearly attack
each other, and where Rivine has been led by Calmar
as to a secure retreat. Here she is seized by Durstan and,
when Ronan seeks to free her, he summons a band of

his followers. As they appear, Rivine stabs herself, crying,

> O, Prince of Morven! guard thy noble life
> From shame, from Durstan; this shall save Rivine.

Ronan attacks him and both are fatally wounded. Rivine laments,

> I have undone thee,
> Blasted thy youth, cut short thy noble life.
>
> .   .   .   .
>
> *Ronan.* 'Tis not thy fault. Fortune has cross'd our love;
> But I would rather be what now I am
> Than love thee less, or yet be less beloved.
> *Riv.* Beloved thou art. I die, give me thy hand.
> *Ronan.* My heart, my soul are thine.

As in his earlier plays Home has here an effective close, and *The Fatal Discovery* contains some memorable passages of dialogue and description. But it has one fundamental weakness. Whatever fraud as a rival lover Durstan had used, Rivine had given herself to him as his bride, and his claim upon her against Ronan is so far justified. Even in the case of Bajazet and his wife, Rowe's Tamerlane had recognized the obligation of the marriage tie.[1] But, as it happened, the fate of the play was not to depend on its intrinsic worth or otherwise. As a protégé of Bute, Home had shared something of the unpopularity of the fallen Prime Minister. The tragedy was therefore produced anonymously, but the secret of its authorship soon leaked out, and after a run of eleven days it had to be withdrawn.

Discouraged by this ill fortune Home waited for four years till he made another dramatic venture, in a fresh field. *Alonzo*, produced at Drury Lane on 27 Feb-

---

[1] See pp. 11–12, above.

ruary 1773, drew its subject from the period when Spain was the battlefield between Christians and Moors. Ormisinda, daughter and heiress of the King of Spain, had secretly married the heroic noble Alonzo. Thinking that he had seen her, shortly after the wedding, playing him false with a handsome youth, he had fled from her to distant lands. Eighteen years had since elapsed and the son of their brief union, Alberto, was growing to maturity. The King, as she tells her confidante Teresa, ignorant of her marriage has announced that she shall become the bride, with Spain as her dowry, of the victor in a duel between a redoubtable Moor, Mirmallon, and a Spanish champion whose arrival at once is expected. The King believes that this will be Alonzo, but a messenger reports that he is an Oriental:

> Clad in the flowing vesture of the east,
> A Persian turban on his head he wears.
> Yet he's a Christian knight. To mark his faith,
> Holy, and adverse to Mahommed's law,
> Before his steps a silken banner borne
> Streams in the wind and shows a golden cross.

Alberto thereupon claims that the champion should be a Spaniard, and that, though young in arms, as a killer of savage beasts he may engage this Moorish dog. The news is brought to Ormisinda, and Home again strikes his favourite *motif* of anguished mother-love.

> My son! my son!
> My hope, my comfort, in despair and death,
> The only star in my dark sky that shone,
> Must thy unhappy mother live to see
> Thy light extinguished?

But it is not to be. The stranger knight declares himself to be the Persian prince, Abdallah, chosen friend of

Alonzo, and the Council decides that he shall fight the
Moor. Abdallah is Alonzo disguised, and to an incredulous friend Velasco he tells the story of Ormisinda's
guilt. Before the duel he declares to the King that he has,
if victor, only 'an earnest and a just request', which he is
assured will be granted. When the Moorish giant has
fallen the King asks his daughter to speak their gratitude
to their saviour. As she voices this he makes his request,
'justice on a great offender', the Princess Ormisinda.

> Here in the presence of the peers of Spain
> I charge her with a crime, whose doom the laws
> Of Spain have wrote in blood: Adultery.
>
> . . . .
>
> [She] Had given her honour to a worthless wretch,
> And driven a noble husband to despair.

The amazed King retorts that his daughter was never
married, whereupon she confesses the secret of her
wedding to Alonzo and his eighteen years' desertion, of
which she speaks in truly poignant lines:

> There is no calendar so just and true
> As the sad mem'ry of a wife forsaken.
> The years, the months, the weeks, the very days,
> Are reckon'd, registered, recorded there.

But she protests that, though she transgressed against her
father by her secret wedlock, she has never in the smallest parcel broken her vow as a faithful wife. Alonzo (still
posing as Abdallah) challenges anyone who will maintain her cause. Alberto takes up the gage of this 'base
defamer of a lady's name'. Before an encounter can take
place the King entreats Abdallah to produce specific
witness of the charge that he has brought against
Ormisinda. Thereupon Abdallah goes out and re-enters
in Spanish dress as Alonzo. Crying 'My husband!'
Ormisinda runs to embrace him, but he repels her,

'Away, thy husband's shame; shame to thy sex!' Alberto runs to attack him and Alonzo draws his sword, but before they can engage, Ormisinda throws herself between them.

> Hold! strike through me!
> You know not what you do, unhappy both,
> This combat must not, nor it shall not be.
>
> .   .   .   .
>
> You have no quarrel. I'll remove the cause.
>   *She stabs herself and falls.*

With her dying voice she again protests her innocence, reveals that Alberto is their son, and discloses that the youth with whom Alonzo thought her guilty was Teresa with her brother's sword and plumed helmet. She takes her husband to her arms with words of comforting forgiveness:

> Had I been
> What I to thee appear'd, thy rage was just,
> A Spaniard's temper, and a prince's pride,
> A lover's passion, and a husband's honour,
> Prompted no less.

Before her dying eyes she has the joy of seeing her husband and son embrace, and of committing the youth to his father's care. But Alonzo passes this trust to the King, and turns his own sword against his dishonoured life.

> Oft have I struck with thee,
> But never struck a foe with better will
> Than now myself.

The Fatal Discovery like *Alonzo* has a fundamental flaw. It is incredible that Alonzo on such a flimsy misconception, without putting it to the test, should give way to such savage rage against his wife, desert her for eighteen years, and return disguised to cover her with open shame. But if this can be overlooked, *Alonzo* exhibits some of Home's characteristic merits. Alberto, the high-spirited youth, reared in ignorance of his true birth, has something of the quality of Douglas, though reserved for a happier fate. Ormisinda, impersonated by Mrs. Barry, filled the part of an appealing martyr-heroine. Yet the play did not attract and had a shorter run than it deserved.

It was not till five years later that Home made another bid for theatrical favour with a tragedy, *Alfred*, produced at Covent Garden on 21 January 1778. He was probably unaware that Thomson and Mallet had anticipated him twenty-eight years before with a masque on the same subject, to which they had given a political colouring.[1] Home, on the other hand, had to meet the criticism that he violated historic truth by making Alfred's motive in visiting the Danish camp in disguise not patriotism but love of his captive betrothed. In his preface to the published play he makes this defence:

> In tragedy, if the subject be historical, the author is not permitted to introduce events contrary to the great established facts of history; for instance, in the tragedy of *Alfred* the hero must not be killed nor driven out of England by the Danes; but preserving these ancient foundations as the piers of his bridge the author may bend his arches, and finish the fabric, according to his taste and fancy . . . the poet's fancy is controlled by nothing but probability and consistence of character—the barriers of dramatic truth.

This is excellently said, but it does not fully vindicate Home's somewhat fantastic development of his plot. The Danish King Hinguar, on the day fixed for Alfred's wedding to Ethelswida, had treacherously attacked the English camp, and in the slaughter that followed it was

<hr />

[1] See p. 158, above.

believed that both had perished. But Alfred had escaped
to Athelney, whence he has now come forth, and he
learns from the Earl of Surrey that Ethelswida is a
prisoner in Hinguar's camp. Alfred at once determines
to learn her fate by visiting the Danish camp in disguise
as a British bard, and when the Earl of Devonshire
betrays anxiety, he assures him:

> I read thy thoughts, but urge me not to hear
> Thy friendly counsels which I cannot follow.
> In great events the agitated mind
> Consults its genius only. Low or high,
> The active spirits in that level flow
> Nor fall nor rise, to act another's counsel.

This is one of Home's striking reflective passages, but
what follows draws too heavily upon dramatic illusion.
Alfred with his music so enchants Hinguar that he begs
his aid in soothing the frenzy of a beloved fair one whose
wits have been crazed by shock. When she enters, fan-
tastically dressed, and intermingling her 'roving words'
with snatches of song, she is no other than Ethelswida.
She recognizes Alfred through his disguise and, when
they are left alone, dropping her pretence of madness
she adjures him:

> Fly from this place of peril; fly with speed.
> Thy presence to us both is sure perdition.
>
> .   .   .   .
>
> Tarry not here; else I shall lose my reason,
> And be the thing I seem.

When the King returns it is to announce a further com-
plication. Though a suitor to Ethelswida, he has already
a royal Danish wife, Ronex, whom he detests, and
who now comes to take vengeance on her supplanting
rival. Meanwhile Edda, one of Ethelswida's attendants,

has confided to Hinguar that her distraction is feigned, and he infers that the supposed bard is her lover. He charges him with being an impostor, whereto Alfred replies that he is the Earl of Surrey who has disguised himself to learn the fate of a much loved sister. It is hard to reconcile this with the traditional conception of the Saxon King, of whom Tennyson wrote, 'Truth-lover was our English Alfred named.' And when Hinguar, still pleading his suit, tells Ethelswida that her pretended brother has paid the forfeit of his life, she blurts out the secret:

> Inhuman monster! hast thou murder'd Alfred,
> And dost thou speak of love to Ethelswida?

Hinguar offers to spare Alfred's life if she will accept his hand, and in desperation she assents, on condition that he sets him free and conducts him to the English camp. To Alfred he offers as a bride his own niece, a 'maid of beauty', to be a pledge of union between their races. Alfred indignantly rejects the proposal, but challenges the Dane to single combat to decide the fate of Ethelswida and of England. Hinguar's answer is 'Thou shalt die, or wed the maid of Denmark.' Within an hour he must resolve, and it is for death. But as he and Ethelswida are having a last interview, Ronex with a band of soldiers headed by her partisan Rollo enters in pursuit of her rival, only to repent seemingly of her rage on learning that she is the princess, Alfred's betrothed.

From this point the plot becomes more and more complicated. A plan by the jealous Ronex to have Ethelswida murdered miscarries. Alfred is set free by English troops. He engages, as he had offered, in single combat with Hinguar and gives him a mortal wound. Believing that Ethelswida has been killed, he swoons after the duel, to revive when she appears, and to proclaim,

> The nations now are one: with Hinguar died
> The enmity of England and of Denmark.

But before this happy issue had been reached the Covent Garden audience had probably found it difficult to follow the entanglements of Home's plot, and the play fell flat. Discouraged by his series of failures in the theatre Home wrote no more plays, though he lived for thirty years more till 5 September 1808. Posterity has been content to concentrate its interest in him solely on *Douglas*. But an unprejudiced survey of his dramatic work as a whole shows that his too loudly acclaimed masterpiece does not monopolize its merits, though they can be appreciated more fully in the study than on the stage.

XIII

ISAAC BICKERSTAFFE—HUGH KELLY

ISAAC BICKERSTAFFE was born in Ireland about
1724. At the age of eleven he became page to Lord
Chesterfield. Coming to London, he became a member of Dr. Johnson's circle, and also an officer in the
marines, but was discharged in ignominious circumstances.

After a prior venture with a 'musical entertainment',
Thomas and Sally, or, The Sailor's Return, produced at
Covent Garden on 28 November 1760, Bickerstaffe
made a great hit with a comic opera, *Love in a Village,*
at the same theatre, on 8 December 1762. It was equally
successful on the stage and in print, and would deserve
fuller notice had it not in its main plot followed so
closely Johnson's *The Village Opera,*[1] with further borrowing from Wycherley's *The Gentleman Dancing-Master.*
Young Meadows, like Freeman, takes up the role of a
gardener in the service of Justice Woodcock, to be near
Rosetta with whom he is in love. Like Betty in *The
Village Opera* she is a girl of good family, who has become
chambermaid to Woodcock's daughter, Lucinda, in
order to escape being forced by her father into a marriage against her will. Lucinda, too, like Rosetta in *The
Village Opera,* is defying Woodcock by engaging herself
to Jack Eustace whom she has met at Bath, whom she
passes off as a music-master, and with whom she is
arranging to elope.

All these entanglements are resolved in much the
same fashion as in *The Village Opera,* though with modi-

[1] See pp. 208–12, above.

fications in detail. Woodcock is the same domineering, testy figure as Sir Nicholas Wiseacre in Johnson's opera. But instead of having a submissive wife he has a shrewd, termagant sister, Deborah. Between them it is 'an established maxim never to agree in anything'. Deborah warns her brother that Eustace is Lucinda's lover and not a music-master, but he retorts, 'What, then you know better than the fellow himself, do you? and you will be wiser than all the world.' She gets wind of her niece's planned elopement and tries to stop it by locking up Eustace in a closet. She turns angrily upon Lucinda.

This is mighty pretty romantic stuff, but you learn it out of your play-books and novels. Girls in my time had other employments; we worked at our needles, and kept ourselves from idle thoughts: before I was your age I had finished, with my own fingers, a complete set of chairs, and a fire-screen in ten-stitch; four counterpanes in Marseilles quilting; and the Creed and the Ten Commandments in the hair of our family; it was fram'd and glaz'd, and hung over the parlour chimney-piece, and your poor dear grandfather was prouder of it than of e'er a picture in his house.

Even after Eustace has declared who he is, she seeks to keep up the quarrel.

Deb. He shan't marry my niece.
Woodcock. Shan't he? but I'll show you the difference now; I say he shall marry her, and what will you do about it?

. . . .

Deb. Why, I'm sure he's a vagabond.
Woodcock. I like him the better, I would have him a vagabond.

This brings the piece to an amusing and characteristic close. An attractive incidental episode is the village statute fair where various types of servants offer themselves for hiring in songs which are among the pleasing airs in the opera.

Love in a Village was followed at Covent Garden in January 1765 by *The Maid of the Mill*. Here Bickerstaffe went for his main plot to Richardson's *Pamela*. Lord Aimworth's choice of a bride in Patty, daughter of the miller Fairfield, instead of the well-born Theodosia, is modelled on that of Mr. B—'s preference of the maid-servant Pamela over a lady in his own rank of life. Both Patty and Pamela have been given an education above their station, but Richardson's heroine has a demure attractiveness which is lacking in the more conventional maid of the mill. Mr. B— is a reformed rake who has begun with an attack on Pamela's virtue. Lord Aimworth is almost insipidly virtuous, and delivers himself of the most irreproachable sentiments. In his first dialogue with Patty he declares:

The degrees of rank and fortune, my dear Patty, are arbitrary distinctions, unworthy the regard of those who consider justly; the true standard of equality is seated in the mind: those who think nobly are noble.

And when, after his announcement of his intention to marry Patty, he is warned of ill consequences attending such an alliance, he retorts:

One of them, I suppose, is that I, a peer, should be obliged to call this good old miller, father-in-law. But where's the shame in that? He is as good as any lord in being a man; and if we dare suppose a lord that is not an honest man, he is, in my opinion, the more respectable character.

One wonders how far such egalitarian doctrines appealed to a mid-eighteenth-century audience. They certainly got no shrift from the moving spirit in the underplot,

Lady Sycamore. At her instigation her husband, Sir Harry, had made their daughter, Theodosia, break off her previously sanctioned engagement to Mervin, in order that she might be free to marry Lord Aimworth. 'Fie, Miss', she reproaches the girl, 'marry a cit! Where is your pride—your vanity? have you nothing of the person of distinction about you?' Whereupon good-natured Sir Harry interjects, 'I am a piece of a cit myself, as I may say, for my great grandfather was a dry-salter.' But Mervin will not take 'no' for an answer, and with the help of a gipsy, Fanny, disguises himself as one of their gang and thus gets speech of his lady-love, and plans an elopement. The secret leaks out, and when Lady Sycamore tells that she saw Theodosia go into the garden the excitable Sir Harry conjures up a vision of her throwing herself into the pond.

'Twas but the Wednesday before we left London that I saw, taken out of Rosamond's pond in St. James's Park, as likely a young woman as ever you would desire to set your eyes on, in a new callimancoe[1] petticoat, and a pair of silver buckles on her shoes.

Sir Harry's rambling fears are unfounded, and while Theodosia is planning to go off with Mervin in a gipsy disguise, Lord Aimworth persuades her parents to sanction the match. And when he reveals that he is going to marry Patty, Sir Harry immediately supplies a precedent:

I once knew a gentleman that married his cook-maid; he was a relation of my own—You remember fat Margery, my lady? She was a very good sort of a woman, indeed she was, and made the best suet dumplings I ever tasted.

Lady Sycamore has some justification in exclaiming,

[1] Variant spelling of 'calamanco'—'a glossy woollen stuff of Flanders, twilled and chequered in the warp' (*O.E.D.*).

'Will you never learn, Sir Harry, to guard your expressions?'

The portraiture of this 'commanding wife', as her daughter calls her, and her voluble husband is the best thing in the piece. But also well drawn are the upright miller, his idle son Ralph, in love with Fanny, and Patty's disappointed suitor. And the words of many of the airs, including quartets or quintets at the close of the acts, are often attractive.

During the following decade Bickerstaffe's prolific pen poured forth with varying success a variety of theatrical entertainments—more light operas, comedies, farces, interludes. Highest in rank among them was *Lionel and Clarissa*, produced at Covent Garden on 25 February 1768 with music by Charles Dibdin. The scene opens not with the titular characters but with Colonel Oldboy and his family. He is a hearty, hard-drinking, roistering Squire, whose high-spirited daughter Diana so far takes after him that when he talks to her of marrying a duke, she replies, 'So my husband's a rake, papa, I don't care what he is.' Her mother, on the other hand, is a peevish *malade imaginaire*, whose first exclamation is, 'Shut the door! Why don't you shut the door there? Have you a mind I should catch my death?' She had prevailed upon Oldboy to let their son be brought up by her brother, Lord Jessamy, whose estate he has inherited, and whose name he has taken. The result was that he had become an astonishingly close prototype of a modern 'apostle in the high aesthetic band'. Is he not the sworn brother of Bunthorne in *Patience* when he remarks to his mother:

That's an exceeding fine china jar your ladyship has got in the next room: I saw the fellow of it the other day at Williams's, and will send to my agent to purchase it: it is the true matchless old blue and white.

This chattering about old china infuriates the Colonel who tells in an air what he most detests:

> A coxcomb, a fop,
> A dainty milksop,
> Who, essenc'd and dizen'd from bottom to top,
> Looks just like a doll for a milliner's shop . . .
> Who shrugs, and takes snuff,
> And carries a muff;
> A minikin
> Finiking,
> French powder-puff.

He thinks Jessamy no fit husband for Clarissa, the daughter of his friend and neighbour, Sir John Flowerdale, who is anxious to make a match between them. Clarissa is secretly in love with her father's protégé, Lionel, an Oxford scholar preparing to be a clergyman, who is instructing her in mathematics and philosophy—another anticipation of a modern fashion. He also is in love with her, but, expecting her immediate marriage to Jessamy, surprises Sir John by telling him that he must return to Oxford.

Diana, too, as she confides to Clarissa, has a secret 'affair'. On a visit to London 'an odious fellow, one Harman', as she puts it, had paid her attentions, and, by getting a bogus letter from a friend of the Colonel, had procured an introduction to him and had arrived on a visit. Harman tells Oldboy that to avoid the consequences of an affair with a citizen's daughter he thought it better to be for a time out of the way. He was also in love with a lady in this county but her father was an obstacle to their happiness. Ignorant that the lady is his own Diana, the Colonel afterwards in her presence advises Harman to carry her off, as he had done with his wife. When Diana protests that this will make a noise in the county, and if he is known to be the abettor—Old-boy interrupts with 'Why, what do I care?' He even offers the use of his post-chaise, at a minute's warning, and a 'hundred pieces', if needed.

Meanwhile Diana undertakes to be mistress of the ceremony in introducing her brother for his 'first audience' with Clarissa. As usual, what most interests him are artistic effects.

Jess. Upon my word, a pretty, elegant dressing-room this! but confound our builders, or architects, as they call themselves; not one of them knows the situation of doors, windows or chimneys.

Diana. My dear brother, you are not come here as a virtuoso, to admire the temple; but as a votary to address the deity to whom it belongs.

It is a first-rate epigram, but the deity declines the votary's tepid admiration. She tells him that, though it means disobedience to the best of fathers, their union is impossible. The venom which often underlies a super-ficial aesthetic gloss reveals itself in Jessamy's outrageous abuse of the girl and Sir John. Clarissa, having rejected him, now confesses her love to Lionel, to whom Sir John imparts his belief, 'Surely her affections are not engaged elsewhere.' Then follows her lover's white lie, 'Engaged, sir? No, sir'—to have coals of fire heaped upon his head by Sir John's offer to him of a small country estate which will make him independent. He reproaches him-self bitterly, 'To impose upon my friend—to betray my benefactor and lie to hide my ingratitude—a monster in a moment—No, I may be the most unfortunate of men, but I will not be the most odious.' He begs Clarissa to see him again, and advises her to make her father happy by submitting to his will in accepting Jessamy. But Sir John has already, through an indiscretion of

Clarissa's faithful maid Jenny, learnt the truth of the situation, and he listens in to the lovers' parting interview. He solemnly reproaches them both for their conduct towards him, and then amazes them—and the audience—by telling Lionel, 'Now, sir, I have but one thing more to say to you—take my daughter; was she worth a million, she is at your service.' It is a highly effective and satisfying *coup de théâtre*.

For another father the same day has a more electrifying surprise. The Colonel has become so engrossed in Harman's plan of elopement that he urges him 'to have a letter ready writ for the father, to let him know who has got his daughter, and so forth'. He even insists on writing it himself—and gets a shock when it returns to him with boomerang effect, and with the news that it is his Diana who has gone off in his post-chaise with the gentleman. In his first fury he declares that the letter was none of his writing; 'it was writ by the devil'. When the pair return, without running away, and ask for pardon, he challenges Harman to a duel. But his wife shrieks, 'If you attempt to fight, I shall expire'; Jessamy calls his sister a perfect heroine for a romance, and Sir John, who has gone through a testing time himself, advises his old friend to make the best of the situation. Oldboy even turns upon Jessamy, who thinks that Harman is being let off too lightly for using him so ill. 'That's as I take it—he has done a mettled thing; and, perhaps, I like him the better for it; it's long before you would have spirit enough to run away with a wench.' This characteristic final outburst of the Colonel is symptomatic of Bickerstaffe's skilfully consistent portraiture of the personages in *Lionel and Clarissa*. Among light operas of its period it might repay revival in a National Theatre.

Bickerstaffe was another of the playwrights of this

period who had contributed to the entertainment of his contemporaries, but whose own career ended in misfortune. In 1772, being suspected of a capital crime, he fled abroad. From St. Malo he wrote in French to Garrick asking for help, which could not, however, be given. As late as 1812 he is reported as living under pitiable conditions.

HUGH KELLY

AMONG the dramatists who carried on into the latter half of the eighteenth century the tradition of sentimental comedy Hugh Kelly was one of the most prominent. Born in 1739, he was the son of a Dublin tavern-keeper through whom he came into contact with actors in the Irish capital. In 1760 he came to London to seek a living by his pen. After some journalistic hack-work and the publication of a novel, *Memoirs of a Magdalen*, he delivered his first play, *False Delicacy*, in September 1767 to Garrick, who produced it at Drury Lane, 23 January 1768. The plot is concerned with the cross-purposes and distresses that arise from exaggerated sensitiveness in love affairs. The chief victims are Lady Betty Lambton and Lord Winworth. She is a young widow who, after a first unhappy marriage, has resolved against another. As she tells the sprightly Mrs. Harley, 'I have frequently argued that a woman of real delicacy should never admit a second impression on her heart.' To which Mrs. Harley, who has been twice widowed, replies, 'Yes, and I always thought you argued very foolishly.' Lady Betty accordingly has declined a proposal of marriage from Lord Winworth, though she loves him and is now disconsolate. Mrs. Harley offers to give him a hint of how matters really stand, but Lady Betty scornfully refuses to make use of 'chamber-maid artifices for a husband'. Mrs. Harley retorts, 'Well, the devil take this delicacy! I don't know anything it does besides making people miserable.'

So indeed it turns out. When Winworth asks for an interview with Lady Betty, and tells her, 'I am at this moment come to solicit you upon a subject of the utmost importance to my happiness', and that 'my happiness, in a most material degree, depends upon your ladyship', she is all agog to hear and reciprocate a renewed avowal of his love. But to her dismay he asks her to be an advocate for him with her bosom-friend, Hortensia Marchmont, whom her father had taken into their household. But Miss Marchmont had fallen in love with Winworth's cousin Sidney, and as he was a man of birth and fortune and she a dowerless orphan, delicacy had prevented her from giving any sign of her feeling. Moreover, she understood that Sidney was plighted to Theodora Rivers, whose father, Colonel Rivers, was a brother of Lady Betty. But it was only the Colonel who had insisted on this engagement, while Theodora's heart was secretly given to Sir Harry Newbury who is arranging an elopement with her.

Here is confusion worse confounded. When Lady Betty intercedes with Miss Marchmont for Winworth, she is secretly delighted when Hortensia declares that it is utterly impossible for her to return his affection. Lady Betty assures her that, instead of being offended by her refusal, she is infinitely pleased. But her friend misinterprets this very eagerness as 'a manifest proof of her dissatisfaction.' After retiring for a time she comes back to ask forgiveness, and to say that she will pay a proper obedience to Lady Betty's commands, and that she will make Winworth, if not a fond wife, a dutiful one. Well may Mrs. Harley interject in an aside, 'Did ever two fools plague one another so heartily with their delicacy and sentiment?' Lady Betty is on the point of revealing her true feeling when Winworth enters, and Miss Marchmont confesses to him that she is compelled 'to break through the common forms imposed on our sex, and to declare that I have no will but her ladyship's', for which 'condescending goodness' Winworth returns ten thousand thanks.

Meanwhile there have been other developments. Colonel Rivers has overheard Sir Harry urging his daughter to elope with him that night. Before the appointed time he reproaches her bitterly with her undutifulness, but he will not keep her with him by force, and he will even give her a promised dowry of £20,000. She is so overcome by his generosity that when Sir Harry arrives with his plain-spoken kinsman Cecil to carry her off, she declares that she can never forsake her father. When the exasperated lover attempts to seize her, Cecil intervenes, protesting that he came 'to assist the purposes of a man of honour, not to abet the violence of a ruffian'—a reproof which restores Sir Harry to his better self. But their problem is solved by none other than Sidney, who informs the highly indignant Colonel that when he aspired to the hand of Miss Rivers, he did not know that her affections were otherwise engaged. 'At that time I did not suppose my happiness to be incompatible with hers. I am now convinced that it is so.' So the way is now open for Sir Harry to wed Theodora without defying her father, and for Miss Marchmont to be united to Sidney without making any sacrifice for Lady Betty. Thus there is no longer need or excuse for false delicacy, and Lady Betty openly makes amends for it:

That I may not be censured any longer, I here declare my hand your lordship's, whenever you think proper to demand it; for I am now convinced the greatest proof which a woman can give of her own worth is to entertain an affection for a man of honour and understanding.

False Delicacy may count as the leading case on a subject favoured by eighteenth-century dramatists—the misunderstanding and mischief caused by a woman's concealment, through wilfulness or modesty or fear of parental disapproval, of her true feelings. It is somewhat curious that the two characters who unselfishly help to bring about the final happy all-round solution, the gay, clear-sighted Mrs. Harley and the unconventional, laughter-loving Cecil, go otherwise unrewarded. But they have lent a lighter element to balance the sentimental and moralizing aspects of the play, and doubtless contributed to its triumph both on the stage and in its printed form. 3,000 copies were sold before 2 p.m. on the day of publication, and this number was increased to 10,000 before the end of the season.

With a handsome sum in his pocket Kelly was able to wait for two years before following up his success with a second comedy, *A Word to the Wise*, produced at Drury Lane on 3 March 1770. In broad outline it repeated the central theme of *False Delicacy*, but with some interesting distinctive variations. Caroline, the daughter of Sir John Dormer, is designed by her father to be the bride of Sir George Hastings, a man of worth and fortune but with an element in him of the coxcomb which is repugnant to Caroline. As she pictures him to her sharp-witted friend, Harriot Montagu, 'he is a Narcissus that constantly makes love to his own shadow, and I can't bear the idea of a husband, in whose affection I am likely to be every moment rival'd by the looking-glass'.

Moreover, as she confides to Miss Montagu, she has
formed a secret affection for Mr. Villars, a young man
of unknown origin, whom Sir John has taken into his
household as a literary assistant. But, not to give pain to
her father, she persuades Sir George, when he comes to
make his formal proposal, to pose not as a rejected suitor
but as one who has changed his mind.

Miss Montagu is contracted to Caroline's brother,
Captain Jack Dormer, a good-natured rake, who has
been attracted by Cornelia Willoughby. Her father and
stepmother are the chief additions in the play to Kelly's
portrait gallery. Willoughby is described by the Captain
as a 'Candide to perfection, who is continually blessing
his stars the more they load him with misfortunes'. His
wife, on the other hand, 'is, as usual, continually em-
bittering every comfort of life, and lamenting the
miseries attendant on mortality'. Willoughby's optimism
can turn even a major family misfortune into a disguised
blessing:

When my son was stolen from me in his infancy, I found
a consolation in reflecting that I had not lost my daughter
too—and though I have never since been able to hear any
account of my poor boy, I am satisfied he was taken from
me for the best.

Now, in a different fashion, Willoughby is running a
risk of losing his daughter. Captain Dormer has induced
her to avow her tender feelings for him, and thus to
deceive her father. 'So', as he cynically tells Villars, 'it
is a maxim with me that a woman who can forget the
sentiments of nature has half an inclination to forget the
sentiments of virtue.' Her ambitious stepmother advises
her to elope with the Captain, and thus circumvent his
marriage with Miss Montagu, and has already packed

up all her things 'ready for an expedition to Scotland'. When Willoughby returns from a call upon Sir John he finds his daughter flown, and summons a coach to follow her 'with that libertine Dormer'. Yet even now he clings to his philosophy, 'Something whispers at my heart that all will still turn out for the best.' And he infuriates his wife by assuring her that 'in the severest trials the truly honest feel a satisfaction which is never experienced in the most flattering moments of a guilty prosperity'.

Cornelia has taken the desperate step, as she lets the Captain know by letter, of running off to his lodgings in Pall Mall, confident that he will carry her to Scotland and make her his wife. But, as he tells Villars, he does 'not feel bound to take more care of a lady's honour than she chooses to take herself'. Miss Willoughby knew that as he was already engaged he could not marry her, and she was therefore 'fair game'. To avert suspicion about her from himself, he will make love against his inclination to Miss Montagu, and ask Villars to look after Miss Willoughby in Pall Mall. She is already repenting her rash flight from home, as she finds that 'the man who declared he only existed for my sake is cruelly industrious to plunge me into infamy'. She begs Villars to be her protector, and with a profusion of moral sentiments he orders a coach to take her where she wills.

Meanwhile Sir George Hastings has to play the part imposed upon him by Caroline of representing to her father that the breach between them is of his making. Here the coxcomb proves that underneath his affectations he is a man of worth. When the astonished Sir John asks him what is the impediment, Sir George replies that a very nice point of honour prevents him from revealing it. The infuriated father challenges him to a duel 'at the Cocoa tree in an hour', and Sir George thus finds that he has to risk his life for a woman who has rejected his addresses, and spoken in contempt of him, but 'be it as it will, Miss Dormer's secret shall be inviolably preserv'd'.

While Sir John is throwing out a challenge his son is receiving one. The distracted Willoughby comes in search of his daughter to the Captain, who also is now repentant, and who conducts him to his Pall Mall lodgings, only to hear from Villars that he has enabled Miss Willoughby to escape from her would-be betrayer. Villars draws and bids the Captain take his revenge—which he does by dropping his sword, taking his friend's hand, and thanking him for having awakened him to a sense of true honour. Nor does the other duel take place, for when Sir John and Sir George are about to engage, Caroline throws herself between them and gives the true explanation of her suitor's conduct. Sir John then declares that he will not make his daughter wretched to show that he is master in his family, which Sir George caps by the dictum, 'There are a great many good fathers who never refuse any thing but happiness to their children.'

Miss Willoughby, instead of returning home, has sought out Miss Montagu, to entreat her pardon for coming between her and Captain Dormer—and to hear her declare, 'I never will marry Captain Dormer. He's not a man to my taste.' But this gay-spirited lady expects him, for his father's sake, to pay her a formal proposal, which she turns into a 'whimsical scene' for Miss Willoughby's benefit. She declares that when he offers adoration he merely means 'my happiness depends upon your being a slave, and I must be eternally wretched without the power of making you miserable'. And is not this, she asks, 'a true translation of all the love speeches

that have been made since the world began'? She then
leads him on, in Miss Willoughby's hearing, to make
light of her attractions, till she comes out of hiding, and
the pair turn him into a laughing-stock. To them succeeds his father with angry reproaches for the shame that
he has brought upon his family, till the Captain falls at
his feet, protesting that his future will redeem his past,
and uttering the sentiment which points the moral of the
play, 'I am now satisfied that nothing can be consistent
with the principles of honour which is in any way repugnant to the laws of morality.'

All is now ready for the final adjustment of love's
multiple cross-currents. Sir John, probably contrasting
his son's wildness with the rectitude of Villars, accepts
the latter as a son-in-law even before it is discovered that
he is Willoughby's long-lost son and displaces Sir
George, who takes the loss smilingly, as heir to a legacy.
The repentant Captain is pardoned and welcomed back
by Cornelia Willoughby and her family. And Harriot
Montagu shows that on her own conditions she will
accept Sir George—'if you can make a tolerable bow to
me, do, but don't let me have a syllable of nonsense,
I beg of you'.

It is a signal tribute to Kelly to say that Harriot
Montagu is no unworthy kinswoman of Shakespeare's
Beatrice. Even more than Mrs. Harley in *False Delicacy*
she relieves the sententiousness of the play, which Willoughby has the satisfaction of ending with a characteristic flourish of optimism.

Providence looks down delighted on the altars of the
worthy, and, however it may command adversity to frown
on the beginning of their days, they will acknowledge with
me that all its dispensations are full of benignity in the
end.

If the success of *False Delicacy* had fostered optimism in Kelly himself, it was now to undergo a severe test. As editor of *The Public Ledger* he was in the pay of Lord North, and his political enemies determined to damn his play, irrespective of its merits. They raised a riot in the theatre on the first night and at a second performance, and though it had many supporters, it had to be withdrawn. It was published in the same year, under its own name, and with a long list of subscribers. But so strong was the prejudice against him that his next two plays, a blank-verse tragedy, *Clementina* (1771), and a comedy of a less sentimental type, *The School for Wives* (1773), were at the time given out under false attributions. They were followed by *The Romance of an Hour*, adapted from a French tale by Marmontel, and by his last comedy, *The Man of Reason* (1776). But the dispensations of Providence were not 'full of benignity' to him in the end, and he died in poor circumstances on 3 February 1777.

XIV

RICHARD CUMBERLAND
ARTHUR MURPHY

ANOTHER dramatist who, like Kelly, made a resounding success with an early play which he never repeated was Richard Cumberland. Son of a Northamptonshire rector who later became an Irish bishop, he was born on 19 February 1732 in the house of his maternal grandfather, Richard Bentley, Master of Trinity College, Cambridge. Educated at Westminster and Trinity, he became secretary to the Earl of Halifax, whom, when Lord Lieutenant, he accompanied to Ireland in 1761. Turning later from an official to a literary and theatrical career he began with a tragedy and two comic operas, followed by a comedy, *The Brothers*, produced at Covent Garden, 2 December 1769, which showed greater promise. This was amply fulfilled in *The West Indian*, produced at Drury Lane on 19 January 1771. The title was taken from the central figure of the play, Belcour, just arrived in London as inheritor of large estates in Jamaica. He is the unacknowledged son of the prosperous merchant Stockwell, who in the opening scene confides the secret of his birth to his clerk Stukely. This is a departure from the usual convention where, as in *A Word to the Wise*, such a disclosure is not made to the audience till the end. Stockwell conceals their relationship from Belcour because he will discover much more of his real character as his merchant than as his father. In their first interview Belcour gives him an insight into its opposite aspects by his frank confession.

I am the offspring of distress, and every child of sorrow

is my brother. While I have hands to hold, therefore, I will hold them open to mankind. But, sir, my passions are my masters; they take me where they will; and oftentimes they leave to reason and to virtue nothing but my wishes and my sighs.

It is not long before he gives proofs of this self-accusation. He becomes infatuated with the beauty of a girl whom he sees by chance in the crowded London streets, and follows her home. She is Louisa Dudley, daughter of a half-pay Captain, and sister to Charles, an ensign. The mother had been the eldest daughter of Sir Oliver Roundhead who, indignant at her marrying an impecunious soldier, had cut the family out of his will. The veteran Captain, to improve his fortunes, is now seeking an exchange into a commission with full pay 'in the fatal heats of Senegambia', but needs a sum of money to equip him for the expedition. Charles appeals for this to his hard-hearted puritan aunt, Lady Rusport, to whom Sir Oliver Roundhead had left his whole estate. But his plea is in vain, though supported by her stepdaughter Charlotte who is in love with the ensign.

The Dudleys are lodging with a Mr. and Mrs. Fulmer, who are in even worse plight than themselves. Fulmer has tried different trades and failed in all. Now he has set up as a bookseller, with the result, as he complains, that 'men left off reading; and if I was to turn butcher, I believe, o' my conscience, they'd leave off eating'. Now Mrs. Fulmer is planning a more disreputable way of earning their livelihood. Meanwhile Belcour arrives in pursuit of Louisa, and, on hearing of the Captain's plight, shows that it was no boast when he called every child of sorrow his brother. He hands the astonished Captain a sealed paper containing his necessary expenses of travel in two hundred-pound notes. Thus

when another veteran soldier, the Irish Major O'Flaherty, who is paying court to Lady Rusport, comes with
a letter from her ordering Dudley to leave London at
once, he is able to give a promise to that effect. Nor is
Belcour his only would-be benefactor. In a stolen interview with Charles Charlotte entrusts him with a box
containing her jewels, to be deposited with Stockwell for
the accommodation of £200. The merchant agrees to
send her the money but hands the jewels to Belcour to
be returned to her.

During their dialogue the West Indian is transported
by receiving a letter from Mrs. Fulmer telling him that
she can arrange an interview with his charmer at her
house. On hearing that she is the daughter of his bene-
ficiary, the Captain, he declares that this is the end of
the matter. Finding that he is 'one of your conscientious
sinners', Mrs. Fulmer plays her trump card. She tells
Belcour that 'sister' to Charles Dudley is merely cover
for 'mistress', and it is in that sense that she is daughter
to the Captain. Belcour eagerly swallows the bait, and
lets Mrs. Fulmer wheedle him out of Charlotte's jewels
which she is to hold in trust for Louisa. The girl begins
to thank him for his civilities, but he cuts her short by
an impassioned declaration of love and an assurance
that 'this good lady, Mrs. Fulmer, has something to
offer in my behalf'. Louisa demands a better proof of the
sincerity of his abrupt professions than ' a little super-
fluous dross', which Mrs. Fulmer interprets to him as
meaning jewels instead of coin.

He tries to atone to his conscience by bringing Charlotte a more valuable case of diamonds than her own,
and when she refuses them, he makes a clean confession.

I cannot invent a lie for my life; and, if it was to save it,
I couldn't tell one. I am an idle, dissipated, unthinking fellow,

not worth your notice; in short, I am a West Indian; and you must try me according to the charter of my colony, not by a jury of English spinsters. Truth is, I have given away your jewels.

His sincerity disarms Charlotte into forgiveness, and when a letter comes from Charles revealing that Belcour is his father's rescuer, she is prompted by his generous action to disclose to him her love for the son, and her readiness, as soon as she is of age, to share her fortune with him. Belcour is struck silent by the sudden entrance of Louisa, to whom Charlotte shows the diamonds in the belief that her own are now with her cousin, who protests that such things are infinitely above her reach. They have been retained by Mrs. Fulmer, who is preparing to make them the means of escape from their creditors.

Still believing the slander about Louisa, Belcour begs from the girl 'love, free, disencumbered, anti-matrimonial love', and takes hold of her. She throws him off, calling for rescue from Charles, who salutes Belcour as 'villain' and bids him defend himself. They begin a fight till, at a cry from Louisa, Major O'Flaherty knocks up their swords, and, finding Charles to be the son of an old companion-in-arms, warns him, 'Never, while you live, draw your sword before a woman.' The Major, outraged by Lady Rusport's callous treatment of her kinsfolk, has forsaken her house. She is now to receive a shattering blow. A lawyer, Varland, informs her that Sir Oliver Roundhead left in his last illness a second will by which his grandson, Charles Dudley, inherited his whole estate. Lady Rusport offers him a bribe of £5,000 to let her destroy the will, and with sundry twinges of conscience he accepts it. But the bargain is overheard by O'Flaherty who threatens Varland with a beating unless he

surrenders the will. The lawyer bids him give it to
Charles Dudley, if he is an honest man, to which the
Major indignantly retorts, 'An honest man! Look at me,
friend. I am a soldier. This is not the livery of a knave.
I am an Irishman, honey; mine is not the country of
dishonour.' Thus Dudley becomes a man of fortune at
the very moment when Charlotte, overcoming false delicacy, offers herself in marriage to him, thinking that he
is still poor, and that she will have enough for both.

In somewhat too-protracted fashion the various
complications are resolved. O'Flaherty bears a formal
challenge from Charles to Belcour, for whom Stockwell
acts as second, in order that, when they meet on the
duelling-ground, he may produce the Fulmers in custody as witnesses to their slander of Miss Dudley, and as
guilty of trying to sell Charlotte's diamonds. Charles
thus withdraws his epithet of 'villain', and Louisa accepts Belcour's now honourably proferred hand. Charlotte and Charles can be united without eloping to
Scotland. Lady Rusport flounces out in a rage, bidding
the pair marry and be wretched. O'Flaherty looks forward to a retreat in his native country, where he has not
set foot for thirty years, but which he thinks worth all
the rest of the world put together. Finally, Stockwell
reveals to Belcour that in him he has found a father
'who observes, who knows, who loves you'.

The West Indian has been called 'the extreme example
of English sentimental comedy', and it took the town by
storm. It had an initial run of thirty nights and was
revived from time to time. It has therefore called for a
somewhat detailed analysis of its elaborate plot. But
today it has lost much of its attraction. For a mid-
eighteenth-century audience a stranger coming from
Jamaica to London had something of the glamour of the

unknown. And he could be credited with blunders in getting to know the ways of the unfamiliar capital city. But it passes reasonable belief that even a novice should be so easily taken in by a Mrs. Fulmer and should persist so obstinately in the conviction that Miss Dudley is a professional wanton. Belcour is one of the least persuasive of the favourite eighteenth-century type, the good-hearted rake. The other characters are on more or less conventional lines except Major O'Flaherty, who brings a refreshingly piquant note into the usually high-flown dialogue. But, whatever may be posterity's verdict, *The West Indian* can claim to have proved 'good theatre'.

Towards the end of the same year, in December 1771, Cumberland ventured into a different field with an adaptation of *Timon of Athens*, but returned in January 1772 to sentimental comedy with *The Fashionable Lover* which, however, failed to repeat the success of *The West Indian*.

Nor, in spite of his indefatigable labours for the stage, did Cumberland ever again repeat his early triumph. Amongst his pieces of various types in the same decade *The Choleric Man*, produced at Drury Lane on 19 December 1774, presents some features of interest, especially in its printed form. It went through three London editions in 1775, as well as one in Dublin. It contained an ironical dedication by Cumberland to 'the high and mighty Sir, Detraction'.

When any play, like this now submitted to the public, meets a favourable reception on its first appearance, the very next morning by break of day out comes your manifesto. . . . They who have been pleas'd, being told they ought not to have been pleas'd, go no more and avoid an error in judgement; they who would have gone stay at home and save their money.

Here is a clue to Sheridan's caricature of Cumberland as Sir Fretful Plagiary in *The Critic*.

The titular figure of *The Choleric Man* is Nightshade, who comes up to London from the country to consult his brother, the lawyer Manlove, about a case against a neighbouring parson concerning a pigeon-house, and gets involved by his temper in serious difficulties. But the main interest is in two contrasted sons, Jack, whom Nightshade keeps with him under severe discipline, and Charles, brought up by his uncle Manlove, whose name he has adopted, with the social advantages of a public school and university education. What distinguishes Charles from most of the gallants in eighteenth-century comedy is that he is also an artist, having studied chiefly in Rome as the grand repository of the antique, and having acquired a collection of paintings. Manlove suggests that this will be a link between him and Miss Laetitia Fairfax, an heiress who is also a painter and has been two years in Italy. He chooses to meet her incognito, and presents himself under the guise of an artistic young man, a friend of Charles Manlove whose pictures he invites her to visit with Mrs. Stapleton, her guardian's wife.

There the ladies have a surprise. Jack Nightshade has taken advantage of his father's absence to follow him secretly to London. Here, to let him pose as a man of quality, Charles lends him a fashionable suit and gives him a handsome sum to spend. Then, for a freak, Jack poses as Charles and receives the ladies in the picture-gallery. In what is apparently a unique scene in the comedies of the period, and one which shows Cumberland's interest in the fine arts, Laetitia comments to Mrs. Stapleton on the paintings as a connoisseur, while Jack takes them aback by his Philistine retorts.

Laet. Look, dear madam, here is grace and dignity, Guido's Lucretia, the dagger in her breast, and in the act of heroic self-destruction. What resolution! what a spirit has the great artist thrown into those eyes!

Jack. Yes, she had a devil of a spirit. She stabb'd herself in a pique upon being cross'd in love.

. . . .

Laet. Do you observe that picture, madam? 'Tis a melancholy story, very finely told by Poussin. It is a view of Marseilles at the time of the plague, with a capital figure of the good bishop in the midst of the group.

Jack. Bishop, madam! That person which you look upon is a physician, and the people round about him are his patients; they are in a desperate way it must be confest.

The ladies can stand no more when Jack gives an immodest explanation of a picture of Actaeon being turned into a stag, in which Laetitia sees the colouring of the Venetian school, probably by 'Tintoret'. Sadly disillusioned, Laetitia will have nothing more to do with this vulgarian. Jack on his part is pleased because, while posing as Charles Manlove, he has been tricked into making love to Laetitia's maid, Lucy, pretending to be her mistress. Lucy has been pressed into this by her brother, Dibble, and under interrogation by Laetitia reveals the secret of the various impersonations. Knowing the truth Laetitia, seen as a painter in her own studio, makes play with Charles by asking his judgement and help about a portrait of Mr. Stapleton till he is forced to confess that he is pleading for himself. It is appropriate that it is in this studio that the final allround explanations take place. Nightshade is aghast at the idea of his son marrying a chambermaid. When reminded that he cannot disinherit him, he shouts, 'I'll live for ever on purpose to plague him; I'll starve the

whelp; he shall have nothing to live upon but rain-
water and pignuts.' But when Manlove offers to keep
him Nightshade retorts, 'I'll forgive him and keep him
to myself', and they go off together. With his 'rival' gone
Charles and Laetitia are free to fall into each other's
arms and thus end a comedy with some unusual
features.

Undeterred by 'Detraction' and by Sheridan's satire,
Cumberland continued to write plays, novels, translations, and an epic till towards the close of his long life
on 7 May 1811.

ARTHUR MURPHY

ANOTHER long-lived and prolific author was Arthur
Murphy. Born in Clomquin, Roscommon, on 27 December 1727, he was educated at St. Omer and began life
as a merchant's clerk. He published *The Gray's Inn
Journal*, 1752–4, became an actor and barrister, and
began writing for the theatre with several farces in
1756–8, followed by a tragedy, *The Orphan in China*,
produced at Drury Lane in April 1759, which went
through a number of editions in print. It was with *The
Way to Keep Him*, a comedy first produced at Drury Lane
on 24 January 1760, in three acts, and extended a year
later to five, that Murphy made his distinctive mark as
a dramatist. Indebted in part to De Moissy's *La Nouvelle
École des Femmes*, he subordinated the stock theme of the
reformation of a married rake by making it dependent
upon a change for the better in his wife's attitude. As
Lovemore, who has been a husband for two years, complains to her:

You could take pains enough before marriage; you could
put forth all your charms, practise all your arts, for ever

changing, running an eternal round of variety to win my affections; but when you had won them, you did not think them worth your keeping; never dressed, pensive, silent, melancholy; and the only entertainment in my house was the dear pleasure of a dull conjugal tête-à-tête.

Thus there is nothing now but a distant civility between them: in the modern phrase, a cold war. Mrs. Lovemore's pert, sharp-witted lady's-maid Muslin tries to rouse her from her tearful passivity:

Lord, ma'am, to be for ever pining and grieving! Dear heart! If all the women in London in your case were to sit down and die of the spleen, what would become of all the public places? They might turn Vauxhall to a hopgarden, make a brewhouse of Ranelagh, and let both the playhouses to a methodist preacher.

And that Muslin herself frequents the playhouses appears from her amusingly perverted reminiscence of *The Taming of the Shrew*. 'Ma'am, was you ever at the play of Catharine and Mercutio? The vile man calls his wife his goods, and his chattels, and his household stuff.—There you may see, ma'am, what a husband is.'

There is another couple estranged on different grounds. Sir Bashful Constant is something of a parvenu. After living in middling conditions he had suddenly come into an estate and a title, had married a woman of quality, and had carried 'the primitive ideas of his narrow education into high life'. Afraid of being an object of ridicule, he stands upon his dignity with his wife, quarrels with her, and keeps her short of money. But 'at the bottom', to use his favourite phrase, he is in love with her and secretly pays her bills.

An intimate of both husbands is the bachelor, Sir Brilliant Fashion, whose name is the index to his role. As Muslin describes him to her mistress, 'He's the very pink of the fashion—he dresses fashionably, lives fashionably, wins your money fashionably, loses his own fashionably, and does everything fashionably.' At present he is following the fashion by making love to both Mrs. Lovemore and Lady Constant. He has also been paying his addresses to an attractive widow lately come from Bath, Mrs. Bellmour. But he has been outrivalled by Lord George Etheridge—none other than Lovemore masquerading, with suitable decorations, under this title.

Sir Bashful and Lovemore in an entertaining scene confide to each other that, in spite of all appearances, they love their wives, but hide this from them and from the world to escape ridicule. And they seem justified when Sir Brilliant enters with the rarest piece of news that Sir Amorous La Fool (the title borrowed from Jonson's *Epicœne*) has got into such a scrape; he has fallen in love with his own wife. Moreover, Sir Charles Wildfire has just made him the hero of a comedy, 'The Amorous Husband, or the Man in love with his own Wife', for which they will have to send in time for places.

But one of the neglected wives takes action. Mrs. Lovemore calls upon the widow Bellmour to inquire about her acquaintance with a gentleman called Lovemore. The widow denies any knowledge of him, but begs to know who he is. Mrs. Lovemore pours out the unhappy story of her husband's alienation from her and his gallantries abroad. Whereupon Mrs. Bellmour administers a surprising form of consolation.

If his affections, instead of being alienated, had been extinguished, he would have sank into a downright stupid, habitual insensibility, from which it might prove impossible to recall him—in all love's bill of mortality there is not a more fatal disorder—but your husband is not fallen into that way. By your account he still has sentiment, and, where

there is sentiment, there is still room to hope for an alteration.

Mrs. Bellmour then proceeds to prescribe the proper
cure. Wives are mistaken in thinking that it is enough
if they are guilty of no infidelity. 'Home must be made
a place of pleasure to the husband, and the wife must
throw infinite variety into her manner. And this I take
to be the whole mystery, the way to keep a man.'

Lord Etheridge is announced and, at the widow's
request, Mrs. Lovemore steps into an adjoining room,
from which she hears her husband making love to
Mrs. Bellmour and her singing a song which he has
written for her. She faints away, and while Mrs. Bellmour is reviving her, there enters Sir Brilliant from
whom Lovemore hastily hides his bogus ribband and
star. But he cannot hide his identity from Mrs. Bellmour
who, though ready to sink into the ground with amazement, still assures Mrs. Lovemore that there is hope of
her husband's atonement.

Lady Constant also turns the tables on her husband
by telling him that she has written to her solicitor to
attend her with articles of separation. With his hand
thus forced Sir Bashful writes her a letter revealing his
ardent passion for her, but, to hide this from his inquisitive servant, he gets it directed by Lovemore, who substitutes a love-letter from himself which she tears to pieces,
thus bitterly disappointing both husband and gallant,
whose laments mingle in an ironical duet. Sir Bashful
declares that he is ready to part from her as soon as she
pleases, and that she is not to believe a word of his letter,
the fragments of which he picks up to keep them safe.

Another fateful love-letter has been sent by Sir Brilliant to Mrs. Lovemore, which she has left in her
dressing-room. In reply she has invited him to the large

rout which, on Mrs. Bellmour's advice, she is holding,
though timorously and with 'an aching heart'. While
the company are engaged at the whist-table Lovemore
comes home in a yawning mood and anxious to go to
bed. When his wife rallies him on being 'everywhere,
but at home, all whim, vivacity and spirit', he retorts,
'Such a description of me! I that am rather saturnine,
of a serious cast, and inclined to be pensive.' Puzzled
by her transformation he is about to follow her into the
card-room when Muslin rushes in with Sir Brilliant's
letter, which Lovemore seizes from her, and which reveals
the falseness of his seeming friend. But his fears for the
honour of his wife thus aroused are dispelled when he
hears her denounce Sir Brilliant for his 'unequalled
insolence'. He angrily rejects the knight's pleas for pardon, and denounces his conduct as the worst thing a
gentleman can be guilty of, and an unparalleled breach
of friendship. But in his turn Lovemore is now to be
unmasked as having committed a similar breach. Sir
Bashful produces his letter to Lady Constant which had
been pieced together again, and which he in vain pretends is a forgery.

Nor is this the end for him. Mrs. Bellmour enters to
greet him as 'my Lord Etheridge', and, after some
badinage between her and his wife, to ask, 'What's become of the star and ribband?' And so 'the gay, the
florid, the *magnifique* Lord Etheridge dwindles down
to plain Mr. Lovemore, the married man!' She is followed by Lady Constant who also denounces him, till
he turns the tables upon Sir Bashful by reading out the
letter telling her that he had been in love with her all
the time. With his real sentiments thus disclosed, the shy
husband 'can't look any body to the face'. And now
Sir Brilliant has his opportunity for retort. 'Sir Bashful,

will you go and see the new comedy with me? Lovemore, pray, now, don't you think it a base thing to invade the happiness of a friend?' Lovemore turns upon him sternly:

Love. To cut the matter short with you, sir, we are both villains.

Sir Bril. Villains!

Love. Ay, both; we are pretty fellows, indeed.

Mrs. Bell. I am glad to find you are awakened to a sense of your error.

Love. I am, madam, and am frank enough to own it.— With sincere remorse I ask your pardon.

With general confession of errors all round, the play ends by pointing two lessons—that men should not allow their passions to violate friendship, and that ladies should learn that 'after the marriage rites, they should not suffer their powers of pleasing to languish away'.

Whether the Drury Lane audience took these lessons to heart may be doubted. The rakes, as usual, come off too lightly. But, as a whole, *The Way to Keep Him* is one of the most attractive of the comedies of its period. Its main theme, as has been seen, is not on stereotyped lines. In its characterization Sir Bashful and Mrs. Bellmour are of somewhat original quality, and the denouement is skilfully worked out. But the chief merit of the play lies in its racy dialogue. It might well bear revival on a National Theatre stage.[1]

Murphy followed up the success of *The Way to Keep Him* by another comedy, *All in the Wrong*, produced at Drury Lane on 15 June 1761. Again he drew upon a French source, Molière's *Le Cocu Imaginaire*, for part of the somewhat complex plot. But once more the naturalness of the dialogue, of which Mrs. Inchbald said 'it never in one sentence soars above the proper standard

---

[1] Meanwhile it has been recently revived by the Arts Theatre Club.

of elegant life', gives the play its air of originality. The central theme is the causeless mutual jealousy and suspicion of Sir John and Lady Restless. Their house looks on the Park, and when Sir John hears that his wife has gone towards the Horse Guards, he is sorely perturbed. And when Lady Restless sees Lady Conquest's well-dressed maid Marmalet taking leave of her own servant Tattle, she is convinced that she is a hussy who has come after Sir John.

She finds still stronger cause for her belief that Sir John is unfaithful in an incident arising out of the under-plot. Bellmont is in love with his friend Beverley's sister, Clarissa, and Beverley timidly dotes upon Belinda. Her father Blandford has, however, arranged with Bellmont's father, Sir William, that the match is to be between their two children. He announces this to the girl in uncompromising terms: 'My power is absolute, and if you offer to rebel, you shall have no husband at all with my consent. . . . If I find you an undutiful girl, I cast you off for ever.' At the shock Belinda faints and falls into the arms of Sir John, who happens to be passing by. She also drops a picture of Beverley which he has presented to her, and which is to be almost as fateful as the handkerchief in *Othello*. Lady Restless, watching from her window, is confirmed in her belief that Sir John is playing her false, and afterwards finding the picture on the ground, keeps it as a clue to tracing his *inamorata*.

In her jealous fury, unaware that Sir John is watching and overhearing her, she exclaims, 'This is really a handsome picture. . . . Why had I not such a dear, dear man, instead of the brute, the monster?', and she kisses the picture. Well may Sir John rush out, snatch it from her, and begin a slanging match in which each mocks and accuses the other. Meeting Bellmont and Beverley in the Park, Sir John, in an entertaining scene, makes excuses for coming close to them, and identifies Beverley as the original of the picture. Beverley recognizes it as the one he gave to Belinda, tries in vain to recover it from Sir John, and feels sure that she is false to him. When Bellmont, to test the matter, asks Belinda to show him the picture, she cannot find it, and Beverley taunts her with his having seen it that day in the hands of the very gentleman to whom she gave it. She retorts by calling him 'the self-tormenting Beverley', and by bidding him 'amuse yourself with your own fancies'.

To make certain, he calls at Sir John's house, where Lady Restless gives him her version of the fainting incident, and convinces him that Belinda is betraying him. On the other hand, Sir John, seeing him come out of his own house, is more certain than ever that he is his wife's paramour. In another of Murphy's skilful, equivocal dialogues each abjures his lady, the one meaning Lady Restless and the other Belinda. Beverley goes to bid farewell to the woman whom he has loved to excess, but she teases and rallies him in an interview which she brings to a triumphant close.

Bev. Take notice, madam, that this is the last time of my troubling you.

Belin. I shall expect you to-morrow morning.

Bev. No, never; by Heaven, never!

Belin. Exactly at ten, your usual hour.

Bev. May I perish at your feet, if ever again——

Belin. O, brave! but remember, ten: kneeling, beseeching, imploring, your hand upon your heart, 'Belinda, won't you forgive me?'

Bev. Damnation!—I have done; I here bid you an eternal adieu; farewell for ever!

But each is subconsciously playing a part. When Beverley tells his valet Brush that to escape from Belinda he is going into the country, Brush slyly hints, 'I suppose a couple of shirts will be sufficient, sir—you will hardly stay them out', to which his master retorts, 'Pack up all, sir, I shall stay in the country a whole month, if it be necessary.' He tears up a contrite letter from Belinda in which she subscribes herself, 'unalterably yours'. He is reproached by his sister Clarissa, who tells the truth about the fainting incident, and bids him go and make his peace with his beloved.

But further complications occur. Sir John waits upon Belinda, to be told that his wife has ruined her with the man she loves. In return he complains that Beverley has given his picture to Lady Restless, and that, on seeing her kiss it, he wrested it from her. Beverley meanwhile has visited Sir John's house to get the picture back, which he only obtains by threatening to draw his sword against the knight, who is more than ever convinced, by finding him with Lady Restless, that he is her paramour.

Belinda, convinced by Sir John of her lover's treachery, decides to obey her father and marry Bellmont. She gives Beverley back his letters and presents, and with a breaking heart says farewell to him for ever. As her maid, Tippet, who still believes in their mutual affection, comments, 'They have got into a rare puzzle, and how they will get out of it is beyond my dexterity.' Indeed it needs all Murphy's dexterity in a too long-spun-out last act to solve the puzzle, to clear up all the misunderstandings, and to leave the two pairs of lovers in each other's arms. A repentant Sir John points the moral, 'Since we have been *all in the wrong* to-day, we will for the future endeavour to be *all in the right*.'

These two comedies will have illustrated Murphy's share of the gift of natural dialogue which is the fortunate inheritance of so many Anglo-Irish dramatists. During the succeeding years he contributed to the Drury Lane and Covent Garden stages plays in a variety of types, comedies, farces, and tragedies, partly derivative, till 1777. A collection of his works was published in 1786, and among his later writings were a biography of Garrick and translations from Latin authors. He died on 18 January 1805.

XV

DAVID GARRICK
GEORGE COLMAN, THE ELDER

DAVID GARRICK's fame is primarily that of an actor, theatrical manager, and adapter of Shakespeare's plays for revival. But he has his own less conspicuous niche as a dramatist, especially in collaboration. He was born in Hereford on 19 February 1717, son of Captain Peter Garrick and his wife Arabella. She was the daughter of a Vicar of Lichfield, and David was first sent to the grammar school of that town, and later to Samuel Johnson's short-lived academy. It was in Johnson's company that he came up to London to seek his fortune in 1737. After a venture as a wine-merchant and some experience as a journalist on *The Gentleman's Magazine*, he began his connexion with the stage with the production of his first farce, *Lethe, or Aesop in the Shades*, at Drury Lane on 15 April 1740. In the following year it was transferred to Goodman's Fields where it had a successful run. It was at this theatre, on 30 November 1741, that Garrick's second farce, *The Lying Valet*, was produced, with himself in the chief part, as an afterpiece to Otway's *The Orphan*. Six weeks earlier he had already established his position as a Shakespearian actor on 19 October by his triumphant performance as Richard III. As Goodman's Fields was not regularly licensed, the play had been announced as part of 'a concert of vocal and instrumental music'.

So great was his success that he was engaged at an unprecedentedly large salary for the season of 1742–3 at Drury Lane, with which theatre he was almost entirely

associated during the rest of his career, becoming
manager as well as chief actor in 1747. In the succeeding
twenty years he appeared in leading Shakespearian
roles, including those in his own versions of *Romeo and
Juliet*, *A Midsummer Night's Dream*, *The Tempest*, *The
Taming of the Shrew*, *The Winter's Tale*, and *Antony and
Cleopatra*. He also provided a number of entertainments
and farces from his own pen, many of which proved
popular. Of special interest among them was *A Peep Behind the Curtain, or The New Rehearsal*, produced on 23 October 1767 as an afterpiece to Lillo's *The London Merchant*.
It was doubtless suggested to Garrick by his success
as Bayes in the Duke of Buckingham's *The Rehearsal*
in 1761. The stage is being prepared for the rehearsal of
the first act of Mr. Glib's *Burletta of Orpheus*. Patient, the
manager, and the prompter, Hopkins, are discussing the
difficulties they meet with.

Pat. Actresses quarrelling about parts; there's not one of
'em but thinks herself young enough for any part; and not
a young one but thinks herself capable of any part.

Prompt. The young fellow from Edinburgh won't accept
of the second Lord; he desires to have the first.

Pat. I don't doubt it.—Well, well, if the author can make
him speak English, I have no objection.

As Glib has only furnished the first act, Patient supposes that in the second act he intends to bring Orpheus
into hell. Glib agrees that he will make him play the
devil there, but he will be stopped for a fine at the gate
by Cerberus, whose three heads will sing a trio, treble,
tenor, and bass—nothing in the world but *Bow, wow,
wow*. Then enter Glib's invited fashionable friends,
Sir Toby, Lady, and Miss Fuz and Sir Macaroni Virtu.
Sir Toby and his wife are themselves amateur actors of
Shakespeare, and, in her opinion, he is the best Romeo

that ever appeared. Sir Macaroni, only half-awake, declares that 'a playhouse in England is to me as dull as a church and fit only to sleep in', and he goes out before the Burletta begins.

It opens with a recitative and air by Orpheus with the refrain, 'I must and I will go to hell for my wife'. His mistress Rhodope seeks to detain him, and they have a duet, accompanied by his lyre, which sends her to sleep. There follows a pastoral scene in which Orpheus by his music sets an old shepherd and a chorus of younger ones dancing till he leads them off together with cows, sheep, and goats on their hind legs. Glib apologizes for not making the houses and trees dance also, as in the old story, but it would have crowded the stage too much.

But, as Lady Fuz now rushes in crying out, there has been other dancing off behind the scenes. Miss Fuz has made the rehearsal the opportunity for an assignation with a distant connexion, Wilson, who had won her heart when he visited Sir Toby's house in the guise of a strolling player. She has slipped out during the performance to where her lover is waiting with a post-chaise and horses. It is the addition of this sentimental background that helps to distinguish *A Peep Behind the Curtain* from the theatrical burlesques in *The Rehearsal* and the more recent *Tom Thumb* and *Pasquin*.

With its author's exceptional intimacy with everything relating to the stage, it has a value of its own. But in the previous year, 1766, Garrick had, in collaboration with George Colman, gained a more notable success in the field of high comedy. Colman was born in 1732 in Florence. His father, Francis, was envoy there to the Court of Tuscany, but died in the next year. Under the protection of his mother's brother-in-law, Lord Bath, George was educated at Westminster School and Christ

Church, Oxford. He was entered at Lincoln's Inn and was called to the Bar in 1755, but was chiefly engaged as joint-editor of *The Connoisseur* (1754–6). Though twenty years senior to Garrick, he became his intimate friend and was thus led to write for the stage.

Garrick supplied the prologue and epilogue for Colman's first theatrical venture, *Polly Honeycombe, A Dramatic Novel*, produced anonymously in one act at Drury Lane on 5 December 1760. Here Colman anticipated Sheridan in the attack on the sentimental novel and its kin, the sentimental play. As has not escaped critical notice, Polly, discussing with her nurse the fashionable novels from the circulating libraries, is a forerunner of Lydia Languish in *The Rivals*. Like Lydia she looks on an elopement as the proper path to marriage. She is settling to run away with Mr. Scribble to escape a union with the man of her parents' choice, Mr. Ledger, who pays his addresses in business-phrases. She rejects them in the whole-hearted fashion that she has learnt from her reading : 'Your sight is shocking to me, your conversation odious, and your passion contemptible.' When her father threatens to lock her up, she comforts herself with thinking of poor 'Clarissa and poor Sophy Western'.

The nurse smuggles Scribble disguised in a livery into Polly's room, where he is discovered and thrown out by her father. Again with the nurse's aid, she escapes with Scribble in a hackney-chaise, but they are overtaken and brought back by Ledger, who now refuses to 'underwrite her for ninety per cent.' Scribble turns out to be only an attorney's clerk and nephew of the nurse. But Polly sticks to her choice. 'Who knows but he may be a foundling, and a gentleman's son, as well as Tom Jones?' Mrs. Honeycombe bids her husband compose himself, but he is left lamenting and appealing to the audience for their sympathy.

The success of *Polly Honeycombe* prompted Colman to another dramatic attempt, under his own name, on a larger scale. *The Jealous Wife* was produced at Drury Lane on 12 February 1761. In his advertisement to the almost simultaneous printed edition Colman acknowledged the help he had received from Garrick's advice 'relating both to the fable and characters'. He also acknowledged his debt to Fielding's *Tom Jones* and several other sources. For this the prologue claimed august precedents.

> Books too he read, nor blush'd to use their store;
> He does but what his betters did before.
> Shakespeare has done it, and the Grecian stage
> Caught truth of character from Homer's page.

But the links with *Tom Jones* can be exaggerated, and the titular character, Mrs. Oakly, with her husband and brother-in-law, is Colman's creation. Mrs. Oakly is in a passion because a letter has arrived from Mr. Russet, a country squire, addressed to her husband's ward and nephew, Charles Oakly, stating that his daughter Harriot has eloped, and that Charles must be privy to it. In her jealous obsession Mrs. Oakly is convinced that Charles is merely a blind for her husband, and his real love for her makes him her ready victim. As he complains to his brother, Major Oakly, she has 'confined me to my house, like a state prisoner, without the liberty of seeing my friends, or the use of pen, ink, and paper'. The Major, who is the linch-pin of the action, advises his brother to foil her with her own weapons. 'Do as you please for one month, whether she likes it or not; and I'll answer for it, she will consent you shall do as you please all her life after.' He promises to be steel and adamant, and offers to dine out with him at a tavern, but gives in to his wife when she objects. The Major becomes also the confidant of Charles, who tells him that it is true that Harriot, whom he loves, has run away alone, to escape marriage with her father's choice for her, Sir Harry Beagle, a wealthy Baronet. He is a sort of junior Squire Western, 'with not a single idea in his head besides a hound, a hunter, and a horse-race'. Charles confesses that he himself, in a drunken bout, has offended Harriot and angered her father by swearing that he would drive Sir Harry Beagle out of the country. So the girl's only refuge is with her aunt, Lady Freelove, who, as the Major warns Charles, is an unprincipled woman of the world, of whom he must beware.

In a highly entertaining scene both Sir Harry and Russet are seen in pursuit of the runaway. The former is much more concerned with the condition of his horse, Snip, and the loss of a favourable chance in a race. The latter is the extreme type of the tyrannical father, blustering 'She *shall* have him. I will make her happy, if I break her heart for it.' Meanwhile Lady Freelove is pressing on the girl another suitor of yet higher rank, Lord Trinket, an affected libertine, who sprinkles his talk with French phrases, and who expounds to Harriot the divergence between Nature and the *bon ton*.

The chief aim of the *bon ton* is to render persons of family different from the vulgar, for whom indeed Nature serves very well. For this reason it has, at various times, been ungenteel to see, to hear, to walk, to be in good health, and to have twenty other horrible perfections of Nature.

But *bon ton* does not prevent his lordship, when left alone with Harriot, from attempting by force to seduce her—from which (by the long arm of coincidence) she is rescued by the sudden arrival of Charles, who fights with Trinket, while the girl again takes to flight. But the peer, in concert with Lady Freelove, pursues his design upon 'this wild little thing', as he calls her. He has procured a naval post for an Irishman, Captain O'Cutter, whose talk is as full of seaman's jargon as that of some of Smollett's sailors. He is in charge of a press-gang, and Trinket engages him to take up Russet and Beagle, whom he describes as a couple of impudent fellows, at an inn in Holborn. With them out of the way for a time, he plots to carry off Harriot. He also directs O'Cutter to take a letter from him to a gentleman who has offended him in a point of honour—Charles.

Harriot has for a time supplanted Mrs. Oakly as the centre of interest, but now the jealous wife visits Lady Freelove, only to have her suspicions of her husband's attachment to the girl confirmed by her ladyship's subtle innuendoes. At this very time Harriot, in all innocence, has run to Mrs. Oakly's house to seek her protection, but, finding her away, she puts Oakly into a quandary by begging him to let her stay a few days under his roof. Mrs. Oakly, returning suddenly, overhears him in his embarrassment offering to take a private lodging for her a little way off, where he will try to visit her every day. Naturally she believes the worst, and comes forward screaming, 'She sha'n't stay a minute!', to which Oakly, his temper aroused at last, retorts, 'She shall stay a minute, an hour, a day, a week, a month, a year! 'Sdeath, madam, she shall stay for ever if I choose it.' While the terrified girl cowers between them her father bursts in and she faints into Oakly's arms. Russet now joins Mrs. Oakly in a duet of abuse of her unfortunate husband, interrupting all his attempts at explanation, till he expostulates, ''Sdeath, you will not let me speak. . . . I wish you were married to one another, will all my heart.'

Throughout the whole of this dialogue Colman shows at his best, but, as Harriot is leaving with her father, he lowers the tone and violates probability by bringing in Charles, who had saved her from Trinket, in another of the drunken bouts which had already cost him dear. But circumstances conspire in his favour. Lord Trinket has entrusted Captain O'Cutter with two letters, one a challenge to Charles, the other to Lady Freelove concerning the plot about the press-gang. With an excess of an Irishman's irresponsibility O'Cutter, without reading the addresses, interchanges the letters, delivering the one for Lady Freelove to Charles, who thus learns that Harriot is with her father in a Holborn inn, and that Trinket again has a design against her. At the inn Harriot has again indignantly rejected Beagle's suit, which he has made in terms proper to a horse. Her tyrannical father insists, 'He shall marry you this very night. I'll go for a licence and a parson immediately.' He hurries out with Beagle and they are seized by the press-gang. But Charles, pleading for pardon, has forestalled Trinket. Against his lordship's drawn sword he produces a loaded pistol, and for the second time saves Harriot from dishonour.

The last act shows Mrs. Oakly, in a frenzy of agitation, railing at three of the servants in turn for not being able to tell her where her husband has gone, giving contradictory orders, and finally announcing that she will dine in her own room. She has departed there when Oakly returns with the Major, Charles, and Harriot. On the Major's advice he does not go near her, and it is to the same shrewd counsellor that Harriot appeals to pacify her father when, released from the press-gang, he comes in with Trinket and Beagle. Tempestuous as ever, Russet will not hear a word from anyone, but bids Sir Harry take her away. Then the Baronet springs a surprise. He has sense enough to see that Harriot dislikes him, and he now follows his race-course instinct.

When one has made a bad bet, it is best to hedge off, you know; and so I have e'en swopped her with Lord Trinket here for his brown horse, Nabob, that he bought of Lord White-Jacket for fifteen hundred guineas.

This astonishing confession is followed by the Major's assurance to Russet that Trinket set the press-gang upon him, and his attempted denial is met by the evidence of his own wrongly delivered letter. This, too, convicts Lady Freelove of her part in the plot, though the pair affect to carry off their discomfiture with nonchalance, as beneath the notice of persons of fashion. Russet's bestowal of Harriot, now proved innocent, on Charles is too sudden to be convincing, as is also her lover's declaration that she has reformed him altogether. On the other hand, when Mrs. Oakly, again changing her mind, joins the company, the recrimination between her and her husband is somewhat too prolonged. Even when she falls into a fit he forbids anyone to help her, 'She'll behave better another time.' When she recovers, Harriot, Charles, and Russet all join in explanations and apologies, and she at last confesses her mistake, but weepingly laments that her husband's love is entirely destroyed. Then he can hold out no longer, but assures her that his affection for her is as warm as ever, and that she needs no forgiveness, while the Major wishes them joy, and takes credit for the success of his somewhat rough medicines.

The Jealous Wife fully deserved the success it immediately won. Though it depends too much on coinci-
dences and sudden conversions, it interlaces its different
threads of interest into a well-knit design. Above all, it
furnishes an exceptional number of first-rate acting
parts. Garrick and Mrs. Pritchard headed the original
cast as Mr. and Mrs. Oakly. With possibly a few cuts
it might well stand revival today.

This test has been successfully passed by another
comedy of which Colman and Garrick were joint-
authors, *The Clandestine Marriage*. The composition of
the play took an unusually long time. Towards the end
of 1763 Colman sent Garrick an autograph draft which
covered in essentials the first four acts and the general
scheme. During the following two years Garrick elabo-
rated the draft, contributing to the creation of Lord
Ogleby, and most of the last act.[1] But, for some reason
never fully explained, Garrick, to Colman's great disappointment, declined to play Ogleby's part which then
fell to Thomas King. And though he wrote the prologue,
attributing to Hogarth's *Marriage-à-la-Mode* the idea of
the play, he left it to Charles Holland to speak it. Here,
even more than with *The Jealous Wife* and Fielding, the
debt is exaggerated. For Hogarth's series of six paintings
depict a sordid and sombre story which might have
suggested a tragic domestic drama, while *The Clandestine
Marriage*, produced at Drury Lane on 26 February 1766,
is a light-hearted comedy, sporting with follies, not with
crimes.

Mr. Sterling, a rich city merchant, has bought an
estate in the country, where the action of the play takes
place, and is anxious to match his well-portioned elder

---

[1] See, for a detailed discussion, the article by J. M. Beatty in *Modern
Language Notes*, 1921.

daughter, Miss Sterling, to a sprig of nobility. He has
been in treaty with the elderly Lord Ogleby for her
marriage to his nephew, Sir John Melvil. Word has just
come that the pair are to arrive that evening, to be
followed next morning by the lawyers who are to draw
up the marriage settlements. Ogleby has also introduced
to Sterling a more distant kinsman, Lovewell, who has
been given a clerical post in his business. Before the play
opens, Lovewell has won the heart of Sterling's younger
daughter, Fanny. Their secret wedding, four months
past, gives the comedy its title, though only indirectly its
main interest. The secret is becoming a burden to
Fanny who tells her maid, Betty, 'I shall never have a
moment's ease till our marriage is made public.' But
Lovewell begs her to delay the disclosure because of her
father, who cares for nothing but money and rank, and
who stands in awe of his widowed sister, Mrs. Heidelberg, whose Dutch husband had left her with an im-
mense fortune. So Fanny holds her tongue, though she
has to bear the taunts of her elder sister who has no use
for love and a cottage:

Oh, how I long to be transported to the dear regions of
Grosvenor Square—far, far from the dull districts of Alders-
gate, Cheap, Candlewick, and Farringdon Without and
Within . . . O dear Beau Monde! I was born to move in the
sphere of the great world.

These ecstatic imaginings are interrupted by Mrs.
Heidelberg entering with the news of the approach of
Lord Ogleby and Sir John Melvil. 'I vow and pertest
we shall scarcely have time to provide for them'; and
looking at her favourite elder niece, 'I am glad to see
you are not quite in a dish-abile.' With her 'pertest' and
'dish-abile' Mrs. Heidelberg foreshadows Mrs. Malaprop

in *The Rivals*, though she confuses not the meaning of words but their pronunciation.

Next morning Lord Ogleby, as described by his valet to the chambermaid, is certainly not a fit sight in 'dish-abile'. 'He must have a great deal of brushing, oiling, screwing and winding-up to set him a-going for the day.' But what makes him a character of distinction is that though a valetudinarian in body he has an alert brain and a caustic tongue. He sees through the weaker sides of Sterling, his sister, and his elder daughter, while he pronounces Fanny delectable. He is bored and wearied by his host's insistence on taking him the grand tour of his estate, and pointing out features and improvements which have the merit for us of throwing light on the mid-eighteenth-century taste in landscape-gardening. The climax comes when Ogleby asks, 'What steeple's that we see yonder—the parish church, I suppose?'

Ster. Ha, ha, ha! that's admirable. It is no church at all, my lord; it is a spire that I have built against a tree, a field or two off, to terminate the prospect. One must always have a church or an obelisk, or something to terminate the prospect, you know. That's a rule in taste, my lord.

Meanwhile the three lawyers have arrived to draw up the marriage settlement between Sir John Melvil and Miss Sterling. They are on their way to their respective circuits, and they pass the time in professional gossip with which Colman as a barrister was familiar. Then there is a sudden, amazing impasse. Sir John has fallen in love with Fanny and has been discovered on his knees before her by Miss Sterling, who hastens with the news to her aunt. Sir John himself tells Sterling that he wishes to marry Fanny instead of her elder sister, and over-comes the merchant's objection by offering to take her with a much smaller dowry. But Mrs. Heidelberg is furious at the slight to her favourite, and threatens to go off to Holland and leave her fortune to her husband's cousin unless Fanny is at once sent away to London.

But she has reckoned without Ogleby, who is inconsolable on hearing this. Lovewell, noting the old lord's partiality for Fanny, urges her to tell their secret to him as the best way out of their difficulties. But in a masterly piece of dialogue the embarrassed Fanny uses such roundabout and equivocal phrases that she leads the infatuated old nobleman to believe that she has rejected Melvil because she is in love with himself. He astonishes Sterling by telling him that he is going to marry into his family—not with his sister, Mrs. Heidelberg, but with his daughter, Fanny. He then breaks the news to the still more astounded Lovewell, and asks 'Why don't you wish me joy, man?'

Love. O, I do, my lord.

Ogle. She said that you would explain what she had not power to utter, but I wanted no interpreter for the language of love.

To add to the confusion Melvil now appeals to Ogleby for his good offices with Mrs. Heidelberg for her consent to his marriage with Fanny.

The imbroglio reaches its peak, and its solution, the same evening in the gallery leading to several bedrooms. In one of these Fanny has been joined by Lovewell, but her sister's maid reports that it is Melvil. Miss Sterling, convinced that they are eloping, arouses her aunt who summons Sterling. The uproar they make brings out from their rooms the visitors—the lawyers concerned about 'a burglarious entry', and Ogleby crying out, 'Where's my angelic Fanny? She's safe, I hope.' When told that his nephew is with her he bids him appear to answer for his misdemeanours, whereupon to the general amazement Sir John enters, not from Fanny's room but 'on the other side'. Then from her room Fanny steps out 'in great confusion' and falls down in a faint, which, again to a chorus of astonishment, brings Lovewell to her aid. To Ogleby's inquiry, 'By what right and title have you been half the night in that lady's bedchamber?', he answers, 'By that right which makes me the happiest of men'; and Fanny puts it more plainly, 'We have been married these four months.' Ogleby takes his disillusionment in the true spirit of nobility. He redeems his promise to support her by appealing to her father to forgive her, which he does, as Lovewell is the peer's relation, while Mrs. Heidelberg grudgingly concurs, 'The girl's ruined. I forgive her.'

The theatrical effectiveness of the last act of *The Clandestine Marriage* can be fully realized only when it is seen on the stage. The play has repeated its original triumph in our own days, at the Malvern Dramatic Festival in 1936, with Mr. Ernest Thesiger as Lord Ogleby, and at the Old Vic in 1951 with Mr. Donald Wolfit in the same complex role.

In the period that followed, Garrick organized the Shakespeare Jubilee at Stratford-on-Avon in 1769; he appeared in a further series of his adaptations, including a masque, *King Arthur*, from Dryden (1770), *Hamlet* (1772), and Jonson's *The Alchemist* (1774). The last of his farces, without musical accompaniment, was *Bon Ton, or, High Life above Stairs*, produced at Drury Lane on 18 March 1775 in three acts and reduced to two on the 27th. It was for the benefit of Thomas King, who spoke the prologue written by Colman. It is a cynical variation on the theme of town versus country. Lord Minikin has made a loveless marriage with a rich wife and is finding solace in the charms of a relative, Miss Tittup. As he expounds the fashionable doctrine of *bon ton*:

> Marriage is not now-a-days an affair of inclination, but convenience; and they who marry for love, and such old-fashioned stuff, are to me as ridiculous as those that advertise for an agreeable companion in a post-chaise.

Lady Minikin is paying him out by encouraging the warm attentions of Colonel Tivy, who is Miss Tittup's *fiancé*. It is a dangerous all-round situation when Sir John Trotley, Baronet, Miss Tittup's wealthy uncle and guardian, arrives from the country. He finds the new London detestable. He even declines Minikin's invitation to dinner.

> You must know, my lord, that I love to know what I eat. . . . Your men and manners too are as much frittered and fricasseed as your beef and mutton; I love a plain dish, my lord. . . . I'll away into the country to-morrow, and leave you to your fine doings; I have no relish for 'em, not I; I can't live among you, nor eat with you, nor game with you.

But, as Minikin has to find and admit, 'the bumpkin is no dolt'. In an amusing scene Sir John comes upon the amorous quartet returning by night from a masked ball and getting mixed up in the dark. He puts an end to the Colonel's dream of a future with Miss Tittup, sends Minikin into temporary exile, and, with the two repentant ladies on either arm, goes forth 'a Knight Errant', to rescue distressed damsels from those monsters, foreign vices and *Bon Ton*.

The play, though of slender structure, forms an interesting link in Garrick's dramatic career, for, as he stated in the first printed text, it 'had been thrown aside for many years' before being altered for performance.

It proved successful both on the stage and in book form beyond its author's expectation. In the next year, 1776, he retired as an actor and as a manager of Drury Lane, selling his share in the theatre for £35,000. Thus well provided for, he survived till 20 January 1779 and was buried in Westminster Abbey.

Though not an actor, Colman otherwise followed the example of Garrick in combining the writing and adapting of plays with theatrical ownership and management. Inheriting from the Earl of Bath a considerable fortune, in 1767 he bought a share of the Covent Garden Theatre and was its manager till 1774. Here he produced a variety of pieces, among them his own farcical comedies, *The Oxonian in Town* (1767), and *Man and Wife, or The Shakespeare Jubilee* (1769), and adaptations of *King Lear* (1768), *Comus* (1773), and Gay's *Achilles*, renamed *Achilles in Petticoats* (1773), the two last with music by Dr. Arne. In 1774 he sold his share in Covent Garden and in 1777 bought the little theatre in the Haymarket which he managed till 1789. Among his productions there were altered versions of Gay's *Polly* (1777) and Beaumont and Fletcher's *Bonduca* (1778). In the same year he published an edition of their works.

An attack of paralysis in 1785 was followed later by a mental affection, but he survived till 14 August 1794. Though he could not recapture after *The Clandestine Marriage* the zest of his earlier work, the versatility of his achievement and his influential theatrical position during his long career make him a notable figure in eighteenth-century drama.

XVI

OLIVER GOLDSMITH
RICHARD BRINSLEY SHERIDAN

WITH Goldsmith and Sheridan, as with Steele and Addison previously, only slight reference is required here to other than their dramatic activities. Oliver Goldsmith was born, probably in 1730, at Pallas in County Longford, son of a clergyman in poor circumstances. On 11 June 1745 he entered Trinity College, Dublin, as a sizar, took his degree in 1750, and afterwards went to Edinburgh to study medicine. In 1753 he set out for the Continent where he spent three years disputing his passage, as has been said, through Europe. On his return to London he tried schoolmastering and journalism, and in 1759 made his first important contribution to letters in *An Enquiry into the Present State of Polite Learning in Europe*, including a chapter 'Of the Stage', which unfortunately gave offence to Garrick. It was followed by *The Citizen of the World* (1762), *The Traveller* (1764), *Essays* (1765), and *The Vicar of Wakefield* (1766).

In 1766 Goldsmith also began his first comedy, *The Good-Natur'd Man*, completed in 1767. But there were difficulties in having it brought on to the stage. Garrick at Drury Lane suggested changes unacceptable to Goldsmith, who then had recourse to Colman, who had succeeded Rich at Covent Garden. He, too, doubtful of its success, postponed its production till 29 January 1768. Both Garrick and Colman were perturbed because Goldsmith was tilting against the dominant theatrical taste. As he puts it in the preface to the published text of *The Good-Natur'd Man*:

> When I undertook to write a comedy, I confess I was strongly prepossessed in favour of the poets of the last age, and strove to imitate them. The term, *genteel comedy*, was then unknown among us, and little more was desired by an audience than nature and humour, in whatever walks of life they were most conspicuous. . . . Those who know anything of composition are sensible that, in pursuing humour, it will sometimes lead us into the recesses of the mean.

In the light of this preface, and similar expressions of Goldsmith's views, modern theatrical critics have, in my opinion, tended to exaggerate the innovation effected by him in *The Good Natur'd Man*. To anyone bearing in mind a number of the comedies previously surveyed various of its features will be familiar. Sir William Honeywood, returning from abroad and keeping watch over his nephew known to him only in early childhood, and revealing himself towards the close of the plot, plays much the same part as the merchant Stockwell towards his son in *The West Indian*. The nephew, afraid to declare his love for Miss Richland till she takes the initiative, is reminiscent of Beverley's attitude towards Belinda in *All in the Wrong*. Croaker's plan to marry Miss Richland to his son Leontine, who is enamoured of his supposed sister Olivia, recalls what has been seen as common form in the relations between parents and children in many comedies of the period. And the pessimist Croaker with his wife who is the very reverse, 'all laugh', have their opposite numbers, so to speak, in the optimist Willoughby with his acid-tempered wife in Kelly's *A Word to the Wise*.

The recognition, as is due, of such correspondences does not imply that Goldsmith has not contributed his own distinctive elements of plot and characterization. Honeywood, 'the good-natur'd man', is, as it were, a comedy Timon of Athens before his downfall. As his steward Jarvis tells Sir William, 'He calls his extravagance generosity, and his trusting everybody universal benevolence.' He chooses to send 10 guineas to a poor gentleman and his children in the Fleet prison instead of repaying the sum to a dunning broker. He refuses to have a servant hanged for robbing his plate: 'It's enough that we have lost what he has stolen; let us not add to it the loss of a fellow-creature.' With such a nature Honeywood falls a victim to his creditors who send bailiffs to arrest him in his own house. This was the scene which, as Goldsmith wrote in his preface, 'in deference to the public taste, grown of late perhaps too delicate, was retrenched in the representation'.

Today this scene, instead of appearing low, is the high-water mark of the comedy. With the tender-hearted bailiffs bribed into posing as Honeywood's friends, and presented as such to Miss Richland who comes to set him free, the dialogue is in Goldsmith's happiest vein.

Miss Rich. The gentlemen are in the marine service, I presume, sir?

Honey. Why, madam, they do—occasionally serve in the Fleet, madam. A dangerous service.

Miss Rich. I'm told so. And I own, it has often surprised me that, while we have had so many instances of bravery there, we have had so few of wit at home to praise it.—I'm quite displeased when I see a fine subject spoiled by a dull writer.

This leads to a discussion by Honeywood and Miss Richland on French and English taste, which the bailiffs interrupt with outbursts against 'the parle-vous'.

Honeywood seeks to explain, 'They draw a parallel, madam, between the mental taste and that of our senses', to which the lady replies, 'I don't see the force of the parallel', and when Honeywood attempts to check their further indiscretions, she shrewdly comments, 'You answer one gentleman before he has finished, and the other before he has well begun.'

When Sir William arrives to release Honeywood he finds himself forestalled by Miss Richland, to whom he confides in secret that he is the house-prisoner's uncle. He also lets her know that he has been serving her interests with the Government who have some powers over her inheritance, and he warns her against a pretender in her cause, Lofty, who is 'quite contemptible among men in power'. Lofty, who has affinity with Beau Tibbs in *The Citizen of the World*, poses as the intimate of the authorities in Miss Richland's case. 'I take my friend by the button: A fine girl, sir; great justice in her case. A friend of mine. Borough interest. Business must be done, Mr. Secretary. I say, Mr. Secretary, her business must be done, sir.' Not recognizing Sir William, he tells him to his face that he procured him his place abroad, of which he speaks in disparaging terms as 'a mere trifle . . . he wanted dignity to fill up a greater'. And when Honeywood is released, Lofty by equivocal answers lets him suppose that he was his benefactor, and in return enlists his favour in a suit to Miss Richland, of whom Croaker is the guardian.

It has been suggested that Croaker has been based on the pessimist Suspirius in Johnson's *Rambler*, No. 59. But Goldsmith has developed the character on his own lines. His first entry is with a wail about 'a country going to ruin like ours. Taxes rising and trade falling. Money flying out of the kingdom and Jesuits swarming into it.'

With Communists substituted for Jesuits a similar lament might be heard today. Domestic affairs are as grievous as public to Croaker. 'My wife has so encroach'd upon every one of my privileges that I'm now no more than a mere lodger in my own house.' But with all his groans he has an eye to the main chance, and he begs Honeywood to influence the heiress Miss Richland in favour of his son Leontine.

Leontine, however, has brought from France a girl, Olivia, with whom he has fallen in love, and whom he successfully passes off as his sister, boarded out ten years ago with an aunt in Lyons. Here Goldsmith makes a heavy draft on the credulity of an audience. The pair find themselves forced to reveal their secret to Croaker, and Olivia asks for his sanction to their union. Thinking that she is referring to a match between herself and a man of large fortune, about which he has heard in a letter from his sister in France, he is only too pleased to assent —till Leontine comes forth to add his grateful thanks, and to appear to his father to be out of his senses. His only course then is to elope with Olivia to Scotland, and Honeywood, now released, comes to their aid with a bill drawn by a friend of his on a merchant in the city, which Jarvis is to get changed. But the bill proves to be not worth a rush, and a letter is written by Olivia's maid to Leontine, asking him to leave 20 guineas at the Talbot Inn till called for. The letter contains the words 'will be all blown up', and, falling by accident into the hands of Croaker, he interprets it as a murderous threat. 'Perhaps this moment I'm treading on lighted matches, blazing brimstone and barrels of gunpowder.' Mrs. Croaker tries to laugh him out of his fear, and they both appeal to Honeywood who sides with each in turn.

All this business with the letter, though apparently

popular with the Drury Lane audience, seems far-
fetched today. Goldsmith is far happier in another of
his cross-purposes dialogues when Honeywood fulfils his
promise of making love to Miss Richland on Lofty's
behalf, and she reciprocates, thinking that he is speaking
for himself—till he amazes her by declaring how happy
she has made his friend, and that friend none other than
Lofty. Meanwhile Honeywood and Croaker visit the
Talbot Inn to seize the miscreant who is expecting the
20 guineas. Croaker is still obsessed with the idea of an
incendiary, and lays violent hands upon the inn's harm-
less post-boy.

He also finds to his surprise his son and Olivia, who
now at last makes it plain to him that she is not his
daughter. Here, too, Goldsmith has a surprise for his
audience; Croaker, instead of bewailing what might
seem a real misfortune, confesses, 'I don't find it afflicts
me so much as one might think. There's the advantage
of fretting away our misfortunes beforehand, we never
feel them when they occur.' Is that the paradoxical
moral that Goldsmith wishes us to draw? Croaker is
confirmed in his forgiving attitude when Sir William
certifies that Olivia is the daughter of the late Sir James
Woodville. He announces that, 'if the two poor fools
have a mind to marry, I think we can tack them together
without crossing the Tweed for it'.

Reformation is in the air, and Honeywood laments
that he has sunk low by too great an assiduity to please.
He tells Miss Richland that he is leaving England, and
that 'among the number of my other presumptions, I
had the insolence to think of loving you'. Lofty, whose
suit he had pleaded, is unmasked by Sir William, and
as a sign of repentance confesses that he had no hand
in Honeywood's release. Sir William discloses that Miss

Richland was his nephew's benefactress, and urges that
to complete their joy she should give him not only
friendship but love, which she admits, after what has
passed, she cannot dissemble. With a touch of the old
Adam still in him Croaker sums up the situation, 'Well,
now I see content in every face; but Heaven send we be
all better this day three months.'

The reception of *The Good-Natur'd Man* was more
favourable than the management had anticipated.
Croaker and Lofty, in particular, attracted the town.
The play ran for nine nights, and went into five editions
in the same year. But, though occasionally revived, it
has not become a classic of the theatre. That distinction
was reserved for Goldsmith's second comedy, *She Stoops
to Conquer; or The Mistakes of a Night*, though it, too, had
a troubled passage on its way to the boards. Finished by
the end of 1771, it was accepted by Colman for Covent
Garden, but he delayed so long in producing it that
Goldsmith offered it to Garrick for Drury Lane. But
through the intervention of Dr. Johnson, Colman,
though still pessimistic about its prospects, and though
two of the cast threw up their parts in rehearsal, brought
it out at Covent Garden on 15 March 1773, to receive
an enthusiastic welcome.

Colman may have been perturbed by Goldsmith's
laying the action of his play in the country instead of
in fashionable London, though here, and in the idea of
stooping to conquer, Farquhar furnished a precedent.
But what chiefly caused misgiving was that Goldsmith
continued his crusade against sentimental comedy. What
figure could be more alien to it than the boorish, tippling
squire, Tony Lumpkin? And could there be more deadly
irony than the comments of his rapscallion companions
when he has sung a song to them in an ale-house?

1st Fellow. The squire has got spunk in him.

2nd Fellow. I loves to hear him sing, bekays he never gives us anything that's *low.*

3rd Fellow. O damn anything that's *low.* I cannot bear it.

4th Fellow. The genteel thing is the genteel thing, at any time.

In one respect, however, Goldsmith follows the contemporary convention by presenting a husband and wife at loggerheads. Mrs. Hardcastle pines for a trip to town, and hates old-fashioned trumpery; Mr. Hardcastle, an addict of the country, loves 'everything that's old: old friends, old times, old manners, old books, old wine', and, in spite of their differences, an old wife. To humour him his daughter Kate dresses herself according to her own fancy in the morning, and in a plain housewife's dress in the evening, which pleases him.

It is in the convention of the period also that Hardcastle tells his daughter that he has chosen a husband for her, the son of Sir Charles Marlow, with every excellent quality, and 'one of the most bashful and reserved young fellows in all the world'. This is scarcely a recommendation in Kate's eyes, but her cousin, Constance Neville, tells her that this is his character 'among women of reputation and virtue', but 'very different among creatures of another stamp'. As Hardcastle has chosen Marlow for Kate, so has his wife chosen Tony, her son by a previous marriage, for the rich Miss Neville. But he cares nothing for her, and her heart is given to Hastings, Marlow's best friend, who is accompanying him on his visit to the Hardcastles' country house.

Whether or not it be true, as seems probable, that Goldsmith himself was led to mistake such a house for an inn, and to treat the proprietor as a landlord, such is the basis of the plot of *She Stoops to Conquer*. It is so familiar both to theatre-goers and readers that a detailed discussion is not necessary. It is the impish Tony who gives the two belated travellers the misleading direction. As neither of them has seen Hardcastle before, they may well mistake his greeting of 'This is Liberty Hall, gentlemen' for the welcome of an assiduous mine host of an inn. And with what gusto Goldsmith shows them concerned with their dress, drink, and supper while Hardcastle pours into their deaf ears his reminiscences of the Duke of Marlborough and Prince Eugene!

The dramatist, as I think, is less happily inspired in letting Miss Neville conspire with her adorer Hastings to keep Marlow still misinformed, and to persuade him that she and Miss Hardcastle have called at the inn after dining in the neighbourhood. But he again shows his mastery in the dialogue between Kate and Marlow. Even with the lady and Hastings helping him out, he can get no farther than declaring that he has been 'but an observer upon life, while others were enjoying it'. And when Hastings deserts him he can only stammer out platitudes and apologize for growing tiresome.

Before they meet again Miss Hardcastle learns from her maid of Tony's trick, and that Marlow has taken her to be the barmaid. She determines to test him by acting the part with him. We have to take it on trust that, with her face hidden by a bonnet, and with her suitor not having dared to lift his eyes to it, he does not now recognize her in her more homely dress. At once he looks her full in the face, pays compliments, and tries to take liberties, which are interrupted by the entrance of Hardcastle, exclaiming, 'So, madam! So I find *this* is your *modest* lover!' She pleads for an hour, to convince him that the description is still true. But the drunken behaviour of Marlow's servants proves the last straw, and Hardcastle orders them out of his house directly. Marlow refuses, 'This your house, fellow! It's my house. This is my house. Mine, while I choose to stay.' The crowning impudence of this sets the supposed innkeeper laughing, and he ironically offers his customer the various pieces of furniture while he keeps shouting for his bill.

At last, Hardcastle's mention of his father's letter gives Marlow an inkling that he may be mistaken, and Miss Hardcastle goes so far as to assure him that this is not an inn, nor is she a barmaid, but a poor relation of the Hardcastle family. So the deception is prolonged, and the mystification of Marlow's double role is kept up till it ends with his father and Hardcastle, to their amazement, seeing him on his knees before Kate with diffident vows, to which she gives a bantering response, but with her father declaring that all will be forgiven.

Meanwhile Hastings and his Constance have had their troubles. They intend to elope, not to Scotland but to France, with Miss Neville's fortune which consists chiefly of jewels. Tony, only too glad to be of help, gets hold of the jewels for them from his mother's custody. Hastings entrusts them for the time being to Marlow who puts them in charge of 'the landlady'—none other than Mrs. Hardcastle—and thus restores them to her. Moreover, she gets hold of a letter from Hastings to Tony, showing that her son is providing a pair of fresh horses for the eloping pair. She turns the tables by ordering the horses to be used for transporting Miss Neville with herself to an austere aunt. All this is in the traditional vein of comedy complications. But it leads up to an unexpected and highly entertaining denouement. Tony, who has hitherto been by turns an ill-fashioned

oaf and an *enfant terrible*, becomes the saviour of the
situation. Ordered by his mother to guard her and
Miss Neville on their forty miles' journey by coach, he
leads them in the dark 'with a circumbendibus' round
and-about, finally lodging them in the horsepond at the
bottom of the garden. Telling his mother that they are
on the notorious Crackskull Common, he puts her in
such a panic that she mistakes her husband for a highwayman. When she is undeceived and reproaches Tony,
he retorts that all the parish says she has spoiled him,
and now she is taking the fruits of it. He has left the way
open for the elopement, but Miss Neville repents of her
agreement to it, and a certificate by Sir Charles Marlow
establishes Hastings as a worthy suitor, and makes need-
less a runaway match.

It was probably Tony Lumpkin and his boon companions that made Colman—as it turned out, without
cause—apprehensive of the success of *She Stoops to Conquer* with a genteel audience. But with the whirligig of
time it is possible that just his part may permanently
keep its hold. With the egalitarian social movement
constantly growing stronger, the time may be coming
when such a contrast as that between Marlow's behaviour
to a lady of quality and to a barmaid may in its turn be
voted 'low'. However this may be hereafter, Goldsmith
survived little more than a year the success of his play,
dying on 4 April 1774.

RICHARD BRINSLEY SHERIDAN

It was early in the following year that another dramatist
born in Ireland was, with *The Rivals* produced at Covent
Garden on 17 January 1775, to begin the short, eventful
career on the stage which brought to a victorious close
Goldsmith's campaign against sentimental comedy.

Richard Brinsley Sheridan, born in Dublin on 30 October 1751, was the second son of Thomas Sheridan and his wife, Frances Chamberlaine. From both sides, especially from his mother, he inherited a connexion with letters and the theatre. After six years (1762–8) of school at Harrow his time was spent chiefly in Bath, where his father settled in 1771, and in London. It was from Bath that he eloped in 1772 with Elizabeth Linley, whom he married in April 1773, after he had fought two duels with her admirer, Captain Mathews. It would seem scarcely to have been merely a coincidence, though this is open to question, that Sheridan called his first comedy *The Rivals*, placed the scene of it in Bath, and made much of an abortive duelling episode.

The unexpected triumph of *She Stoops to Conquer* may have helped Colman's ready acceptance of *The Rivals* for Covent Garden. And it would not be amiss if Sheridan's play had been given as sub-title *He Stoops to Conquer*. Captain Jack Absolute, son and heir of Sir Anthony Absolute, a Baronet of three thousand a year, has fallen in love with the sentimental Lydia Languish who feeds her fancy on the fashionable novels from the circulating libraries. Though, if she marries without the consent of her aunt, Mrs. Malaprop, she loses the greater part of her fortune, she prefers to pay the penalty and to give her hand to a suitor of lowly status. To humour this romantic caprice the Captain has to pose as Beverley, a half-pay ensign, while both his father and Lydia's aunt are eager for him to wed her in his true rank. From this ingenious device of a split personality arise a series of misunderstandings and disputes which might be called the mistakes of a day. Jack Absolute puts his father into a raging passion when he rejects a bride whom Sir Anthony has chosen for him, but goes through a mock

RICHARD BRINSLEY SHERIDAN 347

form of penitence when from a backstairs source he learns that the lady is no other than his Lydia. Mrs. Malaprop welcomes the Captain who tricks her into letting him have an interview with her niece, by way of jest, as the pretended Beverley. It is while overhearing them that Mrs. Malaprop describes Lydia 'as head-strong as an allegory on the banks of the Nile'. It is one of the gems of verbal misapplication that fall every minute from her lips. Among others are 'mistress of orthodoxy, that she might not misspell', 'the very pine-apple of politeness', 'it gives me the hydrostatics to such a degree', 'a nice derangement of epitaphs'. The idea of such high-flown blundering was not entirely novel. But such is Sheridan's virtuosity in exploiting it that Mrs. Malaprop takes rank with some of the comic figures of Shakespeare and Dickens, and we forgive her conduct to Lydia and her elderly infatuation for Sir Lucius O'Trigger.

But the Irish knight thinks that the 'queen of the dictionary' from whom he gets a characteristic love-letter signed 'Delia' is the niece, not the aunt. Another rival for Lydia is the friend of Sir Lucius, the militiaman, Bob Acres, who has trimmed up his dress and hair, and has arrived with a stock of new genteel oaths to pay his court. The fiery Irishman persuades the reluctant Acres to send a challenge to Beverley for supplanting him in the lady's affections, which he delivers to Absolute himself.

Meanwhile Jack's own love-affair has taken a strange turn. Lydia, by calling him repeatedly 'my Beverley' in the presence of Sir Anthony and Mrs. Malaprop, unconsciously gives away his secret, and both of them leave the pair, as Sir Anthony puts it, to fly into each other's arms. But instead Lydia sits sullenly in her chair. All her dreams of a romantic elopement are destroyed, and when Jack implores her on his knees, she taunts him, 'Pshaw! what signifies kneeling, when you know I *must* have you?' She flings back the picture of himself that he has given her, and tells him that she throws the original from her heart as easily. He retorts by declaring that, though all is over between them, he will keep her picture to remind him of what she was, of 'the lips which sealed a vow, as yet scarce dry in Cupid's calendar', but now forsworn.

It is a highly diverting reversal of the usual situation where lovers have obtained their elders' approval of their union, and an ironical shaft at feminine sentimentality.

This is balanced by an exposure of exaggerated masculine sensibility in the underplot. Faulkland's love is returned by Julia whom he has rescued from drowning. But he is constantly fretful because he suspects that she is not as ardent as himself. When Acres reports that while she was in Devonshire she was in full health and spirits, sang gay songs, and joined in country dances, he is at once jealous and depressed. 'My days have been hours of care, my nights of watchfulness. She has been all health! spirit! laugh! dance! Oh! d—ned, d—ned levity!' When he sees her, he gives such a suspicious twist to all her avowals of affection that she leaves him in tears. Even when she sends him a letter, asking him to come to her as soon as possible, he scents 'something indelicate in this haste to forgive'. Well may Absolute, himself so perversely disappointed in his hopes, reproach Faulkland as 'a cautious sceptic in love, a slave to fretfulness and whim'. Yet, when Jack asks him to be his second in the forthcoming duel, he determines to make a final test of Julia's constancy by telling her that he has become engaged in a quarrel which will oblige him to flee from England. At once she declares that she will entrust her person to his honour, and that they will fly together. Now that he has proved her to the quick, he confesses that his tale was a useless device to throw away all his doubts. Again, as with Lydia and Absolute, the unexpected happens. Instead of running into his arms Julia astounds him by retorting, 'I now see it is not in your nature to be content or confident in love. With this conviction—I never will be yours.'

Thus both pairs of lovers are now at odds. But, paradoxically, it is the duel into which Sir Lucius O'Trigger seeks to force the other unwilling participants as principals or seconds that helps to save the situation. While Sir Lucius is trying to bring Acres up to the scratch, and is mistaking Faulkland for Beverley, and drawing his sword against Absolute, David, a servant of Acres, screaming 'Murder, thief, fire!', begs Sir Anthony to stop 'bloody sword-and-gun fighting' in King's Mead Fields. The Baronet arrives on the scene just in time to prevent fatalities, bringing with him Mrs. Malaprop and the two girls now alarmed for their lovers' safety. There are explanations, confessions, and reconciliations all round, and Sir Anthony promises to drink a health to the young couples, and a husband to Mrs. Malaprop.

With the originality of its character-drawing, the dexterous management of its complicated action, and the crispness of most of its dialogue, it should have been plain that in *The Rivals* a new playwright of the first rank had arisen. But the Faulkland–Julia underplot, besides its paradoxical basis, retained much of the traditional high-flown diction. And the first actor of Sir Lucius O'Trigger was miscast. Hence the reception of the play was disappointing. But with a change in the part of Sir Lucius and other modifications *The Rivals* soon gained a well-merited popularity which it has kept till the present day.

Instead of following up this success by another comedy of a similar type, Sheridan, as versatile as he was gifted, succeeded it by a two-act farcical piece, *St. Patrick's Day, or The Scheming Lieutenant*, at Covent Garden on 2 May 1775; and next by a comic opera, *The Duenna*, at the same theatre on the following 21 November. Here Sheridan was entering into the sphere of Gay, but with a difference. Instead of the comparatively simple scheme of *The Beggar's Opera* there was a complicated plot of rival lovers, disguises, elopements, and misunderstandings. The piece takes its title from the imposture by which the Duenna of Donna Louisa passes herself off as her ward, and thus gains the hand and fortune of the rich Portuguese Jew, Isaac, whom her father has chosen to be the girl's husband. Louisa is thus set free to escape, and, after assuming the name of her friend Clara, to be united to her lover, Antonio. Clara is the *inamorata* of Louisa's brother Ferdinand, who offends her for a time by his presumption in entering her bedchamber to prevent her being sent to a convent by her father and a heartless stepmother. But in the end they too are brought together happily.

Sheridan shows much the same skill in *The Duenna* as in *The Rivals* in solving plot-entanglements. The dialogue, especially between Isaac and the Duenna, is well above the average standard of contemporary comic opera. This cannot be said about the words of the songs as a whole, though a few, e.g. those beginning,

> When sable night, each drooping plant restoring,
>   Wept o'er the flowers her breath did cheer,

and

> Oh, the days when I was young,
> When I laugh'd in fortune's spite,

have a charm of their own. With musical setting by the two Thomas Linleys, father and son, *The Duenna* had a very favourable reception. It has been occasionally revived in recent days and, though such a feature as the drinking-bout of the friars is not to modern taste, the opera deserves a permanent place in the theatrical repertoire.

While it was still on the Covent Garden stage Sheridan succeeded Garrick as manager and part-owner of Drury Lane Theatre, which opened under his direction on 21 September 1776 and which saw the production of his remaining plays. After a revival of *The Rivals* on 16 January 1777, he took the surprising step of bringing on the stage his adaptation of Vanbrugh's *Relapse* as *A Trip to Scarborough* on 24 February. His only acknowledgement to his Restoration predecessor was in some lines in the prologue:

> As change thus circulates throughout the nation,
> Some plays must justly call for alteration;
> At least to draw some slender covering o'er
> That *graceless wit* which was too bare before.

How many in the audience recognized that this was an echo of Pope's 'And Van wants grace, who never wanted wit'? It was indeed a slender covering that Sheridan supplied, scarcely warranting the change of title. He changed some of the names, especially Colonel Townly for Worthy, and he shortened Vanbrugh's over-lengthy comedy by cuts in the dialogue and by the omission of the blank-verse passages, a song, and the masque in Sir Tunbelly's house. Otherwise *A Trip to Scarborough* is what now would be considered sheer plagiarism in plot, characterization, and dialogue, many of the speeches in *The Relapse* being repeated word for word, even to Lord Foppington's artificial pronunciation of 'Tam' for Tom, 'tawn' for town, and so forth.

But 1777 was to be Sheridan's dramatic *annus mirabilis*, and he was to make the most gratifying atonement before its close. *The School for Scandal*, produced on 8 May, preceded by about six months *The Critic* on 30 October, but as the latter has backward links it may be considered first.

It was on 7 December 1671 that the second Duke of Buckingham's *The Rehearsal* was produced at Drury Lane, in which Bayes, representing Dryden, presents before two critical spectators, Johnson and Smith, his new play, parodying incidents and dialogue in Restoration heroic tragedies. In *Tom Thumb the Great* (1730) and *Pasquin* (1736) Fielding had carried on in his own fashion the burlesque tradition.[1] Now, a little more than a century after *The Rehearsal*, Sheridan reverted more closely to Buckingham's pattern, though, unlike the Duke and Fielding, his satire was directed more against the general type of contemporary tragedy than against specific plays. Act I of *The Critic* is, in fact, a little comedy in itself. Dangle, who hates all politics except theatrical politics, is reproved by his wife for his lack of patriotism: 'If the French were landed to-morrow, your first inquiry would be whether they had brought a theatrical troup with them.' As far as Dangle has any liking for the theatre it is for truly sentimental comedy of which Mr. Sneer arrives with a specimen together with another comedy with a serious moral, *The Reformed Housebreaker*. He is followed by Sir Fretful Plagiary,

[1] See above, pp. 222–5 and 231–4.

supposed to represent Cumberland, pretending to look upon the abuse of his plays in the newspapers as a panegyric.[1] Then comes the real practitioner in panegyric, Mr. Puff, with the art of it reduced to rule—'the puff direct—the puff preliminary—the puff collateral—the puff collusive—and the puff oblique, or puff by implication'. Puff's elaboration of all these is somewhat too long drawn out before the curtain rises on his tragedy, *The Spanish Armada*, in which there is 'no scandal about Queen Elizabeth', but the daughter of the Governor of Tilbury Fort, Tilburina, is in love with the son of the Spanish Admiral, Don Ferolo Whiskerandos. The other chief figures in the play have become familiar—Raleigh telling Sir Christopher Hatton with his toes turned out things he already knows; Leicester talking in trope, figure, and metaphor; Burleigh in a merely thinking part and meaning volumes by the shaking of his head; the Beefeater who reveals himself to be Drake and 'after the usual number of wounds' kills Whiskerandos in a duel. Whereupon Tilburina enters stark mad in the customary white satin with her confidante stark mad in white linen. As the heroine cries:

> An oyster may be crossed in love.—Who says
> A whale's a bird? Ha! did you call, my love?
> He's here—He's here—He's everywhere.
> Ah me! He's nowhere—

well may Puff ask, 'There, do you ever desire to see anybody madder than that?' and Sneer answer, 'Never, while I live.'

The piece thus rehearsed, with Puff's explanations to Dangle and Sneer of its oddities, is a masterly triumph of fooling. It would probably be more frequently revived were it not overshadowed by the permanent lustre of its

[1] See above, pp. 306-7.

A a

predecessor by a few months in the sphere of high comedy.

Original genius though he was, even Sheridan in *The School for Scandal* could not break entirely away from the eighteenth-century comedy tradition. In the survey of this in the previous pages precedents will be found for several of its chief figures. Charles Surface is the prodigal but warm-hearted libertine. Maria is the heiress who loves him and is won by him, but who has to defy the advances of suitors preferred by her guardian. Joseph Surface is the contemporary man of sentiment, with an admixture of the Restoration rake. Sir Oliver Surface is the wealthy relative who conceals his identity so that he may be a better judge of character. Rowley is the typical devoted family retainer.

It was Sheridan's triumph that on to this conventional framework he grafted novel developments and additions which resulted in a masterpiece of stage-craft. Comedy has always been a vehicle for slanderous tongues, but seldom in such concentrated fashion as in that 'scandalous college' of which Lady Sneerwell is president, and which includes Mrs. Candour hiding her malice under an affectation of good nature; the scurrilous Mr. Crabtree with his poetaster nephew, Sir Benjamin Backbite, who specializes in satires and lampoons on particular people; and for a time Lady Teazle, till she hands back her diploma for killing characters. It may be doubted, however, whether much has been gained by making Lady Sneerwell secretly in love with Charles, and therefore making trouble between him and Maria by bribing Snake to forge love-letters from Lady Teazle to Charles and answering them herself, till Snake finally confesses.

Many comedy libertines have, under a test, shown their better side, but none stands out like Charles Surface auctioning the family portraits to the pretended 'Mr. Premium' supported by Moses, but refusing at any price to part with that of his Uncle Oliver, and thus winning his heart. In contrast is the elder brother, Joseph (always punctiliously called 'Mr. Surface'). Through him Sheridan delivered the death-blow in the campaign against moralizing sentimental comedy in which Goldsmith had been his forerunner. When Joseph, in mock pity for Charles, proclaims 'The man who does not share in the distresses of a brother, even though merited by his own misconduct, deserves——', Lady Sneerwell, who sees through him, cuts him short with 'O Lord, you are going to be moral, and forget that you are among friends'. Yet soon afterwards he assures Maria that 'to smile at the jest which plants a thorn in another's breast is to become a principal in the mischief'. The person who is most taken in by such utterances is Sir Peter Teazle, who declares that 'there is nothing in the world so noble as a man of sentiment'.

Yet at this very time Joseph is the treacherous enemy of his household happiness. The relation between an elderly husband and a young wife, Chaucer's 'January and May', has been a constant subject of satire. But never has it been handled with finer art than in the case of Sir Peter and his seven months' bride. In addition to the difference of age there is that of social standing. Sir Peter has married the daughter of a plain country squire and made of her, as he reminds her, a woman of fashion, of fortune, of rank. Exasperated as he is by her extravagance and choice of undesirable friends, his tender feeling for her cannot help finding expression even after their quarrel. But in her wish to be completely in the fashion she has allowed Joseph to become her lover on platonic terms—with which he is no longer content. So when she rashly visits him in his library he assails her with a subtle seducer's plea till Sir Peter is suddenly announced. There follows one of the classical episodes of the British stage—Lady Teazle hiding behind a screen, and Sir Peter's glimpse of a petticoat, explained by Joseph as being that of a little French milliner; Charles Surface in the hearing of Sir Peter, unseen in a closet, disclaiming any fondness for his lady; Sir Peter seeking to turn the laugh against Joseph by telling about the little French milliner, and, when Charles throws down the screen, their startled cries:

> *Charles.* Lady Teazle, by all that's wonderful!
> *Sir Peter.* Lady Teazle, by all that's damnable!

and the discovered wife's repudiation of Joseph's tale and her promise of amendment.

It is a theatrical climax of the first order, but for sheer technical virtuosity it is challenged by the exploitation of it in the College of Slander. Mrs. Candour and Sir Benjamin Backbite contend as to whether the gallant was Charles or Mr. Surface; Sir Benjamin gives details of a duel with swords, till his uncle corrects this to pistols, but both agreeing that Sir Peter is dangerously wounded—till he confutes them both by walking in unharmed. It only remains for Sir Oliver to reveal himself and affectionately salute Charles, on whom Sir Peter bestows Maria with the wish that they may 'live as happily together as Lady Teazle and I intend to do'.

The triumph of the play was ensured not only by its own merits but by the brilliant acting of the Drury Lane company, headed by Thomas King as Sir Peter, also speaker of Garrick's prologue, and Mrs. Abington as Lady Teazle, also speaker of Colman's epilogue. John Genest even went so far as to say in his *Account of the*

British Stage (1832), fifty years after the play's début, that no new performer had ever appeared in any one of the principal characters that was not inferior to the person who acted it originally. However this may have been, the leading parts in *The School for Scandal* still have a potent attraction for performers of high comedy, and the play keeps its place on the stage as securely as *Much Ado about Nothing* or *As You Like It*. As in them Shakespeare had brought sparkling Elizabethan prose dialogue to its perfection, so Sheridan in *The School for Scandal* had given the finest edge to its elegant eighteenth-century counterpart. Aged only twenty-six, he had still forty years to live, but except for the ill-fated adaptation from the German in *Pizarro* (1799) he devoted himself henceforward mainly to parliamentary and official life. Thus it was that the British stage had to wait for dialogue on a par with his till the early years of the twentieth century, in the plays of the brilliant group of dramatists, headed by G. B. Shaw, W. B. Yeats, J. M. Synge, and Sean O'Casey, born, like Sheridan, on 'John Bull's Other Island'.

INDEX

Abington, Mrs., 356.

Addison, Joseph, 65, 78, 129; early life, 117; Secretary of State, 123; *Campaign, The*, 117; *Cato*, 117–23, 172; *Drummer, The*, 123–5; *Rosamund*, 117; *Spectator, The*, 117; *Tatler, The*, 117.

Aitken, G. A., 70 n., 85 n.

Anne, Princess Royal, 254.

Anne, Queen, 101, 142, 144, 149.

Arbuthnot, John, share in *Three Hours after Marriage*, 175.

Aristophanes, *Frogs, The*, 224.

Aristotle, 7, 23, 149.

Arne, T. A., 225, 334.

Astbury, Joseph, 32.

Atterbury, Bishop, 150.

Augusta, Princess of Wales, 158.

Barry, Mrs. Ann Spranger, 270.

Barry, Mrs. Elizabeth, 16.

Barry, Spranger, 269.

Bath, Lord, 321.

Beaumont, Francis, and Fletcher, John, *Bonduca*, 334; *Maid's Tragedy, The*, 247; edition of works by George Colman, 334.

Behn, Mrs. Aphra, 100.

Bentley, Richard, 301.

Betterton, Thomas, 18, 50.

Bickerstaffe, Isaac, early life, *Lionel and Clarissa*, 288–91; *Love in a Village*, 285–6; *Maid of the Mill, The*, 286–8; *Thomas and Sally*, 284; last years, 292.

Boas, F. S., 193 n., 261 n.

Boccaccio, *Decameron, The*, 162–3.

Bolingbroke, Viscount, 123, 231.

Booth, Barton, 50, 83, 95, 123.

Brereton, William, 270.

Buckingham, Duke of, *Rehearsal, The*, 320–1, 352.

Budgell, Eustace, 129.

Bullock, William, 49.

Bute, Lord, 273, 276.

Canongate Theatre, 269.

Carey, Henry, 207; *Amelia*, 195; *Chrononhotonthologos*, 194–6; *Contrivances, The*, 191–3; *Dragon of Wantley, The*, 199–200; *Dragoness, The*, 200–1; *Honest Yorkshireman, The*, 196–8; *Nancy*, 201–2; *Press-Gang, The*, 202–3.

Caroline, Queen, 152, 158, 179, 226.

Centlivre, Joseph, 101.

Centlivre, Mrs., life, 100–1; *Artifice, The*, 116; *Bold Stroke for a Wife, A*, 111–16; *Busy-Body, The*, 101–5, 108; *Cruel Gift, The*, 111; *Gotham Election, The*, 111; *Marplot in Lisbon*, 105–8; *Wife Well Manag'd, A*, 111; *Wonder, The*, 108–9, 111.

Cervantes, *Don Quixote*, 175, 190.

Chamberlaine, Frances, 346.

Chapman, George, *Revenge of Bussy d'Ambois, The*, 120; *Tragedy of Caesar and Pompey, The*, 120–1.

Chapelle, J. de la, *Les Carosses d'Orléans*, 50.

Charles XII, King of Sweden, 43.

Chastillon, Chevalier de, *Les Amours d'Armide*, 64.

Chesterfield, Lord, 284.

Chetwood, William Rufus, prompter at Drury Lane, 204; *General History of the Stage*, 208; *Generous Free-mason, The*, 205–8; *Lover's Opera, The* 204–5.

Mary, Queen, 65.
Massinger, Philip, 1; (and Nathan Field) *Fatal Dowry, The*, 13.
Mathews, Captain, 346.
Mills, John, 123.
Milton, John, *Comus*, 334; *Doctrine and the Discipline of Divorce, The*, 60–61.
Moissy, A.-G. de, *La Nouvelle École des Femmes*, 309.
Molière, *L'Avare*, 228; *Le Cocu Imaginaire*, 314; *Le Médecin Malgré Lui*, 228; *Le Sicilien*, 78.
Moore, Edward, early life, 255; *Fables for the Female Sex*, 255; *Foundling, The*, 255–6; *Gamester, The*, 257–60; *Gil Blas*, 256–7.
Motteux, Pierre, 50.
Mottley, John, 216.
Murphy, Arthur, early life, 309; *All in the Wrong*, 314–17, 336; biography of Garrick, 318; *Gray's Inn Journal, The*, 309; *Orphan in China, The*, 309; *Way to Keep Him, The*, 309–24; last years, 318.

Nichols, John, 85 n.
Nicoll, Allardyce, *Early Eighteenth Century Drama*, 12 n., 99–100, 123 n., 177 n.
North, Lord, 300.

O'Casey, Sean, 47, 357.
O'Hara, Kane, 225.
Oldfield, Anne, 35, 57, 65, 69, 83, 111, 123, 129.
Old Vic Theatre, 352.
Ormonde, 1st Duke of, 65.
Ormonde, 2nd Duke of, 50–51, 65, 73.
Orrery, Earl of, 51.
Otway, Thomas, *Orphan, The*, 319; Belvidera in *Venice Preserved*, 173.
Ovid, *Metamorphoses*, 178.

Pembroke, Earl of, 150.
Pennell, Margaret, 50.
Percy, Bishop, *Reliques of Ancient English Poetry*, 264.
Peterborough, Earl of, 57.
Philips, Ambrose, 223; early life, 125–6; skill in dialogue, 155; *Briton, The*, 130; *Distrest Mother, The*, 126–30, 227; *Humfrey, Duke of Gloucester*, 133–6; *Old Ballads*, 126; *Pastorals*, 125, 167.
Pilgrim's Progress, The, 172.
Pinero, A. W., *Trelawny of the Wells*, 34, 221.
Pinkethman, William, 69, 170.
Pitt, William, the elder, 262, 267.
Plato, *Phaedo*, 122, 172.
Playfair, Sir Nigel, 184.
Plutarch, 117–18.
Pope, Alexander, 351; on *The Careless Husband*, 91; on Dennis, 148–9; *Dunciad, The*, 100, 126; *Pastorals*, 125; prologue to *Cato*, 122; share in *Three Hours after Marriage* and *What D'Ye Call It*, 174–5.
Porter, Mrs., 123.
Pritchard, Mrs., 328.
Pulteney, William, 133, 226, 231.

Racine, *Andromaque*, 126–7.
Regnard, J. F., *Retour Imprévu*, 228.
Rich, John, 35, 57, 180, 184, 187.
Richardson, Samuel, *Clarissa Harlowe*, 17; *Pamela*, 288.
Rowe, John, 1.
Rowe, Nicholas, 233; early life, 1; *Ambitious Stepmother, The*, 2–8, 12; *Biter, The*, 17–18; *Fair Penitent, The*, 13–17, 18, 27, 31; *Jane Shore*, 24–27, 31; *Lady Jane Gray*, 27–31; *Royal Convert, The*, 21–24, 31; *Tamerlane*, 8–12, 201; *Ulysses*, 18–21; Poet Laureate and burial in Westminster Abbey, 31.